Praise for Kendra Elliot

"Elliot's best work to date. The author's talent is evident in the character's wit and smart dialogue . . . One wouldn't necessarily think a psychological thriller and romance would mesh together well, but Elliot knows what she's doing when she turns readers' minds inside out and then softens the blow with an unforgettable love story."

—*Romantic Times Book Reviews* on *Vanished,* 4½ stars, Top Pick

"Kendra Elliot does it again! Filled with twists, turns, and spine-tingling details, *Alone* is an impressive addition to the Bone Secrets series."

—Laura Griffin, *New York Times* bestselling author, on *Alone*

"Elliot once again proves to be a genius in the genre with her third heart-pounding novel in the Bone Secrets collection. The author knows romance and suspense, reeling readers in instantaneously and wowing them with an extremely surprising finish . . . Elliot's best by a mile!"

—*Romantic Times Book Reviews* on *Buried,* 4½ stars, Top Pick (HOT)

"Make room on your keeper shelf! *Hidden* has it all: intricate plotting, engaging characters, a truly twisted villain. I can't wait to see what Kendra Elliot dishes up next!"

—Karen Rose, *New York Times* bestselling author

BRIDGED

Also by Kendra Elliot

Bone Secrets Novels
Hidden
Chilled
Buried
Alone

Callahan & McLane
Part of the Bone Secrets World
Vanished

BRIDGED

KENDRA ELLIOT

Montlake
Romance

Text copyright © 2015 Kendra Elliot
All rights reserved.

Published by Montlake Romance, Seattle

www.apub.com

Amazon, the Amazon logo, and Montlake Romance are trademarks of Amazon.com, Inc., or its affiliates.

ISBN-13: 9781477825792
ISBN-10: 1477825797

Cover design by Marc J. Cohen

Library of Congress Control Number: 2014943196

Printed in the United States of America

For Dan
My personal tech-speak geek

1

He leaned far over the steel-and-concrete edge of the bridge, breathing deep of the cold, dank scent of the river. At this time in the early morning, the traffic was light. He'd dressed in dark clothing and hugged the shadows to avoid the eyes of the drivers, because pedestrians didn't belong on the Fremont Bridge. He closed his eyes as the metal rail dug into his gut, and he lifted to his toes, stretching out as far as he could.

If I lean a bit farther and give a good push . . .

He opened his eyes and stared down through the night at the water, imagining what it would feel like to fall that far, knowing it'd most likely end in death. It was a 175-foot drop to the water. He'd checked. He'd read everything possible about the bridge before he'd set one foot on it. And standing where someone shouldn't be standing at two in the morning made his head swim.

Cold. Alone. Powerful.

Fearless.

Would it feel like flying?

He could end it here. Toss his intricate plan to the wind.

There was something soothing about the thought. To never worry about anything ever again. Suddenly he understood the appeal of suicide to the people who struggled; they simply wanted everything to stop. Everything.

Still leaning over the edge, he raised his head and looked at Portland's skyline.

Beautiful. Colors and lights.

He had no desire to end things now. He was just getting started.

Will I feel the same way in a week?

He knocked the niggling doubt out of his brain and straightened, losing the dizzying rush from the danger of a moment ago. This wasn't his fault. He'd been given no choice.

He had a job to do. Grabbing the rope, he tied a practiced knot around the thick metal railing and checked for traffic.

All clear.

He grasped the heavy bundle in the vehicle behind him and awkwardly heaved it over the edge of the bridge.

Part of his brain expected a splash, but the rope around the body's neck held strong.

A distant motor signaled someone was crossing the wide span. He raced to grab the orange cones and tossed them through the side entrance and slid the door shut.

He hopped in the van, checked his mirrors, and merged into the lane.

2

"How can they be sure it's not a suicide?" Mason Callahan heard a cop mutter behind his back.

He turned to eye the cop in the navy uniform. Young. "Because it's hard to tie a noose around your neck and crawl over the side of a bridge when your hands and feet are bound."

The cop had the grace to flush. Mason turned away and focused on the victim behind the temporary screen that blocked the view from passing vehicles.

"Not everyone has the keen eye you do, Callahan," Ray Lusco joked beside him. "Takes decades to spot the stuff you do."

"Screw you," Mason replied pleasantly. Ray had been his partner for most of a decade during his time with the Oregon State Police's Major Crimes division. Mason could say anything to Ray. Not that he curbed his mouth around anyone.

Dr. Seth Rutledge pulled a thermometer out from a slit he'd cut into the flesh under the corpse's ribs and studied it. "Well, at least someone made it easy for me," Seth quipped. "No clothes to work around."

The victim had been hanged buck naked.

Mason watched the medical examiner poke and prod at the extremely white body on the shoulder of the freeway over the Fremont Bridge. A boater had called it in two hours ago, saying someone had hanged themselves from Portland's most gorgeous span. Portland police had hauled up the corpse and then promptly called for OSP's Major Crimes. Portland's own detective division was overloaded and had nearly been shut down by a virulent flu bug.

Because the body had been found on a state freeway, Mason figured the case belonged to the Oregon State Police, anyway.

"How long, Doc?" Mason asked. He liked Seth Rutledge. The doctor had smoothly taken over the medical examiner's office last fall, filling big shoes.

Seth wrinkled his nose. "What's the temp out? Thirty-six?"

"I don't know, but it's too damned cold. Especially up here in the wind," added Ray.

"Yes, definitely some major wind chill. Going by his current liver temperature and assuming he's been outside the whole time, I'll say he died twelve to eighteen hours ago."

"No one noticed he's been hanging here all that time?" Mason asked. "That'd put him out here before last night's rush hour."

"He didn't die from hanging," said Seth. "He was dead before that. Someone hung a guy who was already dead."

"What?" asked Mason and Ray in unison.

The medical examiner rolled the man onto his side and showed the pair of detectives purpling streaks down the man's back and buttocks.

Until this moment Mason had only seen the man as he lay on his back. The victim's hands had been tied in front of the body. It'd made the man look peaceful.

Seth pointed at the streaks. "He was on his back for quite a while after he died. Lividity is fixed. If he'd been hung, the blood would have settled in his feet and lower legs. After the heart stops pumping, gravity pulls it—"

"—to the lowest point in the body," finished Ray. "So this is not our murder scene." He sighed loudly and made a notation in his notebook.

Mason squatted next to the medical examiner. "How long would he have been on his back to keep the color from developing in his feet when he was hanged?"

"Somewhere between six and twelve hours." The doctor traced a finger along a white pattern on the dead man's lower back. "This is odd. He was lying on something that whole time that applied pressure to keep the blood from settling. Reminds me of a daisy. I'm not sure what would cause this formation."

Mason studied the twelve-inch-wide floral pattern and waved for the crime scene tech to move in closer for more photos of the back. What had the man lain on? A toy? A sculpture?

Seth scowled at the length of rope around the victim's wrists. Whoever had tied up the man had wrapped padding around the lowest third of his forearms before covering the padding with several feet of rope.

Why protect the skin from the rope if you're going to kill the guy?

Seth gently pulled back on the padding, trying to see underneath. "Dammit. I can see some blood under here, but I don't dare remove the rope until I can do it in a way to preserve the evidence."

A car honked, and Mason was thankful for the screen the Portland police had put up. But it wasn't enough. The police cars and the morgue's van told the drivers that something was up. How many people were slowing to take pictures with their phones?

The morning rush-hour traffic was being allowed to crawl by but was limited to one lane. At first all four westbound lanes over the bridge had been closed as police and techs collected evidence. The lucky commuters driving east cruised over the river on the lower bridge level, unaware of the death on the top level. Mason could almost hear the cursing of the westbound drivers late for work. Rush hour in downtown Portland was rotten on a good day. Throw in a problem on one of the many bridge spans and it got exponentially worse.

In Mason's opinion, Portland could easily use another half dozen bridges. No one got anywhere fast during rush hour. Especially if you had to cross the Willamette River.

As far as bridges went, the Fremont was a good one. It had eight lanes to accommodate commuters, unlike the ancient Sellwood Bridge with its two narrow lanes that made Mason want to close his eyes while crossing. The Fremont was modern-looking and elegant with a single large arch that displayed the U.S. flag and the Oregon state flag at its peak.

Seth eased the body onto its back. He pulled off his thin vinyl gloves and laid them on the man's chest to be taken back to the examiner's office along with the corpse. "I'll have a better time frame for you later this afternoon."

"Slow day?" Mason joked. He hadn't expected an autopsy until tomorrow morning.

"A slow day is always a good thing, in my opinion," Seth answered. "I look forward to the day that I can sit around and read a book in the office instead of counting bullet holes in someone's back."

"But if you just sat in the office you'd miss scenes like this," said Ray, indicating the orange-and-pink sunrise behind Mt. Hood. From the Fremont Bridge, the view was nothing short of spectacular.

Mason grunted. Trust Ray to point out the cup was half full. It was freaking cold for February, and Mason hadn't had enough coffee yet. This call had awakened him an hour before his alarm had been scheduled to go off, and it'd been hard as hell to leave Ava in their warm bed. She'd mumbled and stirred as he'd answered his phone, and then promptly gone back to sleep. They'd been together a few months, and he liked waking up to her face every morning. He glanced at his watch. By now Ava was on her way to the FBI headquarters out by the airport.

The morning could be worse, he acknowledged. It could be pouring rain as he stood outside with a dead body. He'd had his share of those types of scenes.

A distant thumping entered his consciousness and he looked up to see two news helicopters far down the river. The helicopters would have already been in the air for the morning traffic. They seemed far away, but Mason knew their cameras could zoom in close. The temporary screen blocked the scene from the traffic, but a helicopter in the right spot would have a perfect view. He motioned for two uniforms to stand between the helicopters and the naked corpse. Sure enough, both helicopters immediately moved position. "Watch them," he ordered the cops. "Try to keep their view to a minimum." Vultures foiled for the moment, he scanned the rest of the scene.

Why stage this show? The guy was already dead.

Light gravel and usual freeway debris littered the area. He knew the techs had collected all evidence before they'd opened the one traffic lane. The rope around the neck had already been bagged and labeled. The responding cops had cut it off in an attempt to resuscitate, and Mason crossed his fingers no key evidence had been damaged.

Was the hanging symbolic to the killer or victim?

Dr. Rutledge studied the face of the victim. "He looks pretty healthy. Build is in good shape. Took care of himself. No wedding ring."

Mason had already mentally classified the victim. Male, thirties, average build, blond, very pale-skinned. No visible tattoos or large scars. Symmetrical face. But one eyebrow was quite a bit higher than the other, making the corpse look dubious about his last living moments. Mason shifted his position to look at the face square on. *Something isn't right.* He reached out a gloved hand to brush the hair to part on the *correct* side.

"Oh, shit," Ray whispered over his shoulder. "That's Carson Scott. The U.S. representative."

Mason's morning took an abrupt turn for the worse.

• • •

Special Agent Ava McLane lifted the lid of the coffeepot in the break room and cautiously sniffed. Someone had a habit of making the coffee five times as strong as it should be, and she had a hunch that that barista had brewed the current batch. She poured a half inch in her cup, wincing at the black color. She sipped and felt her tongue curl at the bitterness. She sipped again. Not so bad. She filled up her mug and grabbed a bagel to offset the acid en route to her stomach.

Hands full, she headed back to her desk to face her email.Monday morning. No calls overnight had been a blessing. Before her injury she'd worked with the Crimes Against Children division of the Portland FBI office. It often took a strong stomach, but she'd been determined to be the loudest, most ass-kicking voice to investigate the cowards who abused kids. Someone had to stand up for the quiet ones. During her recovery time off, another agent had stepped into her position as one of the Crimes Against Children coordinators, and Ava currently was on a sixty-day temporary assignment to Violent Crimes/Major Offenders, a.k.a. VCMO.

She bumped her upper arm on the corner of her cubicle, sloshed her coffee, and saw stars. Sucking in a deep breath, she clenched her teeth until the pain subsided. Under two months ago, she'd taken a bullet in the arm close to her shoulder. Now a nice slab of metal with four pins held her humerus together. She'd returned to work as soon as her doctor and physical therapist had given her permission to run a desk. "Light duty." No physical stuff.

VCMO involved just as much sitting and staring at a computer monitor and going out on interviews as her previous position. Luckily it'd been her left arm that the bullet had injured. It always ached at the end of the day, but she welcomed the pain.

It meant she'd lived.

Mason constantly said she was lucky the gunman hadn't shot her in the head or neck. It'd been several weeks before both of them stopped having nightmares about Kent Jopek. He'd kidnapped Mason's ex-wife's stepdaughter and then shot Ava during hostage negotiations.

Ava set her food down, eased into her chair, and dug for the Advil in her top drawer. Earlier that morning she'd decided to try to skip any meds, but now she knew she'd hurt all day if she didn't take some. She had just opened her email when her desk phone rang.

"Special Agent McLane," she said around a mouthful of bagel.

There was a pause at the other end of the line. "I'm looking for Jayne McLane. She listed you as an emergency contact," said a raspy male voice.

Ava straightened in her chair. "Jayne? Is she okay? I'm her sister."

"That's what I'm calling to find out. She hasn't shown up for work for the last three days."

Ava slumped back. *Dammit, Jayne!* "I'm sorry. I rarely hear from her. You tried her cell phone?"

"Yeah, it's been disconnected."

"Where are you calling from?" Ava asked, rubbing at her forehead, thankful the Advil was already working through her system.

"Party Mart. She was supposed to be here early for inventory." The man sighed. "But I wasn't surprised since we didn't see her all weekend. I just hired her a week ago."

"She's not very reliable," Ava admitted. That was an understatement. Her twin hadn't held a job for more than a month in the past decade. She was a bit surprised that Jayne had listed her as an emergency contact, but she was possibly the only person Jayne knew with a consistent phone number. "Did she give you the Sixty-Fourth Street address for her home address?"

Why am I asking?

She'd given up on Jayne the day she breezed through Ava's hospital room after Ava had been shot and not asked how she was.

Her twin had worn out her second chances years ago. But Ava kept giving them.

She heard paper shuffling over the phone. "Nah, she listed a place on Walnut."

Ava had no idea where that was. Or whom her sister was living with.

And she didn't want to know.

"If you happen to hear from her, would you tell her to call her sister?" she asked reluctantly. Part of her needed to know her sister was still breathing. A second part asked why on earth she cared.

"Sure. If *you* hear from her, tell her she's fired." He hung up the phone.

Ava pressed her fingers into her eyes, trying to quiet the screaming in her brain that Jayne always triggered. Her twin floated from man to man, job to job, and drug to drug. Too many times Ava had tried to rescue her sister, lent her money, placed her in rehab. Nothing worked.

She hadn't heard from Jayne since her surprise hospital visit. Relief rushed through her that Jayne had been fine last week, according to the Party Mart manager. But what had happened to her now? For Ava's own sanity, she had to place Jayne firmly out of her mind and go on with her stable life until Hurricane Jayne blew in with more destruction.

She ached for Mason, wishing for his solid touch to calm her and his rational words to keep her in check. Nothing else made her as crazy as dealing with Jayne. Mason had been her rock for the last two months, through her shooting, her recovery, and Jayne's current silence. Who could have guessed that the gruff state detective with the cowboy hat would ease her world into a soothing harmony? She'd been running on autopilot before she met him during the kidnappings. They'd made an effective team while holding the distraught family together.

She'd fallen head over heels for him without realizing it.

Now she spent 90 percent of her free time at his home. They'd talked a bit about selling one of their places but neither had pushed the issue. His place was bigger than her condo, and he had a fenced yard for his dog. It made sense to be at his house.

She liked going to his home, knowing that he'd be there. Well, eventually he'd be there. Between their jobs, they worked a lot of irregular hours. It wasn't rare for one of them to get a call in the middle of the night informing them that their presence was required.

"Hey, Ava." Special Agent Zander Wells stuck his head in her cubicle. "Duncan wants you and me in his office in thirty minutes."

Zander was also on temporary assignment to VCMO, from Cybercrimes, his computer skills in high demand.

"What's going on?" she asked.

"Don't know yet, but I think it's important. His voice had that sharp edge it gets when something huge has landed on his desk. He's waiting on some intel before talking to us."

"Thanks. See you then."

The tall agent vanished silently down the hall. Zander was one of the good ones. Deadly smart and a memory like a supercomputer. Pleasant, too.

Thirty minutes? That should be enough time to make a small dent in her email. She tapped on her keyboard, but felt her nerves crank up in anticipation of a hot case.

3

"Representative Carson Scott didn't have the best reputation," commented Mason as he stared at the Google images at his desk in the Portland office.

"That surprises you?" Ray asked. "The only reason I recognized him was because his face was all over the TV last fall during that sex scandal. And he doesn't even belong to our state."

"A lot of people consider Vancouver, Washington, to simply be a Portland neighborhood on the other side of the Columbia River."

"People who live in Vancouver don't see it that way. And I'm sure Scott didn't see it that way."

"Looks like the only thing he could see was women. Usually young ones," muttered Mason. "He's with a different one in every picture. They look about Kirstin's age." The blond U.S. representative looked like James Bond in a tux. No wonder the women liked him. The high eyebrow that Mason had noticed at the crime scene made Scott appear always interested in what was directly in front of him. Mason had heard that women found it sexy.

But he thought it had a touch of Hollywood sleaze.

"I'm sure they're older than my fifteen-year-old," said Ray. "Scott is what, all of thirty-three? It's not unusual to date women in their twenties at that age. But that's what got him all the press last year. Everyone believed that donor's wife when she said they'd had an affair."

"She was credible. Him not so much."

"Then why didn't it cost him his job?"

"Maybe it will cost him come election time—oh, crap—guess not." Mason realized too late. "Anyway, Dr. Rutledge said he hoped to have a cause of death this afternoon. Until then we need all possible views of that stretch of the bridge from the traffic cams. We need to locate any family in the area and find out what he's been doing the last few days."

"I know he was out with McKenna Drake Saturday night,"stated Ray.

"How do you know that? And who's McKenna Drake?"

"I'm looking at his Facebook page. It's public. It shows they attended a movie together." Ray clicked one button on his keyboard. "McKenna Drake. Lives in Portland. Dancer at BlazerDancers. Studied business at the University of Portland."

"BlazerDancers? You mean the dancers for the pro basketball team?"

Ray's gaze was glued to the screen. "Yup. Kirstin's main goal in life is to dance on a professional sports cheerleading or dance team. I've tried to tell her they probably make less than minimum wage and work insane hours."

Mason got up from his desk and walked around to look over Ray's shoulder. Ray was studying the Facebook page of a very attractive young woman with black hair and huge turquoise eyes. Sure enough, the top posting was a link to a movie theater where she'd gone with Carson Scott. "Why do people post where they're at? They're just asking for trouble. *I'm not home, come rob my house.*"

"I'll reach out to her and get her in for an interview. I've already talked to his chief of staff, who's headed in to meet with us. They were headed back to DC tomorrow."

"He has a chief of staff? Why? How many people work for a U.S. rep?"

"Looks like nearly twenty."

"Christ. I want a staff. I *need* a staff." Mason frowned at his messy desk and ignored the extreme neatness of Ray's.

"The question is who wanted him dead?" muttered Ray. "A husband or boyfriend of some woman he flirted with? Someone affected by a bill he voted on?"

"His job opens up a whole other issue," admitted Mason. "Denny put in a call to the FBI the moment we had a preliminary ID on him. Murder of a federal official is their territory."

"I'm all about getting their help. They have a lot more funds and resources than we do," stated Ray.

"Do we have camera footage yet?" Mason walked back around to his desk and opened his email. The Oregon Department of Transportation had said it would email footage from the previous evening and early morning. Mason figured it'd happened in the middle of the night. If he were hanging a body in public, he'd do it during the quietest hours possible. Of course, not all criminals were smart.

"Not yet." Ray yanked at his perfect tie to loosen it around his neck. A signal he was sucked into the case. The detective was nearly a decade younger than Mason and dressed like he'd stepped out of a menswear magazine. Mason's working uniform was jeans and button-down collared shirts. And his boots and hat. Occasionally he'd throw on a sport coat and tie if he had a meeting, but he preferred to be comfortable. Ties weren't comfortable.

Ray answered his phone and found out the chief of staff had arrived. He asked for the chief to be placed in an interview room and slipped his sport coat on. Mason grabbed a freshly sharpened pencil and his notebook.

"What's his name?" Mason asked as they moved down the hall.

"Her. Nissa Roberts." He pronounced it *Nee-sa*.

In the interview room, a red-eyed young woman shook their hands. Mason didn't think she looked old enough to drive, let alone run a congressman's staff. Nissa Roberts was petite, with sleek blond hair that curved just under her chin.

They all sat and Nissa slid a file out of her laptop bag, removed a page, and handed it to Ray. "Here is Carson's schedule from the last two days here in town. Before that we were in DC." She flipped through a few more sheets of paper before passing them along. "This is his DC schedule from last week. It's accurate," she said simply. "And here's a record of his recent votes on bills. I assume you'll want to look through his mail? We separate out the threatening correspondence." She wiped at her nose with a tissue and eyed the detectives expectantly. "What else do you need?"

Mason glanced at Ray, who seemed speechless. *No wonder she's in charge.*

"We're very sorry for your loss, ma'am," Mason stated, wondering if she ever slowed down.

Nissa's lips quivered. "Thank you," she said sincerely. "It's been a huge shock. Carson was like a big brother to me. I loved working for him."

Mason leaned forward and rested his weight on his forearms on the conference table. "Let's slow down for a minute. You've provided us with some great details that we need, but let's just talk for a while."

She leaned back in her chair and exhaled, covering her face with her hands.

"I'm afraid if I stop, I'll crumble," she whispered from behind her fingers. "This is how I function."

Her nails were bitten to red stubs.

Is that recent? Or the chronic sign of a worry-aholic?

"You were the one who let the police and crime scene techs into his home, correct?" asked Ray.

"Yes. As soon as they called me. I have copies of all his keys."
She frowned. "They say he didn't die on the bridge."

Mason didn't ask who "they" were. "That's correct. We're looking for the original murder scene."

"In a way I'm glad to know he didn't die like that. That would
have been horrible."

Mason didn't disagree. Death by hanging could take a long time
unless the neck instantly broke.

"The two of you live in DC, correct? But you have homes here,
too?" Ray asked.

Nissa nodded. "I stay with my parents when we're in town, and
I rent a place in DC. Carson rents in DC, too, but owns a condo in
Vancouver. He travels back and forth a lot. I come about a third of
the time. It depends what's going on in each city."

Ray studied one of the sheets. "He's busy every minute. Especially when he's back there."

"Yes, when he's here, it's usually a sixty-hour workweek. Back
East, even longer."

"But he made time for a movie two nights ago," Mason added.

"He has to have a life at some point." Nissa's blue eyes grew cold,
and Mason wondered how often she had to defend her boss.

"Of course he does. Do you know McKenna Drake very well?"

"Yes. I introduced them. She's a sweet girl." Her eyes thawed a bit.

"Are they romantically involved?" Mason asked.

"I'd say no. They'll usually get together once or twice when he's
in town. But he dates other women, too. He keeps it all at a friendship level. There isn't someone special in his life, detectives. He often
moans that he doesn't have time for a relationship besides his job."

"Not an easy life." Mason understood that all too well. He'd
been divorced for a number of years. Ava was his first stable relationship since the divorce. So far it seemed to work because she was
married to the federal government, and he was deeply involved with
the state. They understood each other's job duties. "What about hate

mail? Harassing phone calls? I assume you keep records of that sort of thing?"

"Yes, definitely. The disturbing ones we forward to the Secret Service, but the rest we hang on to in case of a situation just like this one. I asked one of the guys back East to compile a file for you. I'll forward it when I get it."

"Is there anything you recall off the top of your head?" Ray asked. "When you heard he'd been murdered, where did your train of thought go as far as possible suspects?"

Nissa pressed her lips together and looked at the wall behind Mason. "My mind went in a million different directions. Most of them I immediately discarded as ridiculous." She cracked the knuckles on her right hand, trying to collect her thoughts. "Every vote brings out the weirdos. Sometimes Carson felt like he couldn't do anything right." She looked Mason in the eye. "I often told him to vote as his constituency and his gut directed him and to ignore the haters. There will always be someone with a different opinion."

"Sounds like it wasn't the most pleasant job," offered Mason.

"It was hard." Nissa twisted her fingers. "No one knows this, but he wasn't going to run again. He's been up and down deciding if he wanted to continue, but this past year has simply been too stressful. He was giving it up," she said softly. "It was too bad. He had so many good things he wanted to do, but the process and never-ending public scrutiny were destroying him inside."

"He had a rough time last fall," said Ray, alluding to the affair accusations.

"He didn't do it," Nissa said firmly. "She hit on him, and he rebuffed her. It made her angry. And it ripped up his life for three months. He'll never be the same."

The fire in her eyes surprised Mason. Nissa Roberts was very passionate about defending her boss. It was a good quality in an employee.

If the boss was worth defending.

"You seem very certain," Mason stated. "I know the incident ended on a 'she said, he said' brick wall, and once the authorities decided no wrongdoing had happened, they let it go. But I'd say the general public favored the woman."

"You'd be right. Nothing frustrated Carson more than being unable to prove he hadn't done it. He was guilty from a trial by the press. It heavily influenced his decision to not run next time." She took a tissue from the box on the table and blew her nose.

Mason politely looked away and scanned the schedule of the last two days she'd given them. "This says he was supposed to have a town-hall-type meeting last night. You've noted that he never showed." He glanced up. "Did that surprise you?"

"Completely. Carson is meticulous about his schedule. And the fact that I hadn't heard from him was upsetting. I called everyone I could think of and texted and emailed him a dozen times." She dabbed at her eyes. "Now I know why," she said softly. "Have they said how he was actually killed?"

"No. We're hoping to hear from the medical examiner this afternoon." Mason paused. "Do you possibly know if he had life insurance? Or who the beneficiary might be?"

"He has life insurance through the Federal Employees'. I think it was about three-quarters of a million. I don't know who will get it. I assume one of his parents."

Ray made a notation. They'd reached out to the parents earlier that day and spoken to a brother. The parents were distraught, but the brother understood the detectives needed to speak with them. He'd promised to call back later that day.

Mason hated to disturb immediate family when they'd had a crushing blow, but murder couldn't wait. The first few days were crucial to solving a case. And family was always ruled out first.

"You haven't offered any names or suggested a direction for us to take this investigation. There's no one in particular that jumps out in your mind as having an ax to grind?" Mason asked.

Nissa shredded the tissue in her hands, her gaze on the mess. "No. I'll let you know."

Ray and Mason exchanged a glance. He wondered if the woman either wasn't confident in her suspicions or had something she was keeping to herself. Mason slid a business card across the table. "Thank you for your time, Ms. Roberts. Please call if something else occurs to you."

The three of them stood and began walking out the door. "Oh, Ms. Roberts. I know you were going back to DC tomorrow, but would you mind staying in town a few more days? There's a good chance we'll need to talk with you again. Just to clarify some things." Mason gave the young woman a polite smile.

She paled and nodded. "Of course."

Mason and Ray watched her head down the hall, high heels clicking on the tile.

Ray sighed. "I think we seem trustworthy and competent. Why do people hold back on us? Don't they know we're the good guys?"

"Give her time. I think we'll be hearing from Ms. Roberts very soon."

"Ready to take a look at Carson's condo?"

"Let's go."

. . .

The Vancouver cop holding the scene log outside Carson Scott's condo barely twitched an eyebrow at Ava's and Zander's FBI badges. "This is getting bigger every moment," he commented as Zander signed. "Scott being a member of the U.S. House of Representatives pulls your agency into the investigation, the location of his body pulled in OSP, and our little department covers the ground his home stands on."

"The more, the better, I always say," Ava stated. The cop didn't seem resentful; he was just stating the obvious. Jurisdictions did make investigations complicated. Usually the FBI waited until it was asked for assistance by other police departments, but the murder of a congressman fell directly under the FBI's umbrella. She signed the log and froze as she recognized two names farther up.

Well, this will be interesting.

"Our day just developed a new twist, Zander." She pointed the pen at Mason's name.

"He caught the case?"

"Looks that way."

Zander's forehead crinkled. "Is that a conflict?"

"Personally, not at all. But Duncan's opinion might be different." *Dammit.* Duncan had better not yank her from this case. She was eager to get to the bottom of why a congressman had been murdered and left hanging in such a public manner. *I want this case.*

"Maybe we better give Duncan a call," Zander suggested half-heartedly as he studied her face.

"Let's go inside first and see what's up." Ava marched forward, not letting Zander put doubts in her head. Perhaps Duncan wouldn't have a problem. She'd proven in the past she could work with Mason Callahan. Of course, they hadn't been an involved couple when the Kent Jopek case had started.

Assistant Special Agent in Charge Ben Duncan had met with Ava and Zander that morning, to break the news of the young congressman's death and to give them their new assignment. Ava had been stunned.

"They hung him? Off a bridge?" Zander had asked.

"Looks like he was already dead," said Duncan. "Somebody wanted to make a statement with this scene. And just because he's a congressman doesn't mean it's politically driven. Keep your mind open in that regard."

"The nudity bothers me. Someone had a reason for leaving him like that. We might need to get BAU involved," Ava added, referring to the Behavioral Analysis Unit on the East Coast.

Duncan agreed. "We will. I'm going to send them preliminary findings, and we'll pull them in for a deeper analysis if we don't get results soon. I'm hoping we have a stupid murderer here who makes your job easy."

"Our killer's not stupid," Ava had stated to Zander on the way to the victim's home. "No one saw him leave a naked body on a bridge. At least no one has come forward yet."

Now Ava slipped the thin elasticized booties over her shoes, her upper arm complaining as she bent over. She bit her lip and shifted her notebook to her right arm, avoiding eye contact with Zander. A little twinge of pain helped keep her awake, right?

Carson Scott's condo was a two-level unit in a string of connected townhome residences. The moment they stepped through the front door, they had a sweeping view of the Columbia River. "Nice place," Zander muttered as they moved through the spacious foyer, which opened into a high-ceilinged great room with floor-to-ceiling windows to take full advantage of the riverfront property. The sky was a clear blue, turning the water the same shade. Portland hotels and condos stood five hundred feet away across the water.

Inside the home the decor was white and silver. Lots of mirrors and an odd mix of vintage furniture and ultramodern accessories. Off to the left, a gleaming silver kitchen caught Ava's eye. She looked away. Luxury kitchens were a weakness of hers. She didn't cook much, but she had an affinity for specialty countertops, glass tiles, and professional appliances that she'd never get her money's worth out of. She'd rather install a unique stone countertop, or buy a Wolf range, than pick out jewelry.

Someday . . .

From her right, voices moved closer, and a group of men came down the hall, deep in discussion about a computer.

"I'm telling you not to touch it! Don't even unplug it. Let one of the computer forensic guys look at it first."

Ava's heart sped up at Mason's commanding voice. He was a take-charge type of guy. If he saw something that needed to be done, he did it. Or politely kicked the butt of the guy who should have been doing it. He didn't tolerate laziness or waste. She saw he was carrying his cowboy hat in his hand. The hat and cowboy boots had taken some getting used to, but now she couldn't imagine him without them. They represented his old-fashioned character and values.

He worried about their twelve-year age difference, but she brushed it aside.

The heart didn't ask one's age.

The group stopped as they spotted Ava and Zander. Surprise showed on every face but Mason's. He gave a small grin, his brown gaze locking on hers. "I wondered who'd be the lucky ones from the FBI. Zander, good to see you again." Mason shook the other agent's hand.

Ava greeted Mason's partner, Ray, and nodded at the other officers as Mason made quick introductions. She fought to act casual.

She'd nearly moved forward to kiss Mason in greeting. The rueful look in his eye told her he was having the same struggle. She caught Ray watching the two of them and biting back a grin. He knew they were in the early stages of their romantic relationship.

"I assume the murder didn't happen here," Ava said.

Ray shook his head. "We're still looking for the primary scene." He gestured for Ava and Zander to follow him down the hallway toward the bedrooms. "It looks like he left with every intention of coming back." Ava stepped into a slightly disheveled master bedroom. She scanned the area. The bed was unmade, the door to the walk-in closet was open, and the blinds were closed. She surveyed the closet. Men's shoes and men's clothing. A few free weights. She moved into the attached bathroom. One well-used toothbrush stood in a holder on the counter, and a T-shirt and pair of underwear were on the floor next to the shower. She tried not to ogle the five showerheads at different levels in the custom tile shower. Carson Scott used Head & Shoulders shampoo and what smelled like Ivory soap.

"It looks like he lives alone?" she directed at Ray.

"That's our impression. There's no women's stuff like he has a girlfriend occasionally stay. That fits with what his chief of staff told us. She said he dates but no one special."

Possibly another male?

She didn't speculate out loud but tucked the thought away for consideration later. Zander took a second look in the walk-in closet.

Next to the master bedroom was a home office. A nice desktop and a laptop sat on the wide desk. The office had the usual equipment: printer, shredder, whiteboard, and ergonomic chair. The unusual sight in the office was the three shelves of trophies. Ava stepped closer to read them. Baseball. Rugby. Tennis. Swimming. Every date was more than ten years old. Some closer to twenty.

Carson couldn't let go of the glory days.

The old mementoes struck her as odd for someone who'd achieved Carson Scott's high level in politics.

Zander reappeared. "All the clothing and shoes in the closet are the same sizes. It strongly suggests he's living alone. Unless they both happen to wear the same size sport coat and shoes."

Ava mentally slapped her forehead. *Why didn't I think of checking that?* "I guess he's not like a woman who keeps a fat wardrobe and a skinny wardrobe."

He gave a small smile. "I'll admit to keeping a loose pair of sweatpants handy. I know if I'm reaching for them, it's time to increase my daily running distance." Zander then looked at Ray. "Mason is right to insist on waiting for the computer forensics people to look at the desktop before unplugging it. Do you know if someone supplied his passwords?"

"His chief of staff had some of them. She didn't know if it was everything." Ray stepped out of the room to take a phone call.

Zander studied the silent desktop, and Ava wondered how badly he wanted to start mining its hard drive.

"That's like looking at a juicy burger, isn't it?" she prodded the computer geek.

Zander gave her a slow smile. "A rib eye, maybe."

"Steak?" asked Mason.

Ava turned around; she hadn't heard him enter the room.

"What's Duncan going to say about us both on this case?" Mason asked the two of them in a low voice. "My commander won't care, but I suspect yours might take issue with it."

"We've proved we work well together," Ava said.

"You'll have to come up with something better than that. He's going to pull you off the case."

Her chin went up. "Not if I can help it. Have you heard from the medical examiner yet? Is there a cause of death?" She was determined to push forward until she was in so deep that Duncan would hurt the case if he removed her. The twinkle in Mason's brown eyes told her he knew exactly what she was doing.

"Duncan doesn't have a chance, does he?" Mason asked Zander.

"Nope," Zander answered with a sigh. "We're setting up a command center back at our building. We'd appreciate any information you've already collected." At the abruptly cool look on Mason's face, he continued rapidly, "We're not stealing the case, but you know as well as I do the murder of a congressman is firmly under our jurisdiction. We'll want the continued support and skills of OSP to add to our investigation."

Zander would make a good politician.

"Who wants to go to the morgue?" Ray asked from the doorway. "Dr. Rutledge would like to talk to us." He studied the shuttered faces of Zander and Mason. "All of us," he said firmly.

• • •

Zander followed the group out of the condo. He'd wanted this case from the moment Duncan had told them about it. The indignity forced upon a public representative had set his blood boiling, but he'd kept it inside. That was how he operated. He knew his fellow agents thought he had the patience and temper of a priest, but the truth was he simply knew how to hide his feelings. Inside he was often fighting the urge to hit something. Instead he funneled that energy into his job.

He'd been a software engineer for a decade before he'd decided to apply to the FBI. Now with ten years under his belt as an agent, he'd created a reputation for being streamlined and getting shit done with no fuss.

He liked the sound of that.

Sitting in front of a computer calmed him and helped him focus. The feeling that he could create something with software language was soothing. Give him a bank of data and he could pull whatever was needed. Give him a tech problem and he'd sort the logic through his head until he saw the means to a solution. It was the same mind-set he applied to his current work.

He loved working in the Cybercrimes division, but he had to admit that being on temporary assignment to VCMO was giving him a thrill. All his past assignments had been important. But this was a big one. Solving the murder of a congressman had grabbed his focus like nothing else. It was a good shake-up from his usual assignments, for which he spent the majority of his time behind a desk. He'd been getting stale. Working that kidnapping with Ava before Christmas had shown him he needed to step out from the office.

The kidnapping case had also moved him directly into Special Agent McLane's circle. Their paths had occasionally crossed when she'd worked Crimes Against Children. He'd gotten to know a detail-focused agent. And an attractive one. He'd held back, knowing an office romance wasn't an ideal situation. Then he'd had a front-row seat to watch her fall for Detective Callahan.

He liked Ava. When he'd seen the sparks start to fly last December, he'd waited, wondering if her and Mason's attraction would last. It had. It ate at him that he hadn't acted initially, but he liked Mason Callahan. It was hard not to. He was a straight shooter without a big ego and Zander respected that. Together, Mason and Ava were a good thing.

He stopped at his car and waited for Ava to join him. She was talking quietly to Mason. Zander had read that cats saw more wavelengths in the electromagnetic spectrum than humans. If he had the eyes of a cat, what would he see surrounding the couple? Because with his inferior human eyes it was apparent that waves of affection-based energy flowed between them.

He grinned. It pleased him that Ava was happy. Over an impromptu beer a week after the kidnapping was solved, OSP Detective Ray Lusco had told him Mason hadn't fallen for anyone in years. The linebacker-size detective had been optimistic for the couple's future.

But if Mason hurt her, Zander was going to hurt him back.

4

Two months ago he'd been told he'd be dead in a year.

He'd seen too many doctors, all of them stunned at the growth in his brain and the amount that had metastasized to his other organs. He wasn't feeling any pain. Yet. The doctors had promised it would come. Soon.

How could this happen to someone his age?

God's wrath.

He'd spent the first weeks in denial and lashing out at everyone around him. He'd quit his job. Why continue to work in a position he hated? He had some savings. Enough to feed himself and get by for a few years. It was oddly freeing. He could go live on the beach in Costa Rica if he wanted. He didn't have close family to take care of. No one relied on him but his cat.

One of his motivations for survival pushed her head into his hand, searching for a scratch. He scratched at her neck and down her back to her happy spot in front of her tail. She arched her back in bliss.

Becky down the street would take her in when he was gone. The cat spent half her time over there anyway. He added a discussion with Becky to his mental "things to do before I die" list. The list wasn't that long. And that fact depressed him a bit. Most people must have had long lists. People they wanted to say good-bye to, places they wanted to visit, goals they wanted to achieve.

But every time he came up with something to add to his list, he realized it wasn't important. In the great scheme of life, what truly mattered?

Writing the great American novel?

Seeing the Taj Mahal in person?

Skydiving?

Nope.

None of those held any appeal. One month ago his philosophy had been that life was about doing the right thing. That a person should be able to look back on his life and see that he'd treated others with dignity and respect. And that if he'd made a mistake, he should own up to it and correct it.

But when the men he'd trusted tried to kill him, his philosophy had abruptly changed.

That was the drawback to secrets. People wanted them to stay secret.

No exceptions.

He'd started down a path the other night, the one these men's actions had forced him to follow. They'd have no one but themselves to blame in the end.

Why didn't they listen to me?

5

"I was right about the padding around the wrists," Dr. Seth Rutledge said with a confident nod. "His wrists had been slit. He'd bled out and then been cleaned up and bandaged."

Mason identified with the medical examiner's satisfaction; he understood that great feeling when a hunch turned out to be correct.

He, Ray, Ava, and Zander stood in attendance as Seth showed them the long vertical slices in the wrists. Mason had seen people who'd tried to commit suicide by cutting across the wrist, but he'd never seen a case where it had worked. No doubt it worked sometimes, but he'd been told death needed a deep cut down the wrist, not across. Apparently Carson Scott's killer knew the same fact.

"Look how clean these cuts are," Seth continued, twisting the arm toward his stoic audience. "No hesitation at all. Whoever did this clearly succeeded on his first try. Usually with suicides there are several attempted cuts first. Murders, too. Our killer made a long cut, getting a wider section of the ulnar artery for a quicker bleed-out. If he'd just done a small cut at the wrist, it would have taken much longer."

"So someone knew exactly how to do it?" Ava asked. She'd moved to the front of their little group and bent close to get a good look at the arm. Mason noticed she had no issues with getting right next to the table, compared to the three male detectives, who kept a polite distance.

"And had no fear," added Seth.

Cops handled the medical examiner's office in different ways. It'd taken Mason years of internal struggle to calmly handle an autopsy. He'd learned when to look away. Some detectives embraced the procedure and found it fascinating, and it appeared Ava was one of them. Other officers heaved over a garbage can. Mason had always kept his cool, but it wasn't easy.

That smell.

Thankfully today's autopsy had already ended when Dr. Rutledge called them in to review preliminary findings.

"Can you tell what was used to make the incisions?" Zander asked. He had a notepad in hand and had been taking notes as Dr. Rutledge spoke. Mason wondered if he was using the notepad as a crutch to focus on instead of the dead body with the giant stitched incision in its chest. Mason often did the same thing.

Seth held up the arm again. "After the first half inch at the start of the cut, it's exactly the same three-quarter-inch depth for the remaining six inches." He raised a brow at the group, clearly waiting for guesses.

"A utility knife of some sort," said Ava. "Something with a guide to keep it from going deeper."

The other detectives nodded, and Dr. Rutledge appeared pleased.

"So we're looking for a very bloody scene," suggested Ray. "Unless he kept the blood contained in some way."

"Yes." Dr. Rutledge nodded. "I would expect arterial spurting from the incisions, but perhaps your killer was prepared for that."

"There's still a chance Carson killed himself," Ava argued. "Obviously he didn't hang himself, but you've found a cause of death that could be self-inflicted."

"Look up here." Dr. Rutledge took a step toward the head of the body and indicated the skin of the upper arm. With a long-handled, tweezers-like tool, he picked at something microscopic stuck to the hair on Carson's arm.

"Tape residue," identified Ava. "He was bound for the actual cutting of his wrists."

"The residue is across his palms, too."

"Wouldn't there be some white blanching marks on the backside of his arms? From them being tightly bound while the remaining blood settled?" asked Ray.

Mason remembered the odd white pattern on Carson's back.

"There aren't any. His arms may have been taped tightly for the cutting, but once he'd passed out from the blood loss, the suspect may have removed it. I've submitted tissues and fluids for toxicology. Those reports I'll have back in a few days."

"Did you get a narrower time of death?" Zander asked.

"Yes. Between noon and four P.M. yesterday. Does that help?" Seth offered.

"Every bit helps, Doctor," answered Mason. "What about—"

"Seth? Oh, excuse me." Dr. Victoria Peres had stridden into the room. The tall forensic anthropologist scanned their group and made eye contact with Mason and Ray. "Detectives, nice to see you again." She smiled, and Mason fought not to jerk in surprise.

Seth made introductions while Mason took a good look at the woman. He'd dealt with the "Bone Lady" on several investigations, but he'd never seen her smile so easily. Ever. She had a reputation for being prickly and cold. It must have been her new relationship with the medical examiner. Or old relationship. The two had recently been reunited after years apart.

A medical examiner and a forensic anthropologist. Mason wondered what their dinner table conversation was like.

She pulled Seth aside for a quick consult while the four detectives waited.

"I wonder if we'll find the blood," Ava murmured. "Do you think our killer let it spill out at our crime scene or carefully controlled it?"

"Do you think he wanted the blood for something? Maybe to drink or for a ritual?" Ray asked. Mason gagged slightly. Trust Ray to consider the macabre.

Ray's mind worked in different directions from Mason's. It was why they made a good team. Between the two of them they could consider more avenues than either could working alone.

"Did someone make a formal identification?" asked Zander. "Obviously we all recognize him from TV, and I'm comfortable moving ahead based on that, but what about a relative or with his teeth?"

"We've already compared his dental records," said Seth as Dr. Peres headed toward the door. She waved good-bye to the group, and Mason dumbly raised a hand in return. He and Ray exchanged a shocked look.

"Without a doubt, it is Carson Scott," finished Seth.

"Anything else we need to know, Doctor?" Ava asked.

"Not until the labs come back. I'm confident he died from exsanguination. Whether or not there was a chemical element involved remains to be seen. The trace evidence is ready to be sent to the FBI lab. I'm including the ropes and padding. Nail scrapings, residue samples, hair combings. He was pretty clean from my view, but I'm curious to know what you find on a microscopic level. Someone at least *tried* to clean up any evidence."

Ava gave a confident grin. "They always think they've eliminated the evidence."

· · ·

"This has been a long day," Mason stated, stretching his arms above his head. Ava heard his back crack as he twisted it back and forth.

"Definitely," she agreed, and took another sip of wine. The two of them sat in Mason's warm living room with a fire crackling in the fireplace and the dog softly snoring beside them on the sofa. It'd be a typical romantic evening in most homes, except for the paperwork strewn across the coffee table and the crime scene pictures on their two laptops.

Ava enlarged the photo of the odd white shape on Carson Scott's back. Something danced just out of her memory as she tried to make sense of the pattern.

Is it simply a flower?

She rotated the photo, hoping the change would shake its identity loose in her brain.

"That's driving me batshit," added Mason, glancing at her screen. "It looks like a happy daisy embedded in his back. It's wrong on many levels."

"Mmmm," she agreed. She opened up the thumbnails of the hundreds of shots of the scene. "I wish I'd been present at the scene on the bridge." She slowly clicked through the pictures. Again.

"I don't get it," Mason muttered to himself as he read the report from the medical examiner. "Why did someone risk hanging the guy? Who is he sending a message to?"

Ava nodded. If they knew the answer to that question, they'd have their suspect. "The list of people to talk to is growing. We have phone interviews scheduled with his staffers from back East. There's his friends and family in the area. We still haven't been able to track his movements on his last day. Hopefully the computer forensics guys can tell us when he last emailed or was online."

"No luck tracing his phone?" Mason asked.

"No. According to his wireless carrier, it's off. We've got the ball rolling to get his cell phone records from the last few days and to see what cell towers picked up his location. The command center might have received this information by now. We'll know more in the morning."

"People will start coming forward with sightings of him from yesterday or the day before."

"Yes, the evening newscast will definitely trigger more calls. Then we get to sort the nuts from the real reports." Ava almost wished Carson Scott's death hadn't been made public. Her office had told her the hotline had lit up after the early news. She was thankful she wasn't on the phone taking tip after tip. It was going to be bad enough investigating them all. Luckily, with the task force that was coming together with the FBI, Oregon State Police, Portland police, and Vancouver police, there should be plenty of manpower.

"Ray just forwarded me the bridge video he got from the transportation department," Mason said. He clicked on his keyboard and leaned closer to his screen. Ava slid across the couch and pressed against his side for a good look. The clip loaded and they were treated to a calm black-and-white scene with the occasional vehicle crossing the bridge.

"Which way are we looking?" Ava narrowed her brows.

"West. The one-way traffic is moving away from us."

She studied the cars. The image quality was too poor for her to identify most of the makes or models, let alone get a plate number. Finally a white van passed under the camera and crossed the span, slowing as it reached the end of the huge arc that covered most of the bridge. "Dammit. We're too far away," she muttered. The van pulled to the side of the road and switched on its flashers. A few more cars crossed, ignoring the van off to the side. A figure stepped out of the driver's door and set up two construction cones behind the truck. Ava and Mason both leaned closer.

He was simply a silhouette. The camera was at least a hundred yards away.

"No one's going to look twice at a van with cones. What's on the rear cargo doors? It looks like some sort of logo?" Ava asked without taking her gaze from the screen.

"Too far to tell."

He wouldn't use a van that told us who he is. The logo is probably fake or misleading.

The driver slid open the side door closest to the edge of the bridge. The driver stopped and stared off the side of the bridge toward the water and city. He leaned over the side, looking down. Ava sucked in a breath, expecting someone else to leap out of the van and push him over. Even at this distance, she could tell he was perilously close to falling.

"What the hell's he doing? Admiring the view?" Mason swore under his breath.

The driver vanished into the van, reappeared, and worked at the rail of the bridge.

He stepped back, checked the traffic, and then moved into the van. He appeared seconds later with a large burden. He awkwardly flung part of it up on the rail and gave it a push. Wasting no time, he grabbed the cones and flung them into the van. His right blinker politely flashed as he merged into a lane and drove toward the city.

Mason and Ava both leaned back into the couch cushions. "Holy shit, that was fearless," said Mason, shaking his head. He restarted the video.

Ava watched, wondering what was going through their suspect's mind. "He had to know there would be a camera. He probably knew exactly where it was, but there was no way to choose a place on the bridge that wouldn't be caught on film. He managed to pick a location about as far away as he could but still get the punch of hanging Scott from nearly the highest point."

"I want to know why he leaned over so far. I thought he was going to try to fly," Mason added. "Your BAU department is going to have a blast picking this guy's brain apart."

"Methodical, prepared, and cautious," commented Ava. "But then there's that moment where he lets go and simply enjoys the height and thrill." She shuddered. "Heights and I aren't friends. No thrills for me."

Mason looked at her. "I didn't know that. Like bad enough to avoid ladders and amusement park rides?"

"Tall ladders, yes. Amusement park rides don't bother me. Unless they go upside down. I won't ride on anything that takes me upside down." She watched the clip silently play out. "I hope they can make out the logo. It's probably fake, but whatever is on there will give BAU some more fodder to chew on."

"Could just be a stolen van," Mason surmised.

Ava considered that. "I think that's too risky. I bet it's his. Or belongs to someone who doesn't mind him using it. I'm sure our tech guys are already working on this video, trying to get a plate and make on the van."

"We need to check the nearby camera views for passing shots, too."

She nodded. "Hopefully they can catch a clearer view."

Mason started the clip for a third time and they silently watched it together.

She and Mason often spent their evenings discussing cases. While she'd been off the job recovering, listening to him talk about his daily work had kept her sane. To feel human and not useless, she had a need to process and discover and think and speculate. It was essential for her to feel like she was constantly moving forward, not spinning her wheels. Her return to the job had brought her own cases into their evening quiet time. Other couples might go to movies, but she and Mason liked to dig into their files and break them down together.

What is wrong with us?

Or were they perfect for each other? She hid a smile. The lawman-cowboy had turned out to be the yin to her yang. He exuded a confident, relaxed state that helped keep her occasional emotional turmoil under control. He rarely allowed his feathers to ruffle; she was learning to do the same.

Bingo shoved his muzzle under her elbow and rested his head in her lap, creating an effective block to her keyboard. She ruffled his silky ears, and he gave a soft doggie sigh. Ava wasn't the only one who'd recently found a quiet haven under Mason Callahan's wing.

"Have I mentioned I enjoy our evenings together?" she asked.

Mason didn't look up from his screen. "One time or a dozen. Your previous life must have been really dull if this is pleasurable."

"No, I was usually working by myself and stressing over Jayne— Oh! I didn't tell you I got a call about her this morning." She updated him about Jayne's latest job loss.

He shook his head. "Are you sure you're twins?"

"Right now the resemblance is a bit lacking."

He grinned at that. He'd seen the old photos in which Jayne was clearly her identical twin.

"You'd look more like her these days if you unnecessarily lost twenty pounds, dyed your hair platinum blond, and couldn't hold your hands still while you talked. She'll never have your voice, though." He gave her an admiring look.

It'd taken her decades to accept her voice. It was low and a bit throaty. All her life, men had responded to it like she was some phone-sex worker.

"Are you worried about her?" Mason asked, setting his laptop on the coffee table and reaching for his bottle of beer.

"No more than usual, I guess. It never surprises me to hear she lost another job, but I haven't gotten a text or a call since she came to the hospital on Christmas. That's a bit of a long stretch for her. She must have found a man that occupies her time." *Or keeps her stoned nonstop.* "She'll reach out when she wants something."

"Yeah, like another car to steal and wreck." He mashed his lips together.

His sense of honor had been shocked when Jayne "borrowed" and totaled Ava's sedan the previous year. Ava had been angry, but not as stunned as she could have been. Jayne had stopped surprising her long ago. If she let Jayne's actions get to her, she'd have multiple ulcers. She took a large swallow of her wine. "Did I tell you about the time my mother broke up with one of her boyfriends?"

Mason looked up, instantly interested. Her childhood with her nutty twin and single mother contrasted with his stable, rural, working-class background.

"I don't know how long they'd been together. My mother's relationships rarely lasted more than a few months. This must have been a long one because she let him take us out for ice cream on his own. But I guess it was circling the drain because first he took us to get our hair cut."

"Oh crap." Distrust filled Mason's gaze. "What happened?"

"We were about four. We both had long, dark hair that my mom would braid or put in ponytails. He told the hairdresser to cut it short." She swallowed the lump in her throat. "We looked like little boys. He promised us the ice cream if we sat still for the haircuts. I can still see my long hair on the floor under the chair."

"That's simply cruel," Mason said softly.

"My mother cried when he brought us home. Then she screamed at him, and he smiled and left. Her tears made Jayne and me cry. I thought I'd done something wrong. I didn't understand that adults could be so mean. I remember wearing headbands with bows and flowers for a long time after that as she tried to make us look girly." Her voice shook, and she stared at the fire.

She hadn't rehashed that incident in a long time. Shame washed over her as fresh as when she was a child, and it kicked her in the gut. Stress-triggered adrenaline pounded through her limbs. She started to drain her wineglass and abruptly set it down.

No superficial help.

She wasn't Jayne. She didn't drown her emotions and fears in drugs and alcohol.

It's your first glass; lighten up.

One glass was her limit. Always.

Jayne was proof that Ava had the genetics to fall into addiction. They had identical DNA. Only by the grace of God was Ava not an addict. She glanced at Mason. He'd watched her set down the wineglass.

"You are not her," he stated, holding her gaze. It was his mantra for Ava. He knew becoming her twin was her greatest fear.

Wired stress still pulsed through her body from the shameful childhood memory. Part of her brain screamed for her to drink to bury the memory, make it vanish. Instead Ava pulled the memory back out and studied it. "He shouldn't have done that to children."

"No, he shouldn't have. And it was aimed at your mother. It wasn't a punishment for you." He spoke slowly, emphasizing his words, awareness of her anxiety in his gaze.

She licked her lips, willing the quivering in her gut to settle. Mason reached for her. She shoved her computer and Bingo off her legs and crawled onto his lap, burying her face in his neck and inhaling deeply. His masculine scent quieted her, and she wanted to crawl under his clothing to feel his skin touch hers. She pressed her lips against his throat, feeling the tiny prickle of stubble. Her hand slid under the collar at the back of his neck, and she massaged his shoulder. She felt his body suddenly attune to her needs.

"Are we done with work for the evening?" she asked, feeling the two of them fall into harmony.

"Absolutely."

He wrapped an arm under her legs and pushed to his feet, lifting her in his arms as he stood. She clung to his neck and held his brown gaze.

"It's bedtime."

6

Mason had been inside the Portland FBI offices a few times. They were in a large, modern-looking building with manicured grounds and a serious metal fence. He'd now gone through the small security shack, where two guards had scanned him and checked his weapon. Then one of the guards had walked him to the front doors of the main building and politely told him to have a nice day. Ava had met him in the lobby and escorted him up in the elevator to the command center.

The large room was full of computer stations. Half of which were already manned and collecting information. A wall of windows let in the February sunshine, trying to convince employees that it was warmer than forty degrees outside. Mason's goal this morning was to find out what the FBI had gleaned overnight. ASAC Ben Duncan nodded at Mason from across the room, where he was deep in discussion with three other agents. Mason felt a sense of déjà vu from December, when Duncan and the FBI had set up a command center in Lake Oswego while they searched for his ex-wife's stepdaughter.

The FBI had the power to throw a ton of resources at a crime, which Mason's state department did not. A tiny piece of him resented that he and Ray would have done all the legwork of the initial investigation if Carson Scott had turned out to be Joe Public. Instead Scott's position and death commanded the strongest investigative force in the country.

Mason put away his ego. Anyone who could solve Carson Scott's murder was more than welcome. This morning he was to sit in on the interview with McKenna Drake, the woman Scott had seen a movie with the evening before he vanished. He followed Ava to a smaller room down the hall from the command center. Inside, McKenna was already talking with Zander Wells.

McKenna Drake was stunning, and Mason tried not to stare when she glanced up at him with huge turquoise eyes. *Contacts?* The eye color was definitely unusual, but Mason had a hunch that it was real. The woman's black hair was long and styled in the thick, loose ringlets that movie stars wore these days. She was tanned, and glowed with that "I'm an athlete" sheen that hard-exercising people in their twenties often displayed. Upon closer inspection he noticed her eyes and nose were red. She clenched a tissue in her hand, and Zander had placed the tissue box within easy reach.

"Ms. Drake was just telling me that she's known Carson Scott for about a year. They met at a fund-raiser and have gone out socially a few times," Zander explained.

"Call me McKenna, please."

Mason and Ava pulled out chairs and sat. "Did you talk to or receive any messages from Carson after your movie?" Mason asked. The beautiful woman shook her head.

"Did Carson ever mention to you any fears or worries he had for his safety?"

"He was always worried."

"He was?"

"Yes," McKenna stated. "Everywhere we went, he was concerned about who was trying to take his picture or shake his hand. He hated having people approach him in public when he wasn't 'on the clock.'" She made air quote marks with her hands.

Mason raised a brow at Ava. This sounded like a different man from the one Nissa Roberts had worked with. According to her, he had been a devoted public servant. But she'd admitted he had been done with politics. Maybe she'd downplayed his actual feelings about being in the public eye.

"Was he like that before the scandal last fall?" Ava asked.

McKenna tipped her head in thought. "I'd say it got worse after that. He didn't want to go out much last fall. He was terrified of being seen in public with me even though I was single." She wrinkled her nose. "He wasn't thrilled that I was a dancer for the Blazers, but I have an MBA. Anyone who plays the airheaded cheerleader card with me usually shuts up pretty quick when they find that out."

"It's unusual that you find people with that sort of degree in your profession," Mason agreed.

Turquoise eyes gleamed. "I have a plan. My time as a dancer will support the image of the gym and dance studio I plan to run. My name will be synonymous with fitness."

"Was being seen with Carson part of that plan?" Ava asked quietly. "The sight of a good-looking congressman on your arm can get someone a lot of publicity. Especially a man that the tabloids and reporters like to talk about?"

McKenna's gaze rapidly shifted to anger, and Mason was thankful he wasn't sitting in Ava's chair. Ava deflected the visual blow with a raised brow. Clearly she'd been expecting the reaction. Guilt flashed across McKenna's face as she realized she'd let her buttons get pushed.

"It may have started like that. He's famous and powerful. Who wouldn't want to be seen with him? But once I got to know him, I genuinely liked him. He's one of the good ones, you know? Down to earth." She gave a small laugh, flashing perfectly white teeth. "He went into politics because he actually thought he could help people." Her voice cracked, and she visually deflated. "I liked Carson. He was fun."

"Did it bother you that he dated other women?" Zander asked.

McKenna snorted softly. "It did. Any woman would want to be exclusive with him. But he made it clear he wasn't looking for a relationship. He was a good friend who'd call when he was in town."

"Any odd occurrences during your evening out a few days ago?" Mason asked. "Did anyone unusual bother him? Did he seem stressed over something? Did he mention having to meet someone the next day?"

"I've racked my brain trying to remember anything like that. I knew he had a town-hall-type meeting to attend the next day, but he didn't seem stressed about it. Nothing out of the ordinary happened during that night."

"What time did you last see him?" Zander asked, making a note on his pad.

"It was around eleven. He dropped me off at my place. We'd gone to the restaurant after the movie and had a few drinks and a bite to eat. He wasn't drunk at all," she added hastily. "Neither of us was."

"Which vehicle was he driving?" continued Zander.

"The Ford Explorer."

Mason flipped back through his pages of notes and looked at Ava and Zander, who were doing the same thing with their notes. "I don't have an Explorer registered to him. There wasn't one at his place, either." He swore. "At least not in his parking spaces. We need to check the lot's other spaces. What color was it?" he asked McKenna.

"Umm . . . silver, I think."

"He has a BMW Three Series registered. And it was at his place when we were there," Ava added. "Had you seen the Explorer before, McKenna?"

"I don't think so. Seems like he usually drives the BMW."

Zander pulled out his phone and stepped out of the room.

"He's requesting the lot at Carson's condo be checked for the vehicle," Ava explained to McKenna, who nodded.

Zander immediately stuck his head back inside. "We've got another body hanging from a different bridge. Let's go."

. . .

"We're in the middle of nowhere," muttered Ava. She pulled her coat collar tighter around her neck. It had to be ten degrees cooler out here than in the bustling city of Portland.

This time their killer had picked a quiet country bridge instead of the busy center of the biggest city in Oregon. It'd taken her over an hour to drive to the location. Several things were consistent with the first murder. The victim was a white male who appeared to be in his thirties. He was naked, hanging off the bridge, hands and feet bound, and had the odd circular daisy pattern on his back. The main differences were the rural location and the ball gag in the victim's mouth.

Kids in the rural city of Vernonia had found the body two hours before. The bridge stood in a quiet wooded area on the edge of town. It was a typical-looking, green-painted metal truss bridge that supported two lanes of traffic. A narrow concrete sidewalk lined each side and gave a leafy view of a microscopic creek below.

Small crowds of locals had gathered behind the yellow tape at each end of the bridge, watching the FBI, the Oregon State Police, and the tiny Vernonia police force. Ava counted four Vernonia police officers and wondered if that was the extent of the department. The local officers seemed to gravitate toward Mason, asking him questions about the Portland death, and tiptoeing around her and Zander, who wore jackets with FBI emblazoned across the back.

It must have been his cowboy hat and boots. More familiar.

Ava focused on the victim at her feet.

Do we have a serial killer?

The question reverberated in her head.

Generally the definition of a serial killer included three victims. But the common elements between the two deaths had Ava wondering who was next. "Did anyone recognize him?" she asked the local cop behind her. He didn't look older than twenty-three, and she attributed the lack of color in his face to the sight of the body. He shook his head and swallowed hard before speaking.

"No, ma'am. We all took a good look and no one knows him. Between the four of us we know most folks around here. He's not a politician? We figured he'd be another famous guy."

Ava carefully studied the face, seeking something familiar. Death steals the character and leaves its victim an empty shell. The physical features remain, but the personality is gone and with it his essence, that vital piece of the person that distinguished him from the masses. Death evens out the playing field.

She didn't recognize him.

"He doesn't look familiar to me, either," said Seth Rutledge. The medical examiner was beside her on one knee, peering closely at the ball gag.

"You didn't mind the drive out here to examine this case?" she asked him.

"Heck no. As soon as I heard another guy had been hung from a bridge, I wouldn't let anyone else come. This one's piqued my curiosity."

She understood how he felt.

"What do you see?" Ava asked the doctor, wanting his first impressions.

"It's a lot like before. It appears to be the same type of tape and padding around the wrists. I checked and his wrists were slit in the same way as the first body," Dr. Rutledge said grimly. "The lividity is on his back, so once again he was undisturbed while he lay on his back for several hours after he died. And you saw the blanched floral pattern, right?" He glanced to see her nod and went on. "It's similar to the one on Carson Scott's back. What's new is the ball gag. I don't want to take it out until we have him back in the office."

"Seen many of those?" Ava asked quietly.

Dr. Rutledge gave her an amused glance. "Every time I think I've seen it all, something new surprises me. People cram anything in every possible orifice. But yes, I've seen ball gags. Not always in the mouth."

Ava snorted. "Nice. Thanks a lot. There's a mental picture I can't get rid of."

"It adds a sexual element to the crime that wasn't present at the other. Although the tied hands and feet could also indicate an interest in bondage that I hadn't considered at the Scott autopsy. There wasn't any sign of sexual activity with Scott," added Dr. Rutledge. "Of course I'll check to see if the killer took it further than is at first obvious here."

Rape? Her stomach churned.

Mason squatted on her other side. "The local police say there aren't any cameras around, and so far no one claims they saw a vehicle stopped near the bridge. I told them to ask about vans passing through, saying it's a logical vehicle for transporting a body. I didn't tell them white. I don't think we should put that fact out yet."

"Agreed," said Zander from the other side of the body. "If we have to, we can distribute the video of the Fremont Bridge to the networks, but doing it this early is going to create a mudslide of false white van sightings."

"Any idea on the time of death, Dr. Rutledge?" Mason asked.

"I can tell you he died yesterday. I assume he was hung off the bridge in the middle of the night or early morning. I'll get you a closer time frame by tomorrow. I'd say the timeline resembles the Scott case in that he was dumped about the same number of hours after his actual death."

"So while Portland was being shocked by the death of a congressman, our guy was quietly preparing his next victim," Ava stated. "It has to have been done by the same guy. We haven't released enough details for someone to imitate the first death. This scene is too close to be a copycat."

"Unless someone talked," added Zander. "A lot of people got a look at Carson Scott. Cops, crime scene techs. I'm not ruling out a copycat yet."

"I think the lab reports will state the tape and padding came from the same source. It looks damned close to my eye," said Dr. Rutledge. "Those two things should strongly indicate this man was killed by the same person who murdered Carson Scott."

"I wonder if the victims knew each other," Ava said. "They look close to the same age. Both clean-cut. Decent shape."

"This boy is blue-collar," said Dr. Rutledge. "He's no politician."

All three investigators looked at the medical examiner expectantly. Dr. Rutledge uncurled the body's stiff fingers, and they nodded in agreement. The man's hands were black under the fingernails and in the lines. The palms and fingers were heavily calloused. Ava leaned closer and sniffed. "Cars. I can smell oil or tires. He works on cars. Daily."

"Yep," said Mason. "Hard to get that stuff off. Smells more like tires to me."

"Definitely not a politician," said Zander. He pulled a notebook out of his pocket and made a notation.

"How are we going to identify this one?" Mason questioned. "Ask for missing mechanics?"

"This guy has a tattoo," the examiner pointed out. Seth shifted the right leg to expose the back of the calf. The skin was dark purple with lividity, but Ava could see the outline of a dragon. "You can release that information. That should narrow down the missing person reports."

Ava exchanged a glance with Mason and Zander. Both men nodded.

"I'll have the office put the word out," she said.

Who are you? And why did he kill you, too?

7

Mason parked on the street in front of his home and watched in his rearview mirror as Ava guided her bureau vehicle into the driveway. He'd never parked in his single-car garage because it was too crowded for a vehicle. When Ava had started spending the night, he'd given up his driveway parking space for her car.

If he parked behind her, she'd be trapped if she needed to leave in the middle of the night.

It was one of the small changes he'd made to ease her way into his life. It wasn't a big deal. In fact, altering his bachelor frame of mind to relearn how to live with a woman hadn't taken much effort. At one time he'd liked being married and meshing his life with a woman's. His ex-wife had rarely had complaints; she'd simply hated that he worked so much. She'd felt like a single parent raising their son.

She'd been right.

With Ava it was just the two of them. They both worked crazy hours and looked forward to the moments they did have together.

He liked the softer element she'd brought to his life. Now his towels matched. His couch had useful pillows and warm throws.

Every night she set the coffeepot to brew, so he woke up to fresh coffee and someone to drink it with. When he'd lived alone, he could
have programmed the pot, but he'd always forgotten and never
wanted to wait for it to brew. He'd usually hit the drive-through
coffee place.

He couldn't explain how it felt to share the nice little things with
someone.

Who would have thought that sharing a cup of coffee in the
morning would be one of the highlights of his day?

She stepped out of her car, and it struck him how beautiful
she was. She wasn't glamorous; she was girl-next-door wholesome.
Dark-blue eyes and a warm smile. She usually kept her brown hair
in a conservative ponytail for work. When she was home, she let it
down so it constantly got in her eyes, and she'd impatiently tuck it
behind her ears. As soon as Mason had professionally worked with
her clever mind and heard her low laugh, he'd been hooked tighter
than a cat's claw in a knitted throw. She was the whole package.

So why is she with you?

He stomped on the annoying fear. It cropped up occasionally,
but when she smiled at him and held his gaze, his stomach did weird
happy things and that one fear vanished.

The age difference doesn't matter.

Now she gave him one of those smiles as she waited for him
in the driveway and the misting rain dotted her hair with sparkles
from the streetlight. They'd stopped at a nearby pub for a quick dinner after a long day of following leads on Carson Scott. The second
body still didn't have a name, but the evening news had brought up
the calf tattoo, and he knew the body would be identified within a
few hours.

"Zander called me on my way home," Ava said as he approached.
"Dr. Rutledge let him know that the second victim wasn't sexually
assaulted. In fact, he believes the ball gag was placed after the victim
was dead."

Mason made a face. "So what was the point of the ball gag?"

"That's what we need to find out." She gave him a kiss and took his hand, leading him to the front door. It was nearly ten P.M. Bed sounded tempting.

They stepped into the house and Mason waited for Bingo to come do his skittering welcome-home happy-dog dance across the wood floor.

No dog.

"Bingo?" Ava called as she unwrapped the scarf from her neck. "Jeez. It's freezing in here."

She was right, but Mason could hear the furnace running. *Did the pilot light go out?* It was rare but it happened. "Bingo!"

A distant bark drew him through the house to the rear door in the kitchen. Bingo was on the back deck, barking to be let in. Someone had slid the short bookshelf from his dining nook in front of the doggie door, effectively blocking it. Three of the small glass panes in the upper half of the door were shattered, letting in the icy air. Mason drew his weapon.

Someone has been in my house.

He quietly moved out of the kitchen and gazed down the hallway to the three bedrooms and two bathrooms. His house wasn't big. One level. And he'd already seen that the living areas were clear. His ears strained as he listened for someone moving in a bedroom.

"Mason?" Ava froze, spotting him focused down the hall. She was beside him in a split second, her weapon ready. "What happened?" she asked quietly.

"Bingo's doggie door is blocked from inside. Someone broke the glass to get inside."

"Can you hear anything?" she asked softly.

"No."

He listened for another five seconds. "Hey!" he said loudly. "You've made the stupid mistake of breaking into the home of a police officer who has his weapon aimed your way. Come out of the room backward. Hands where I can see them."

Silence.

He repeated his order.

Blood pounding in his head, he started to move down the hall. Ava followed.

One bathroom checked. Two bedrooms checked.

The door to his master suite was closed. "God damn it," he whispered, staring at the hollow core door. It was always open. Hugging the wall, he reached across the door, turned the handle, and pushed the door open. It silently swung in and the mirror above his dresser reflected a view of an empty room. Minus his big-screen TV.

He exhaled.

A quick check of the bathroom and closet and under the bed confirmed that no one was in his home.

He stared at the empty TV brackets on the wall, his mouth in a tight line.

Call the police.

"Shit," swore Ava. She opened the nightstand drawer on her side of the bed. "My necklace is gone. The one with a ring on the chain. It was my mother's. It wasn't worth much but it's all . . ." Her voice trailed off and an odd look crossed her face.

"What is it?"

"Jayne took it," she said matter-of-factly. She'd wiped all emotion from her face. "If I find out she sold it . . ."

"You think she did this?" Would Ava's sister break into a home just to take a necklace? His gaze went back to the empty wall. And a TV?

"How'd she know where I was staying? Oh, dammit. I need to go check my own place. Fuck! I wonder what she's done there!" She pressed the heels of her hands against her eyes. "She doesn't understand that *you don't steal*! Not from anyone! But God damn it, you really don't *steal from your sister*!"

She was shaking. Mason crossed the room and pulled her into his arms. "We can't be certain it was her. Besides, you know she's not right in the head."

"I know! But it still hurts! I need to fix it. She can't live like this! She's obviously with someone who's pressuring her to come up with money. She couldn't have taken your TV alone; someone was with her. It's the drugs. She's using again and now she's stealing to support her habit. I've got to get her back in rehab."

Mason doubted rehab was the answer. Ava had already paid twice for her twin to attend with no results. "Let's make a police report and let them deal with it. Do you have a neighbor you can call to check your windows and doors first?"

"Yes." Ava pulled out her phone and wiped her nose. "Dammit, she makes me so angry!"

Mason kissed her cheek. He placed a call to the non-emergency police number and reported the break-in. He slipped on some vinyl gloves and did a quick check of his own drawers and the closet. Someone had emptied his mug of loose change and clearly rooted through his clothing, searching for hidden treasure. A series of impatient barks drew him back to the kitchen. He snapped a few photos of the broken glass on the floor and then swept and vacuumed the area. He wasn't concerned about destroying this particular evidence; he primarily didn't want to pick glass out of Bingo's paws. The criminals had left plenty of other evidence behind.

He finally let in the demanding dog. "Some protector you turned out to be." He scratched at the dog's ears. "I bet you welcomed them."

He'd thought twice before installing the doggie door, but with his schedule, he couldn't leave the dog inside all day. He'd bought the smallest door Bingo could fit through. Only a four-year-old could have broken in using the pet door.

But I bet they tried it first. He smiled. There were probably prints all over the frame of the flap. Had his criminals been smart enough to wear gloves? He'd know soon enough.

Ava stepped into the room and Bingo stood on his hind legs, placing his paws on her stomach, begging for attention. She rubbed his chest. "Not a guard dog, are you?" She looked at Mason. "Ready to install that alarm system yet?"

"Why bother? Now I really don't have anything to steal."

"Good thing you carry your laptop with you," she said.

"Damn right." What if this had happened on his day off and he hadn't been home? His work laptop would have been long gone. Maybe he *should* get an alarm system. "I need to check the garage."

She followed him out to the detached garage. "I called my neighbor. She checked my doors and peeked in my windows. Nothing has been disturbed. I guess I don't need to rush over tonight to check my condo."

"You still think Jayne is behind this?"

She sighed. "I don't know. I assume any thief would grab what jewelry he could find. Knowing it was my mother's made me instantly think of Jayne. It wasn't much, just a small sapphire in a gold setting. Was anything else missing in the house?"

"Nope. Whoever it was didn't make much of a score. They got a single TV. I've never been one for buying expensive toys."

He unlocked the heavy door to the garage, thankful there wasn't any glass to allow a break-in. His valuable equipment was here. His ATV and power tools and the gun safe.

"No expensive toys, eh?" Ava rapped a knuckle on the ATV and then pointed at the gun safe. "They'd have to bring in heavy hauling equipment to steal that. What's it weigh?" Ava asked as he opened the safe.

A quick scan told him nothing had been disturbed in the garage or safe. "Nearly a ton."

She snorted.

"Did you try to call your sister?" he asked.

"I tried yesterday after the guy from Party Mart called. Her cell has been disconnected."

"Do you have another way to reach her?"

"No."

Mason closed the safe and turned to look at Ava. She had her arms wrapped around herself as if she were freezing. She wouldn't meet his gaze. "You've had times before when you had no way to get ahold of her, right?"

She nodded. "It makes me feel lost. Like I'm the one out there without a lifeline. I'm here and safe with you while she's flapping around in the wind. I can't help but feel guilty and that I need to do something."

Mason put his arms around her and buried his face in her hair. In the few months he and Ava had been together, he'd seen nothing that ripped her apart the way her twin did. Not a bullet in her arm or gazing at the face of a murdered congressman. It was Jayne who broke her down.

Ava was the strongest woman he'd ever met, but her twin caused fracture lines in her core. Mason ached to fix them, but he was at a loss when it came to Jayne. They'd agreed she should leave her twin to do her own thing. That Ava had gone above and beyond the efforts of any sister or saint in her attempts to help. But Jayne still reeled her in.

He didn't know what to do.

Mason heard a car pull up out front and the faint crackle of a police radio. He kissed the top of her head. "We'll find her."

• • •

At work the next morning, Ava checked to see what sort of hits she'd received on her VICAP search. She'd plugged in the basics of Carson Scott's murder, searching the country-wide violent crime database for other post-death hangings in which the wrists had been slit and the limbs bound.

Nothing.

Congratulations. You have the start of an original freak show in your town.

She scowled and finished off the latte she'd bought at the Starbucks down the street. She decided to make another request, specifying the second body's ball gag and slit wrists. Perhaps her first search had been too narrow. Her brain felt divided into a hundred pieces. That was normal for her workday, but today a huge piece labeled Jayne was occupying a larger section than it deserved.

Ava had stopped by her condo before work. Her neighbor had been right. Her place hadn't been touched. Maybe she'd jumped to conclusions about Jayne. She'd packed more clothing to add to the growing wardrobe she kept at Mason's, and she'd glanced through a few bare cupboards and wondered if she should sell her home.

A small chill touched her spine. It was a big step. A topic she and Mason had danced around for the last few weeks. She'd originally "moved in" because she needed help with her injury. And because she'd fallen head over heels for the detective. She suspected the bullet in her shoulder had simply sped up the timeline.

Four weeks ago he'd told her he loved her, and she'd immediately returned the sentiment. She'd known she was in love with him since before she'd been shot, but had been too scared to be the first person to say it. Her last relationship had soured in a mighty big way. She'd been burned and reluctant to play the game again. Especially with another cop.

Now she'd jumped in with both feet.

Should I sell?

"Shit." She filed the question away for later. She didn't have to make a decision right now. But did Mason believe she wasn't selling her place because she thought the relationship would fail?

Of course he didn't. They'd been together a little more than two months. He had to expect her to keep her place a while longer. They could use it as a rental. Maybe Jayne needed—

Stop!

The last type of renter they needed was one like her sister.

Did Jayne break into Mason's house?

Zander stopped at the entry to her office. "You hear the identity of the second body?"

"No, what do they have?" Ava's brain rapidly shifted gears back to the murders.

"Last evening a woman called the tip line whose ex-husband has a tattoo on the back of his calf. She'd called his work and he hadn't shown up Sunday or Monday. She gave me the name of the dentist to forward to the medical examiner to request digital dental films."

Zander's bright eyes told her he was saving the best morsel of the story for last.

She bit. "Where's he work?"

"Universe of Tires."

"Sounds like a good match. Did he work or live out toward Vernonia?"

"No. That's the odd part. He actually lives in Oregon City, and his store is even farther south in Canby. Someone made a special trip to take him all the way to Vernonia."

"Possibly that's our unsub's stomping ground. You said the woman is the ex-wife? So she doesn't know what he's been up to for the last few days."

Zander leaned against her doorjamb and crossed his arms. "That's right. Her name is Laura King. I called her back last night after the lead first came in and asked. She said he's been staying with a friend and gave me his number. She also emailed me a photo. I think we found her ex-husband, Aaron King."

"Show me," Ava requested. She got up and followed Zander back to his desk and waited while he pulled up his email. He opened a photo of a man holding a huge salmon on the deck of a fishing boat on a gorgeous sunny day. "Oh, I think you're right."

The man grinned at the camera, proud of his catch. Life shone in his eyes, but Ava recognized the facial features of the body they'd found the day before. "His hair is a bit longer in the photo." She leaned closer to the screen and pointed at his lower leg. "Is that some of the dragon's tail coming around the side of his leg?"

"I noticed that, too. Yes, our guy's tattoo shows up that much when viewed from the front."

Ava sighed. "What're his stats?"

"Assistant manager at Canby Universe of Tires. Age thirty-five. No kids. Divorce was finalized less than a month ago."

Hearing "no kids" made Ava feel the tiniest bit relieved. Her brain started to process the new man's information. Carson Scott had also been single with no kids. Close in age and build. "Did you ask Laura if Aaron knew Carson Scott?"

"I haven't. She's going to be here soon for an interview, and then we can start putting the pieces together." He spoke faster in his excitement.

Ava felt it, too. They'd just moved a step closer to finding out who their killer was.

"Did you hear the president made a statement about Carson Scott?" Zander asked.

"No. But that makes sense considering his position. What'd he say?"

"Hardly anything. 'We're saddened, yada yada, praying for his family, yada yada.' He didn't even go on camera. He simply did a press release."

"What? For the death of a member of Congress? That seems a little cold."

"You haven't read what the public is saying about the case online, have you?"

"Oh, crap. I can just imagine what's being said. I know better than to look online. You shouldn't read that stuff, either. Are they accusing the other political party of having him murdered? Or was it done by terrorists?"

"No, the rumor that's flying around in cyberspace is that it was a twisted sex crime."

Ava wished she were surprised. "Because he was naked, right? People really need to get over themselves. Is that why the president simply did a press release?"

"Probably. When the second body turned up, the stories and comments shot into overdrive. Bondage and S&M and all sorts of weird suggestions are circulating about the two men together. I suspect the president is putting some distance between himself and Carson Scott. His aides are probably worried that a political scandal will be associated with Scott's death."

"We don't even know if the two victims crossed paths!" Ava fumed. "Some days I hate the Internet, I really do."

"There are a lot of bored people out there who like to add their two cents to everything."

"Is there a press conference scheduled?" she asked.

"Yes, Duncan set one up for tomorrow. He got calls from both the Portland and Vancouver mayors. People are worried there's a serial killer wandering around."

"There is," Ava stated. "Well, we're pretty sure there is. To hell with it. I *know* we've got a serial killer."

"They're calling him the Bridge Killer in the press," added Zander.

"Seriously? A name already?" She thought for a moment. "I wonder if that makes him want to continue to use bridges, or do the exact opposite and change it up. Some people don't like their actions taken for granted."

"Hopefully we'll solve this before we find out."

"The question is, 'Who's next?'" said Ava. "Someone doesn't create elaborate scenes for us to find and then simply stop; they're enjoying the attention and our shock."

"It bothers me that the second body was found so soon after the first. Usually there's a bit of a cooling-off period for the killer. If that twenty-four hours was his cooling-off period, I don't want to know what he's like when he's on a roll." Zander shook his head.

Ava's personal phone vibrated. She checked the screen and moaned. "Oh, crap. What's the date today?"

"The eleventh," answered Zander.

"I'm in trouble," she muttered, and moved down the hall for some privacy.

"Hello, Corinne," she answered.

"Ava. Where are you? You're fifteen minutes late."

Ava rubbed her forehead. "I know. I totally forgot our appointment this morning. I don't know if you've watched the news—"

"Do you want full use of that arm or not?" Corinne asked. "You can't miss physical therapy. You're making good progress, and I don't want you to slip behind."

"I've been doing my daily exercises." *Except for the last two days.*

"Uh-huh. I hear that from everyone."

"Do you have an opening tomorrow?" Ava asked. She tentatively moved her left arm, trying some of the movements Corinne had taught her. Pain shot through her arm, and she gasped.

"Testing your arm, Ava?"

"Maybe. Just seeing how things feel."

"Babying your arm isn't doing yourself any favors."

"I know. I've had two murders dumped on my plate in the last few days, so I've been a bit busy," she snapped. "I'm sorry," she immediately added. "I'm frustrated. And I want my arm as close to normal as you do. What about tomorrow?"

"I'm booked solid all week. Let's keep your standing appointment for next week. If I get a cancellation before then, I'll let you know. Don't slack off on your homework this week, or you'll be crying double next week."

Corinne wasn't exaggerating. Ava was driven to tears at least once every session. She ended the call.

I can't miss physical therapy. She carefully moved her arm in a slow, large circle, feeling the healing muscles and bone shoot pain directly into her brain.

She'd never had an injury before. No broken bones, no sprained ankles. This was a new experience, and it affected how she got dressed, how she slept, and how she moved. Every. Single. Day.

In other words, it was a giant pain in the ass.

Zander caught up with her. "Hey," he said. "Aaron King's ex-wife is here. She brought Aaron's roommate with her, which saves us some extra time, and I have a prelim from the medical examiner. You want to take a look before we go talk to them? The dental records have confirmed it's him."

"I'll look while we walk." Ava held her hand out for the paper in his hand. "Who is the roommate?"

"Gordon Oleson."

She scanned the short email from Seth Rutledge. He'd confirmed that the cause of death was exsanguination, and the odontologist had matched the dental films to Aaron King's teeth. Seth had attached a headshot of the victim to show the ex-wife if she wanted to confirm visually. Ava looked it over. Aaron King's skin tone was definitely wrong, but there wasn't anything gory or shocking in the photo. He appeared to be sleeping in bad lighting.

"Think they'll ask to see this?" Ava asked, lengthening her strides to keep up with Zander's long ones.

"I hope not. Let's not offer unless the ex-wife seems to need to see it."

Ava nodded. Some people had to see death to accept it. "I suspect she'll want to go out to the ME's building."

"Has Duncan said anything about you working with Mason? They officially added Mason to the task force, right? Him and his partner, Lusco? I think part of the press conference today is going to show all the departments that are contributing to the search for the congressman's murderer."

"Duncan didn't really say much. He let me know that he was aware of Mason's and Ray Lusco's roles regarding Congressman Scott's murder, but he didn't bring up any concerns over the two of us working together."

"Good. They're working on finding the van, correct?" Zander must have noticed she was nearly running; he slowed down.

Ava caught her breath. "I know that's part of what they're working on today. Their department recently got some great video enhancement software that rivals what ours back East can do. Hopefully they can get some fast results."

"How's the arm?"

"Sore. Stiff. Some days I put my sling back on in the evening to give it a break. It's amazing how bad it can feel after a day of doing absolutely nothing."

He stopped outside the door to the waiting area. "Ready to talk to Ms. King?"

"Absolutely."

8

Mason nodded and tried to look as if he understood what the video technician was talking about. Charley was excited and in full geek-speak mode. He was demonstrating how he'd added and removed layers of the feed to enhance the image, and Mason was about to lose his patience.

Just tell me what you found!

Ray Lusco was also doing a lot of nodding and frowning, but Mason suspected he understood about as much as Mason did. The tech's hands flew across his keyboard, lightening the image and zooming in on the van as it sat parked on the Fremont Bridge.

"This was the best I could do from this angle," Charley stated. The image of their murderer and the back of the van suddenly filled the screen and the killer slid open the side door to his van. Charley froze the video as the man turned in the direction of their camera.

Mason leaned closer. The killer was still just a shadow. He couldn't make out any features except his nose and chin. "You can't get any more?"

Charley shook his head. "From this shot our guys say he's about six feet two and two hundred pounds. The cap he's wearing makes hair color hard to guess."

"We don't want guesses," muttered Ray. "We also can't tell what he's wearing. What's the make of the van?"

"Ford Econoline. Relatively new. We haven't narrowed the year yet because there's been little change in their body style."

"What about the license plates?" asked Mason.

"Unreadable," said Charley. "I think there's something blurring them. Maybe a plastic cover? Whatever is over them is enough to look normal if he's driving past you, but makes any enhancement from a distance impossible."

Our killer is a planner.

"And I can't read what it says on the back door of the van in this clip. The logo is actually words, not just an image," said Charley.

Mason could hear the glee in the tech's voice; he clearly had something good to share.

"*But* I found a view from a traffic camera on the 405 freeway right after he drove off the bridge," added Charley. "I've been working with that one, and I think I've got something."

"Good. I knew they were searching camera footage in the immediate area. Did they spot him anywhere else?"

"So far they've only discovered this one extra clip." Charley set another video in motion, and Mason watched as a white van sped by, the driver's side to the camera.

"The logo was on the driver's door, too," Mason stated. "Not just on the back."

"Now watch." Elation rolled off the tech.

On the screen the van abruptly froze, enlarged, lost its grainy quality, and came into decent focus. Ray moved closer to the screen to read the print on the driver's door. "Oh, crap."

Mason briefly closed his eyes. Portland didn't need this.

He'd read CITY OF PORTLAND in big type on the door, with THE

CITY THAT WORKS below that. He couldn't make out the two small red roses that framed the phone number on the third line, but he knew they were there. He'd seen the logo a thousand times on city vehicles.

"I'll find out if they're missing any vehicles." Ray pulled out his cell phone and stepped out of the video room.

"They might not have any missing vehicles," said Charley. "Perhaps there'll be no oddities in their logs at all if this guy works for the city and regularly drives a van."

"You think he put something over the license plate but didn't do anything about the logo? I bet he had some of those magnetic car decals made up. Or he stole them. He knew good and well that we'd see the city logo on the van, so I suspect that lead won't go anywhere. What he managed to keep hidden were the plates. Why?" Mason stared at Charley.

"Because they're actually relevant?" he said slowly.

"Bingo. Now to figure out why. Either he owns the van or knows the person who does. Or finding the actual van will tie to him *somehow*." Mason's mind sorted through possibilities, wishing they had video from Aaron King's murder. He looked at the image of the side of the van again. The driver was barely visible.

"That doesn't help us identify the driver, does it?"

Charley shook his head. "I've tried everything. I've even got a call in to the developer of this software to see if there's a trick I'm not aware of, but I wouldn't hold my breath."

"Can you show the part where he's leaning over the edge of the bridge again?"

The tech nodded and tapped his keys. Mason watched as the killer leaned way out over the water. "Can you get closer?" More key tapping, and the image zoomed in. Charley made some adjustments to the graininess of the shot, then sliced out those ten seconds of video and set them on a slow loop to run over and over. Their killer remained a faceless silhouette, only the profile of his nose and chin visible, but Mason could feel the man's excitement from the height and risk of his position.

"Looks like an adrenaline junkie," Charley commented. "He's not scared. Look how he pushes out as far as he can go."

Mason nodded, his gaze never leaving the figure. Why take the risk of stretching out that far? Was he enjoying the thrill of the hunt?

The danger of the position made Mason's stomach drop every time he watched.

Someday he'd ask the killer why.

. . .

Ava liked Laura King, but she didn't like Aaron King's roommate, Gordon Oleson, at all. Not one bit. And Zander seemed to have similar feelings.

Laura had been quietly crying as Zander and Ava guided her and Gordon from the waiting room to an empty interview room to talk. Laura King's damp blue eyes shone with the innocence of a hurt kitten. Gordon had slouched, his hands shoved in the pockets of his pants. Anger and frustration radiated from him.

They'd settled around a large table while Ava and Zander spent a few moments answering Laura and Gordon's questions about Aaron's death. Gordon seemed to get angrier with each question they could not answer. He wanted results. Now.

"We're still investigating," Ava repeated to the man. "His body was just identified this morning, and we had agents and police immediately on the scene. They're still there, interviewing everyone."

"You're probably spending more time on the Scott murder. A congressman is a lot more important than my friend, in the eyes of the FBI."

Ava counted to ten. "Both men are important. And we suspect they were killed by the same man. If we find Carson Scott's killer, we'll find Aaron's."

"If Carson Scott hadn't been a congressman, the FBI wouldn't even be involved," Gordon shot back. "Probably the hick cops from Vernonia would be handling Aaron's death. They couldn't find their ass with a mirror."

"Is that how you'd prefer it?" said Ava. "Do you want us to step away from finding out who killed your friend? Or are you going to give us some help?"

"You're not making any sense," Laura said to Gordon. "Who cares *why* the FBI is involved? They are, and I'm grateful! Now *get over it* and answer their questions."

Ava liked her even more.

Gordon was clearly the type who lashed out in anger when he was upset and didn't pay attention to how ridiculous he sounded.

"I'm very sorry for your loss," she said to Laura, focusing her interview on the woman and letting Gordon stew until he could act like a human. "When was your last contact with Aaron?"

"He'd sent me a text last week, asking if he could swing by Sunday after work to pick up some tools he'd left behind. I agreed, but he never showed up."

"You didn't ask him why he didn't show?"

She shrugged. "You don't know Aaron. He's not reliable. I wasn't surprised that he didn't come by. I learned a long time ago not to make plans based on what he suggests."

Ava wrote the date down on her notepad. Sunday night was the night Carson Scott had been hanged off the bridge. "His boss told you he didn't show up for work on Sunday, right? Nor on Monday?"

"That's correct," Laura said as she glanced at Gordon. "How come you didn't do anything when he didn't return to your place Sunday night?"

Gordon raised one shoulder. "Really? He's an adult. If he decided to spend the night somewhere else, it's none of my business."

Laura flinched and looked away.

Ava exchanged a look with Zander, who lifted a brow. Ava wondered if Aaron had spent the night elsewhere during their marriage without informing his wife.

I've been there, Laura. You did the right thing by throwing him out.

"When did you last see Aaron?" Zander asked Gordon.

"Sunday before he left for work. I was up when he left."

"He didn't mention plans for after work?"

"Nah. I don't think we spoke."

Zander glanced at his notes. "How long's Aaron been living with you?"

"Aaron's been staying on my couch for about a month. He's trying to save to get his own place, but his money gets sucked up by his spousal support." Gordon shot a glare at Laura. She ignored him and stared straight ahead.

The man's anger gave Ava a headache. She was about to separate the two of them and talk to Laura on her own. She and Laura both deserved a break from Gordon.

Zander laid down his pen and leaned forward, holding Gordon's gaze. "I've about had it with your anger directed at us and Laura. She's here to help us figure out what the hell happened to Aaron, but you seem to be here to make a stink about something else. It's time to get over it and use some common courtesy. If you don't want to talk to us, tell me *now.*"

Ava bit her cheek. *Go Zander!*

Gordon stared back at the agent for a full second and then looked down at the table. "Sorry," he muttered.

"Laura, the medical examiner told you he confirmed it was Aaron, right?" Ava asked.

The woman nodded as fresh tears streamed. "Yes, he called me after the dental records were verified."

"I know Zander asked you last night if Aaron knew Carson Scott and you said you didn't think so. What about you, Gordon? Did Aaron ever mention meeting a congressman?"

Gordon shook his head. "I know the mayor of Canby brings her car into his Universe of Tires center. That's the most important person he's told me about."

Ava wondered if Carson had ever needed to get his car serviced in Canby. She scratched a note. Vancouver and Canby were nearly an hour apart. Carson would have needed a good reason to go that far south into Oregon.

It was her job to find that reason.

"Did Aaron have friends in the Vancouver area? People he'd go visit?"

Laura shook her head. "Not that I'm aware of. Neither of us ever went over there."

Ava nodded. It wasn't uncommon for the residents of the Portland metropolitan area to rarely cross the bridges over to Washington. Vancouver was a relatively small city. She'd lived in Portland for two years before she'd crossed the border into Vancouver during a drive to Seattle. Someone could blink and miss it.

"Did Aaron have any enemies? Someone who'd do this?" Zander asked.

Laura and Gordon glanced at each other. Laura shook her head. "Not that I know of. Aaron was pretty easygoing and wasn't the type to anger anyone."

Gordon shifted in his seat. "I know he had an argument with a guy outside of a bar a few weekends back. The guy parked too close to Aaron's truck and dinged the passenger door when he got out. Aaron was in his truck at the time and confronted him. It didn't come to much. Aaron was steamed when he got home, and I know he'd snapped a photo of the guy's license plate, but I think that was the end of it. He didn't mention it again."

"You let our people into your apartment this morning to start their search, right?" Ava asked. "Was Aaron's truck in the lot?" Checking her paperwork revealed Aaron drove a Toyota Tundra.

"His truck hasn't been back since he left for work Sunday morning."

Ava scowled. Carson Scott's vehicle had been left in his lot at his condo. But McKenna had said he'd been driving a silver Ford Explorer, which they still hadn't found. What had their killer done with the men's vehicles?

Ava liked having vehicles involved in her cases. They were hard to hide and often easy to track. Now they were searching for two different ones.

A task force email from Mason that morning had said that the white van on the Fremont Bridge had had a City of Portland logo on the back and side doors. Further digging had revealed no missing vans from the fleet. The fleet manager had stated that several employees drove their vans home, but claimed the one on the bridge wasn't theirs. He could tell by looking at the bumper and wheels. Yes, they used Ford Econolines, but not like that one.

The City of Portland had dozens of the large magnetic sheets featuring the city logo, but tracking them was impossible. The fleet manager had said they were stolen off the vehicles all the time. Most of the vehicles had painted logos, but some used the magnets.

Zander asked Laura and Gordon a few more questions and then thanked and dismissed them. He walked them to the door and then fell into his seat with a sigh. "Gordon is the type of guy who will never get anywhere if he doesn't stop looking for someone to blame for every little thing. Man, I wanted to smack him a few times."

"I know the type," agreed Ava. She scanned the photos of Gordon's apartment that the crime scene techs had just uploaded. "What a shit hole. How do people live like that? Is that a male thing? The women I know clean their dishes occasionally." She turned her laptop for Zander to see. He grimaced at the photos of the filthy kitchen and bathroom. She clicked on another photo of a couch in a living room, with two pillows and a couple of wrinkled blankets. She noticed the pillows didn't have pillowcases. *Dust mites.* "Aaron hasn't slept there since Saturday night and no one's picked up his blankets?"

"Gordon doesn't strike me as the type to be disturbed by a few blankets and pillows."

"Good point."

Plates, cups, and soda cans were stacked on the end table next to the couch. "I hope they find something. I don't care what it is."

"Aaron couldn't be more different from Carson," Zander observed. "These are two very different men, outside of their age."

"We need to figure out where their circles connect. I don't know if we need to be looking deep in their past or in their recent history."

"We've checked the obvious history: schools, cities, jobs, family," said Zander. "Nothing intersects. Both have lived in the Pacific Northwest all their lives; that's about as close as we've come at the first glance. They don't even belong to the same political party."

"Then we slow down and look deeper," said Ava. "Friends and acquaintances are the hard ones to investigate. They're fluid and constantly changing for most people."

"Or they have nothing in common but our killer," Zander said. "We both know that's not how it usually works."

"We'll find the connection." She sighed and stretched to pop her spine.

"What was up this morning? You looked like you wanted to strangle someone when I first saw you."

Ava had to think backward for a brief second. "You haven't heard the latest episode in the story of my twin."

Zander brightened. "Fill me in." Ever since she'd gotten to know Zander on their last case, he'd been interested in her stories of her wild sister. He claimed his family was too boring and he had to live vicariously through hers.

He could have it.

. . .

Ava parked in front of the old apartment building where she'd last picked up Jayne to give her a ride to a "job interview." She sat silently in her car, watching the rain slide down her windshield. She could still turn around. She looked in the rearview mirror and wiped a speck of mascara off her cheek.

Jayne's eyes stared back at her.

She blinked and saw herself again. When they were younger, she'd have days when she wasn't sure where she stopped and Jayne began. Jayne's experiences would become her own. They'd told each other everything, to the point where it felt like they shared the same history.

Later on, she'd realized she'd dreamed about incidents that'd never happened to her; they'd happened to Jayne, but when Jayne had described them, Ava had placed them into joint memory banks. Once she'd explained it to a therapist as a hive collective. Like the Borg on *Star Trek*: each individual mentally dipped into a common cache of memories and claimed it as her own.

If it'd happened to Jayne, then it'd happened to her.

Until things changed. Looking back, Ava believed Jayne's brain had shifted to a different path around puberty. She'd always been the attention seeker and selfish one, but in junior high she'd moved to a different level. Ava had started keeping things to herself, forming her own person, not wanting to be completely connected to a person who wasn't . . . kind.

Ava stepped out of the car and pulled up her coat's hood. Without knowing which apartment her sister had lived in, she searched until she found one with a dirty MANAGER sign next to the door. She knocked and waited. The apartment complex was old and tired. Toddler bikes and plastic garbage bags crowded some of the patios.

The door opened, and a skinny, gray-haired woman peered over her reading glasses at her. The manager sucked in her breath at the sight of her as Ava was smacked in the face with the odor of cat litter boxes. Apparently lots of them.

"It's about time you—" The woman cut off her angry sentence and squinted at Ava. "You're not Jayne." Curiosity spread across her face and she stepped closer.

Ava pushed back her hood, preferring to get her hair wet rather than be mistaken for her twin. She smiled. "No, I'm looking for Jayne. By your reaction to me, I assume she's long gone?"

"Are you a sister?" The woman continued to peer at her face, then swept a gaze over her from head to toe. "You can't be."

"I am her sister. Does she no longer live here?" Ava asked patiently. The woman seemed stunned by Ava's appearance. *How bad does Jayne look?*

"No," the manager said slowly. "She's been gone for at least a month. Skipped out on two months' rent, but at least I got to keep the deposit." She frowned and her eyebrows came together. "I'm entitled to keep the deposit and last month's rent. She's supposed to give notice and she didn't. And it took me a week to get that place back in shape."

Did she break your microwave, too? "I'm not here for money, and I'm sure she owes you quite a bit. I'm just trying to find her. She's vanished and her cell number no longer works. I assume she didn't leave a forwarding address?"

The woman chortled, her eyes crinkling over her glasses. "That girl's not the type to leave a forwarding address. The last thing she wants is for people from her past to keep up with her. She likes a *fresh start*."

Ava flinched at the phrase. Jayne had used it all the time. She was always seeking her next *fresh start* and leaving everything else in a ditch behind her. It was a good sign that Jayne had split for what she believed to be greener pastures. "I see you spent some time talking with Jayne."

"Many times." The manager's face softened. "She's not a bad girl, just misguided."

Ava raised a brow. "For someone she owes money to, you're very kind. You don't have to sugarcoat Jayne for me. I know exactly the type of person my sister is. Count yourself lucky that she didn't burn down a building."

"Do you want to come in for a minute? I can dig out her old application and see if there's something useful on it for you." The manager stepped back, giving Ava a clear view into her pea-green living room. Two cats contemplated Ava from their post on top of a china hutch, their tails swishing.

"Oh, no. I can't stay." Ava wished she wore a watch to glance at. The cat box odor was making her ill, and she felt a bit guilty she was stealing time from her bridge murder cases. "Do you know where Jayne worked or know someone in the complex that she spent time with? I can come back if you find the application." She dug out a business card and handed it to the woman.

"The FBI?" She stared harder at Ava. "What's she done now?"

"The only thing she's guilty of is being my sister."

"Oh, honey." The woman gave her a pitying look. "If you believe that, you're too gullible to work for the government. Why don't you go down the street to Harold's Bar?" She gestured to the south. "One block down on your left. Jayne spent a lot of time in there, and I'm sure she talked to everyone more than she should have."

Ava thanked her and started to turn away but glanced back. "Jayne didn't tell you I worked for the FBI?"

"Honey, she didn't even tell me she had a sister. I wouldn't have believed it if I didn't see you with my own eyes."

Stunned, Ava nodded, her throat tight, and she strode down the walkway.

I stopped telling people about her years ago. Why am I hurt that she's done the same?

9

He flipped through several pages in his journal, stopping to read an entry here and there. He'd kept one on and off for several years, but he'd never been as consistent as the last few months.

> December 1
>
> I have three days off this week and an appointment with my eye doctor. I think I need a new prescription for my glasses. Sometimes I have to squint at the freeway signs and I know I didn't used to. Maybe it's time to consider laser surgery. The thought of a laser cutting through my eyeball makes me sick, but I swear I'm tired of dealing with glasses and wish it'd all just go away. My right eye is getting really bad.

He paused and covered his left eye with his hand and stared out the window. Since then he'd learned eye surgery wasn't an option for him. The blurriness had continued to worsen in his right eye. Just like they'd predicted it would. His eye doctor had increased the prescription twice since the December journal entry, and his insurance hadn't covered the second time. Damned if he would pay for it again when there was no point. Besides, some days it wasn't as bad as others. He'd been warned about that symptom, too.

> *For the first time since I was in school, I'm taking a week off at Christmas. LA, here I come! Sunshine, Disney, and beach. The Oregon rain is driving me nots this year. I'm craving sunshine.*

He rubbed a finger over the word "nots," hating the error, and wishing he hadn't written the entry in pen. The LA trip had never happened, and he still hadn't received a refund from the website where he'd booked the trip. Not that it really mattered, but it was the principle. They'd said they'd mail him a check in six to eight weeks.

He wasn't in a hurry.

He read farther in the journal, noting the more frequent mistakes. It'd affected his speech, too. When talking to the cat, he heard odd words coming from his mouth, but in his mind, he spoke the correct ones. It'd scared him at first, but his doctor said it was to be expected.

A soft voice spoke in his head: *You don't know what fear is.*

She was right. His fear was nothing compared to hers. And giving her what she needed had provided a purpose in his last year of life. He'd spent too many years feeling sorry for himself and living a lie. Once he'd seen the light of what he needed to do, he'd been on the road to peace.

The path before him was clear. He'd crossed several bridges and was approaching his goal.

He'd spent the last few months working on his plans. So much analysis and planning. But it was paying off. He'd watched the news and seen the gleam in the eyes of the reporters. Even as they said how awful the murders were, they couldn't hide their pleasure at sharing the gruesome news. Everyone was interested in death.

Especially when someone important had died in a publicly horrifying way.

He'd researched before he dealt the cuts of death. The Internet was packed with articles on how to properly slash a wrist. There were some twisted and sick people out there. He'd learned he had to cut deep and long to create an effective exit for the blood. Blood spatter reports had warned him about what to expect from that first cut. He'd stumbled across blog posts that talked about the hesitation cuts on the wrists of timid people who tried to commit suicide.

You've made a decision, one post read. *Now don't be a wuss and leave evidence that you had doubts. Show them you meant it! Your dead body will tell the story to the medical examiner. Make it a powerful one and be fearless about your choice.*

Fearless. He liked the word; it felt powerful on his tongue. He'd been a coward in the past. But now he'd learned to be fearless. And his new path would prove it.

He'd known the Fremont Bridge would get the public's attention. He'd chosen it because it was Portland's jewel of a bridge. It had the most traffic, stood the highest, and gleamed the brightest. Sorta like Carson.

He snorted.

The country bridge was for contrast. In the same way that Aaron was different from Carson. He'd also selected the quiet location out of caution, in case residents were watching for odd activity on the downtown Portland bridges. He'd liked the rural feel of his choice. His reconnaissance before Aaron's hanging had shown a lack of cameras. Completely different from his research about the Fremont Bridge. For that mission he'd known cameras would see him from a few locations, but he'd chosen his route for minimal exposure; he couldn't be caught.

Yet.

It'd been a quiet, less stressful night for hanging a body. He'd peered over the edge of the Vernonia Bridge, but it hadn't compared to the rush he'd received from the Fremont. On the Fremont, his life had been in his hands. With the push of his toes, he could have ended everything. But he'd chosen to follow his plan.

It wasn't about him anymore.

10

Harold's Bar was the epitome of a dive. Up close Ava saw the outside walls hadn't been painted in this century, and the bricks held decades of grime that nearly hid their original red shade. The obligatory beer signs glowed, beckoning the rush-hour commuters to spend a few bucks before heading home.

Ava hesitated and glanced at the time on her phone. She had a task force meeting in an hour. *It'll just take a few minutes. I'm already here.*

Go in. Ask a few questions. Leave and get back to work hunting a killer.

Decision made, she pulled open the door. Smoking in Oregon bars had been banned since 2009, but she encountered a strong wave of cigarette odor that leaked from the floor, walls, and ceiling. The building was dimly lit, with a half dozen patrons sitting on stools at the wooden bar along one side of the small room, their focus on two TVs above the glass bottles of liquor. Her stomach growled as she picked up a heavenly spicy smell from the kitchen. Sort of a mix of Thai and Mexican.

She wouldn't stay long. Her hunt for Jayne had taken more time than she'd expected. She had a murderer to find. That was her job.

I can't completely turn my back on my sister.

No one sat at the tables scattered about the small room. In the far corner was a raised platform for a band to entertain a minuscule dance floor. Her ears ached at the thought of live rock echoing off the walls in the cramped space.

Was she getting old?

She stepped up to the bar as the bartender slammed the cash drawer and turned to greet her. He froze, but his gaze rapidly swept from her hair to her chest, lingering too long.

He knows Jayne.

Light finally dawned in his eyes, and he grinned.

He wasn't unattractive if you didn't mind super-scrawny guys who looked to Billy Ray Cyrus for their grooming inspiration. Ava would have bet big money that the bartender had once embraced the mullet, but now he sported Billy's lank, chin-length hair and soul patch.

"Well, if it ain't the FBI!" Soul Patch announced to the closest customer. The senior citizen on the stool glanced at Ava, clearly wasn't impressed, and went back to watching his TV.

Ava flashed her best Jayne smile for the bartender. "I see Jayne's mentioned me."

Soul Patch braced his hands on the bar, his smile broad. "She might have bragged her twin was an FBI agent a time or two. So you're what Jayne would look like if she was a brunette and role-played being a good girl." He leered.

Ava's irritation level shot up to boiling.

She handed him her card, all friendly pretense gone. "Her cell phone's been disconnected. Have you seen her recently?"

"Seen how much of her?" He winked and took the card.

Oh, Jayne. You didn't.

Soul Patch's concentration on her chest indicated that Jayne had. She sighed and raised a brow.

He glanced at the card. "Ava McLane. Jayne told me the two of you'd been named after actresses."

The senior citizen who'd dismissed her a moment before turned his head and took a longer look. Ava stared back.

"You don't look anything like Ava Gardner," the senior stated. "At least Jayne tried to look like Mansfield."

"I don't try to look like someone else," she said, nearly biting her tongue. "Have *you* seen Jayne lately?" she asked the movie buff.

Movie Buff shrugged and turned his attention to the TV.

Nice friends you've made, Jayne.

"Do you know where I can find her?" Ava questioned the bartender.

Soul Patch stroked his chin. "Well, she hasn't been in much since she lost her nearby apartment. Before she moved, she was in here almost every night. I'd say she popped in late one night about three weeks ago. She had a guy with her that I didn't know and was hanging all over him." He gave a sly grin. "She was clearly trying to make me jealous, but I didn't give a rat's ass. She's been used too hard, you know?"

Ava stared at him. "You do realize you're speaking of *my sister*? You could at least pretend to have some manners." Fury clouded her vision. "Just because you fucked her, you think that makes you better than her? I bet you hit on anything that comes through that door without dangly bits hanging between their legs."

"Miz FBI just nailed you!" Movie Buff gave a smoker's laugh. "She read you like a book." He wheezed and looked at Ava with admiration.

"Shut up, Oscar," Soul Patch snarled. He met Ava's gaze, his flirtatious manner gone. "I don't know where Jayne is. I had the impression that she's living in downtown Portland now. Maybe with a bunch of other people. Or else in a shelter."

A shelter? Ava's heart dropped. What had Jayne gotten into?

"She said she was living in a shelter?" She tried to keep her words steady. Had her abandonment of her sister left Jayne with no other option?

I didn't abandon her. She became impossible to be near.

NOT. MY. FAULT.

Soul Patch frowned as he wiped the bar with a damp rag. He appeared to be exercising some memory cells. "I don't recall that she said those words. It was more of an impression, maybe. Or else someone else said she was."

Ava's heart slowed in relief. "You have my card. Please call if you hear about her or she comes in." She slid one to Oscar the movie buff. "You, too." He glanced at the card and ignored it.

Thanks for your concern.

Soul Patch slid his into the front pocket of his jeans. "I'll keep it somewhere warm and safe." He gave one last attempt at a flirty smile.

Ava bit back her retort, nodded at both men, and escaped out onto the dark, wet street, feeling guilty for taking personal time to search for Jayne. She needed to get back to her search for a killer.

• • •

Mason looked again at the clock on the wall behind ASAC Ben Duncan. One minute until the meeting started.

Ava would be late if she didn't hustle. Four other agents plus Zander Wells and Ray were making small talk as they waited for Ava to show up for the task force update. The small meeting room in the FBI building was adjacent to the command center where tips on the Carson Scott and Aaron King murders were flowing in. Mason pretended not to notice as Ben glanced at the time on his phone and then looked in his direction.

Ava's last text had said she'd be on time.

She pushed open the door, and Mason's heart did a tiny jump from the excitement that always struck him when she walked into a room, and from relief that she'd made it. Would his heart always speed up when she appeared or would that fade away with time? A little voice told him that joy was here to stay.

She smiled at the men in the room, her tired gaze lingering on Mason.

Something was up.

It showed in the tightness of her lips. He'd learned to pick up her tiny tells over the last two months, and right now she looked the way she did when her pain meds had worn off or something had unsettled her. She'd given up the prescription meds six weeks ago, so something had upset her. He gestured at the chair next to him and she set her bag on it, pulling out a notepad and her tiny laptop before moving the bag to the floor. She slid into the seat with a tired sigh. The other men settled into their chairs and waited for Ben Duncan to organize his notes.

"What happened?" Mason asked in a low voice.

Tired blue eyes met his, and she squeezed his hand under the table. "Nothing big. I'll tell you when we're done," she whispered. "Don't worry."

Mason reluctantly gave his attention to Duncan as he wondered what'd exhausted Ava.

One person did that to her: Jayne.

He set aside his suspicions as Duncan asked him to update the team on the results from the van footage on the Fremont Bridge. Mason recapped his visit with the lab. "We've kept quiet the fact that there's a City of Portland logo on the side of the van. Is that something we want to release to the media?" he asked. "Word will eventually leak out. I asked the fleet manager to not talk about it, but we know how that goes."

"Chances are it was a removable logo," said Zander. "Our unsub probably assumes we've caught him on camera and seen the logo. I doubt he's driving around with it on there."

"But we haven't ruled out that it's a city employee," said another agent.

"So has our guy stupidly let us see him, or is he leading us astray with the logo?" Zander asked.

Duncan nodded. "I want more insight into what his behavior indicates. I've asked for a BAU consult, so someone will be here tomorrow. We've got two dead men and I really don't want any more."

"Has anyone considered why he's using the bridges?" Ava asked. "Maybe that's more of a question for the specialist tomorrow, but could the bridges mean something to him? What is the purpose of displaying the men on a bridge?"

Mason sat up straighter. He hadn't even considered the why of a bridge. He'd just assumed their unsub had an affinity for using them. *How did I not ask that question?*

"Bridges are associated with power," said Ray. "Height and grandeur."

"I wouldn't call the bridge in Vernonia grand," said Ava. "But go on."

"They symbolize a connection, bringing things together, and providing a path," Ray added.

Mason hid a smile and scanned the other agents in the room as they stared at Ray. Ray didn't have the type of brain his linebacker body suggested. He was smart and sensitive and into artsy stuff that made Mason want to yawn.

"I dated a girl who did tarot cards. One of the symbols was a bridge." Ray glanced at the other agents, two of whom immediately started Googling tarot cards on their tablets.

"'A bridge to rise above the difficulties,'" read one agent.

"'A sign of divine intervention,'" added Zander. He looked up with a stricken expression. "Please don't tell me our unsub thinks he's God."

"'A connection between the harmony and misery in your life; you are at either end of the bridge. Which direction are you walking toward?'" read the first agent.

Maybe he's just fond of bridges.

Mason cleared his throat. "We can't guess what's going on in his head. I think we should keep in mind that the bridge *might* have meaning and not get hung up on it right now."

"Isn't there a hanged man in tarot?" Ava asked.

"Yep," said Zander as he tapped on his tablet. He spent a few seconds reading the explanation. "He hangs upside down by a foot. That's definitely not our guys. There's another divine association with the hanged man card, *or* the card could mean exactly the opposite . . . sheesh. I don't understand this at all."

"Stick to your day job," said Duncan.

"I'm looking to see if something else from these cases refers to a type of card in the deck," said Zander. "Holy cow. There's seventy-eight cards." Zander raised his gaze. "I don't know if this is something we should be spending time looking at or not."

"Let's approach BAU with it. See if they find it credible. If there's seventy-eight cards, it could be just a coincidence that a bridge and a hanging are both on there," said the ASAC.

"The symbolism associated with bridges outside of tarot is across the map," said Ava, studying her laptop. "Personally, I think it's less important to our unsub compared to the hanging and stripping the bodies of their clothes."

"Humiliation," stated Mason. "And the ball gag on the second body upped that ante."

ASAC Duncan nodded. "I agree it's very strong, and it adds a personal touch. I know Special Agent Euzent from BAU will bring it up tomorrow. Moving on." He glanced down at his notes. "Are we getting anywhere on the victims' vehicles? What about the Explorer that McKenna Drake said Carson Scott drove the evening he picked her up?"

Ray raised a hand. "Turns out it belonged to his parents. They said he borrows it when he has something large to move or goes to the mountains. And no, we haven't found it. We have BOLOs out on both victims' vehicles."

"Do they know why he borrowed the SUV this visit? He wasn't going to be in town that long," Ava stated.

"They said he bought a mirror for his place," Ray replied. "One of those big standing mirrors you lean against a wall. I noticed one in his living room when we were there Monday."

Mason had no memory of a mirror, but Ray would notice something like that. Mason did remember the two huge flat-screen TVs.

"We haven't found their clothing and cell phones," Ray continued. "Requests to their wireless providers revealed that Carson's phone last pinged a tower near his home Saturday evening, and it's been silent since then. Aaron King's wireless carrier lost touch with him near his store on Sunday morning. I need to add these to the timeline in the command center. Can we go take a look at it?"

Mason agreed. The conference room was nice and quiet, but he needed the timeline in front of him to keep track of all the aspects of the case. "The last known ping of both men's phones could tentatively be used for an idea of when they went missing. No one's come forward and said they saw Carson Scott after his date with McKenna Drake on Saturday. It's possible he wasn't nabbed until sometime on Sunday."

The agents stood and left their computers on the table to file into the command center. In the large room, a dozen agents occupied phones and computer monitors, processing leads.

"If Aaron's cell phone went silent Sunday morning, and we use that to mark his abduction time, that means our unsub held both men captive and alive at the same time," Ava said as she placed a finger on the timeline whiteboard while Ray added a notation of both victims' last cell phone transmissions. "The ME put Carson Scott's death on Sunday between noon and four P.M. I wonder if the two men saw each other."

Mason stared at the time during which both men were missing but neither had been killed. "Why snatch another victim before you've killed the other? Typical serial killers need downtime, right?"

Zander nodded. "And who says he only took two guys? Maybe he's holding a few, doling out the deaths one at a time."

Ava sighed. "Thanks, Zander."

"Have we come up with any connections between the two men?" Ben Duncan asked. "Give me something good here."

"Both used Bank of America but opened their accounts at different branches," said one of the agents. "Both had Chevron gas cards. According to their bank and credit card statements, they haven't eaten at the same restaurant or been at the same theater at the same time. We're still digging."

"Keep at it. I want to know why this guy killed a congressman and a divorced Universe of Tires employee. We need that connection," finished Duncan.

Everyone nodded.

"Tomorrow we've got a press conference and a meeting with Special Agent Euzent. Attending the press conference is optional; the meeting is not."

More nods.

"Go home and get some sleep," said Duncan. "Hopefully I won't be seeing any of you on a bridge in the morning."

Mason walked back with Ava to the conference room to get their things. He waved good-bye to Ray, who looked intent on getting home to his wife. "Now can you tell me what happened this evening?"

Ava shoved her laptop in her bag, her gaze on her task. "I went looking for Jayne."

Mason was silent. They'd had a few discussions over the last two months about whether Ava should reach out to her sister. They'd always agreed at the end of the talk that Ava was better off staying away from Jayne.

"How come?" Mason asked.

"I wanted to know if she was the one who broke into your home. And I was worried," she added softly. She finally looked Mason in the eye. "I should have told you what I was doing."

"So I could talk you out of it?"

Her lips curved up. "Yes."

"Maybe I've pushed too hard for you to stay away. She is your sister, and I've always tried to let you be the guide in our discussions. I wanted to support your decision, not talk you out of something. What did you find?"

She was silent for a few moments as they walked down the quiet hallway of the center. "I went to her last apartment and talked to her landlady. She skipped out on two months' rent."

Mason didn't say anything. No surprises there.

"Then I went to a bar where she used to hang out a lot."

"Nice place?" he asked.

She snorted. "What do you think? They told me she'd been in once recently, and they got the impression she was living in downtown Portland. Possibly in a shelter."

"What?" Images of overcrowded, dirty shelters popped into his head. "Seriously?"

"Well, the bartender wasn't sure. He did say she might just be living with a group of people."

"That might not be much better."

"I know," she said. "I'm not certain I want to keep looking. I'm scared of what I might find."

Mason sighed. He'd been holding back the contents of an email he'd received earlier that afternoon, wanting to talk about it to Ava in person. It was time.

They stepped out of the building, and Ava pulled up her hood. Mason put on his hat. He stopped her before they stepped out from under the overhang into the light rain. "Portland police ran the prints they pulled off the break-in at our place."

"Already?" Ava's gaze told him she knew what he was about to say.

"I told them to compare them to your sister's. They had hers on file."

"Yes, she's been arrested a number of times. Oh, no. Do I want to hear this?"

"One set of prints was hers. The other set belongs to a dirtbag named Derrick Snyder. His arrest record could fill a library."

Ava held his gaze, her face blank. He couldn't tell what she was thinking.

"Say something," he said.

"God damn it. *I knew it!*" Despair filled her features and she spun away, pressing her fingers against her temples. "Ohhh, I'm going to strangle her. But first I'm going to make her tell me what she did with my mother's ring." She stopped and met his gaze, anguish in her eyes. "Oh, Mason. I'm so sorry I brought her into your life. I can't believe she's done this to you."

"It's just a TV."

She laughed without humor. "It's not the TV. We both know that. It's the violation of *your home.* Aargh!" She looked up at the wet, dark sky, fists clenched at her sides. "What am I going to do with her? You don't know how angry this makes me!"

"Yes, I do!" He grabbed her arms and held her still, making her look at him. "I get it. She's more than one person should ever have to deal with. She's a hurricane, an earthquake, and a tropical disease rolled into a female form. Whatever she touches suffers and breaks. But do you know what is the worst for me? Seeing how she tears you to pieces. I don't care that she broke into my home. I *should* have had an alarm system and better locks, and now I'll get off my lazy butt and do what I should have done a decade ago."

She stared at him, eyes wide, listening intently.

"What's most important to me is that you're happy. I want to destroy what hurts you." His grip tightened on her arms. "But when it's your sister that's hurting you, what can I do to fix it? I've never felt so helpless in my life and it's unbelievably frustrating. I can't order you to stay away from her, but *damn*, that's what every cell in my body is screaming!"

He breathed hard, waiting for her reply.

"So we agree we're both angry," she said softly. "And completely at a loss for what is the right thing to do."

Mason leaned forward, resting his lips against her forehead. "I'll do whatever you want to do. This is your fight, and I'll support you every step of the way," he said quietly, ignoring the deafening voice in his head that wanted to order her to drop the search for her sister.

No good could come out of locating Jayne.

But what Ava needed came first.

11

He circled the fat man tied to the chair.

"You know, Joe, this was one of the hardest decisions I've ever made," he said. "I liked you. I liked you a lot. Carson and Aaron were dicks. I can see that now, but you were one of the good guys. Why'd you let yourself get caught up with them?"

Joe couldn't speak. The ball gag in his mouth blocked his words, but his eyes screamed out his thoughts. *Don't kill me!*

"It's too late, Joe. I'm truly sorry for that. But you had your chance. All of you had your chance to set this to rights and you did the opposite!"

Joe's eyes bulged.

"What? You didn't agree with Carson and Aaron's plan?"

The tied man frantically shook his head.

"Are you trying to tell me that you didn't have a part in my beating in downtown Portland in January? I got the shit kicked out of me. And that guy was about to slit my throat when I managed to kick him in the balls. Do you think it's a coincidence that happened a week after I contacted everybody?"

Joe looked confused.

He studied him. "I know Carson was behind it. He has connections." Joe still didn't seem to know what he was talking about. "You see this?" He pulled aside his collar and showed the healing gash on his neck. "Before he died, Carson swore he didn't hire the guy, but we both know Carson is the king of liars. He coached us, remember? His motto was always 'Deny, deny, deny.'"

Joe nodded, his eyes wary.

"I *trusted* you guys! I thought you all were taking me seriously when I called us together. I thought we had each other's backs. Imagine my shock when I figured out what they'd done. Aaron told me I had it coming. He didn't deny it. He and Carson had agreed it was the only way to quiet me. But look who's quiet now!"

The man wildly shook his head.

"They left you out of that aspect of the plan?"

He nodded.

"I guess that makes sense. You wouldn't be much help, and the fewer people who knew they'd hired someone to kill me, the better." He sighed, shaking his head.

Joe shook his head, muted squeals coming from his mouth.

"You feel remorse for what you did way back then?"

More distressed nods.

"Well, why the *fuck* didn't you remedy the situation when I offered you the chance?"

The large man's body shook with sobs.

"Everybody wants to make it right after they've been caught. All those criminals that cry with remorse at their trials are only crying because they got caught. Not because they destroyed someone's life. You've been caught."

Joe's chin rested on his chest as tears streamed down his fleshy cheeks. He'd put on a lot of weight in the last decade. From the looks of it, eating and watching TV were about all he did.

"Were you able to let it go? It looks like Carson and Aaron moved on just fine with their lives. They had the personalities to put the past behind them, but your life has sorta gone to crap. Is that what happens when you're eaten up inside by guilt?"

Joe didn't look up anymore. He'd given up pleading with his eyes and simply stared at the floor, letting the tears soak his old T-shirt. Joe gave a low moan, which he took as a positive reply to his question.

"Good. Then deserved you part you . . ." He stopped, shook his head to straighten the words in his brain, and slowly stated, "Then you got part of what you deserved. I'm here to deliver the rest."

Dammit. Joe had looked up during his messed-up sentence, a question in his eyes. He swallowed and stood straighter, slipping the utility knife out of his pocket. Joe's gaze immediately went to the tool, and his curiosity about his speaking problem vanished. The chair shivered under his big frame.

That's better.

Sometimes he couldn't think of the word he wanted to say. Sure, everyone had that problem occasionally, but *every single day*? He'd said, "You thank" to the grocery store clerk yesterday and received an odd look in return. He had laughed it off and immediately corrected the phrase, but his face had burned as he'd left the store.

It's getting worse.

Since the diagnosis he'd avoided all social situations. No dating, no beers with friends, no casual discussions in bookstores. In his mind he'd gone dark. He did everything he could by using the Internet now. Banking, shopping . . . thank God for the chat features on most websites. People were used to seeing typos during chats. It was the errors that were spoken out loud that made people stop and stare.

His meeting that Joe had attended two months ago had been one of his last "social" situations. It hadn't gone well. But it'd forced his hand and eased his mind about what he had to do.

Years of asking God for forgiveness hadn't helped. Now he realized it hadn't helped because he'd been asking for the wrong reasons. He'd sought forgiveness to make himself feel better. He'd been selfish. He'd tried to correct one sin with another.

Isn't that exactly what you're doing now? The question inside his head spoke in the female voice.

No, he told the voice. *Now I'm making things right. I gave them the chance to correct it and they refused. I had no choice.*

Everyone has a choice, she replied.

I know what I have to do. I've seen what has to be done.

Very well, she answered. *Thank you, Troy.*

He listened a moment to see if she'd return. She was often his conscience, and he loved to hear her say his name. For years he'd ignored her nagging small voice that'd tried to guide him when he was faced with moral dilemmas. It wasn't until Christmas that he'd finally started to reply. He found it oddly comforting to speak with her.

He blinked and realized Joe was staring at him with questioning eyes. Troy glared at the restrained man, laid his blade down in full sight, and opened up one of the blue tarps, spreading it on half of the carpet.

Fearless. The word rang through his mind, focusing his actions, centering his thoughts. He knew what he had to do; hesitation was not an option. He'd rehearsed every step and prepared for every surprise. Tonight's job had required more modification to his vehicle than a stolen magnet on the side doors or a smoky cover over his license plate. He'd welcomed the challenge.

Joe started to thrash against his restraints, making his chair scuttle to the side. Troy ignored him and pulled out a new roll of duct tape. If Joe tipped over, it'd only make his job easier.

The man wouldn't be leaving of his own accord.

12

Mason wondered if ASAC Duncan's parting words last night had jinxed the task force. Looking at Zander Wells's expression as he stood on the other side of the third dead man, he believed Zander was thinking the same thing.

Victim number three of the Bridge Killer had been found nearly forty miles east of Portland on the stunning Bridge of the Gods, which crossed the Columbia River. Mason wished he could see a pattern in the choice of bridges, but the killer had chosen a central city bridge, and then one west of the city, and now one to the east. Were north and south next? Would there be two more victims?

They had a killer with a clear plan. Now if they only had the blueprint to that plan.

"God damn it."

Ava glanced at him.

"Did I say that out loud?" Mason asked. "Who the fuck is next?"

"He's escalating by increasing the abuse to the bodies," said Ava, studying the victim's shaved head and torso lacerations. "At least he hasn't sped up how quickly he's killing them."

"Don't say that out loud," muttered Zander.

Too late.

The corpse's head had been shaved unevenly, leaving a jigsaw puzzle of hair and white scalp. The body had the wrapped wrists of the first two deaths, but this one also had lacerations to the chest.

"Did this one fight back?" Ava directed her question to the medical examiner. "Is that why there are cuts on his chest?"

Seth Rutledge shook his head. "Defensive wounds are typically on forearms and hands as the victim tries to protect himself. Look at how clean his arms are." He leaned close to the body, peering at one of the slices in the chest. "These cuts are too symmetrical. See how similar in length each one is? And they almost form a perfect upside-down triangle on each pec. Someone carved these after death."

"So besides hanging a naked body that's had its wrists slit and has the pattern on his back, this one has the ball gag from the second death and adds damage to the chest along with shaving its head. Did I miss anything?" Mason asked.

"The pattern on the back is a bit different," said Dr. Rutledge. "There's a band that goes straight across as if there was a two-by-four also pressing into his back." The doctor gestured at the men to help him roll the victim onto his side. The man was very large. It took four of them to allow Mason and Ava to peer at his back. Sure enough. The daisy pattern was very clear on the victim, but it was marred by a white line that crossed his back near the height of his armpits.

"And once again we've got a male who looks about the same age. But this one clearly doesn't hit the gym or avoid McDonald's."

"Could one person have hung him?" asked Ava. "I couldn't wrestle with a body this size, but could a really strong man?"

The men eyed the corpse. Zander shook his head. "There's no way. Either he had help or rigged a way to move him."

Mason tried to visualize a way for one man to move the corpse. "I can't see it. A pulley of some sort, I guess. But that would take some custom adaptations to the van and a lot of preplanning on our guy's part."

Ava lifted a brow at him.

"Yes, I know. Clearly our guy has planned far in advance. What do we have for identifying marks to release to the press?"

"Weight will probably be close to three hundred and fifty pounds," said Dr. Rutledge. "Black hair, blue eyes, and he's wearing a partial denture to replace several molars on his mandible. A casual friend might not be aware of that fact, but a spouse would."

Mason glanced at the victim's fingers. No ring. And no sign that a ring had been removed. His fingernails were decently clean—not an automotive industry employee. At least not an employee that was hands-on with the vehicles. Would finding his identity help pinpoint the link between Carson Scott and Aaron King? Was this guy active in politics? "Anything else? No tattoos on this one?"

Dr. Rutledge grimaced and shook his head. "We'll have to rely on the weight. I'll have an accurate number for you later."

Mason stood up and stretched his back. When Ava's work phone had rung this morning, neither of them had been surprised. But why had the killer picked this bridge? He scanned the high forested hills on both sides of the river. The morning was cloudy, but the sun peeped through to shine on the Columbia River. The bridge was one of Oregon's most beautiful. A steel truss bridge, it looked like a delicate children's toy that spanned the river. It wasn't a solid-looking, heavy-duty structure like those of the last two hangings. The Bridge of the Gods had always reminded Mason of the old Erector Set he'd had as a child.

"There's a camera at the tollbooth," Ray stated. "It's set to capture images of the drivers and their license plates, but he could have driven onto the bridge from the Washington side, turned around after disposing of his victim, and skipped the tollbooth. That's what I would have done. The small rise at the crest of the bridge in the center keeps the operator from seeing this end of the bridge."

"It's definitely not a busy bridge," added Ava. "I bet they don't have more than a few dozen vehicles cross each night."

Mason nodded. The bridge was in a remote area. The tiny town of Cascade Locks sat at the foot of the bridge on the Oregon side, and a heck of a lot of not much was on the Washington side. In his opinion, the bridge was one of the highlights in the Columbia River Gorge. The river spanned the boundary between Oregon and Washington and showcased miles of steep, forested mountain slopes and waterfalls.

Ava stared up at the metal framework. "It's truly gorgeous. I've driven out this way once since I've lived here, but I've never crossed the bridge. I remember seeing it from the highway as I drove along the Columbia. Why did they name it the Bridge of the Gods?"

"I believe it was an Indian name for a dam that was created by a landslide farther west of here," answered Ray.

"Did they destroy it when they made this real bridge?" Ava asked.

"I think the Columbia River eventually wore it away. I don't know who decided to carry on the name with the modern structure," said Ray. "I heard Charles Lindbergh flew under it one time."

Mason looked down at the water. Suddenly the bridge didn't seem nearly high enough. The thought of aiming a plane between the bridge and the water made him dizzy. "Seriously?"

"I'm pretty sure it's true."

"Is there a sexual aspect to this death, Seth?" Ava asked the medical examiner.

"Not that I'm seeing, but"—he gestured at the cuts on the chest—"this has a different tone to it. If our victim were a woman, I'd say there was a sexual aspect. The upside-down triangles almost create breasts on him."

Mason moved to stand at the feet of the victim and get a view from a different angle. "I see what you mean. But if I were trying to make him look more female, I would have made the triangles right side up."

"The upside-down triangle is a female symbol," Ray began.

"Jesus Christ," blurted Mason, glaring at Ray. "You're a handy walking Wikipedia, Ray, but I'm disturbed by your knowledge of certain topics. Why don't you know hockey stats or John Wayne trivia?"

"Actually, I can quote a lot of John Wayne." Ray looked hurt. "But hockey has never held much appeal for me."

Zander laughed, and Mason raised a brow at him.

"You two are like an old married couple," Zander said with a grin. Mason tried to remember if he'd ever seen such a broad smile on the serious agent.

"How long have you worked together?" he asked.

"Too long," they stated in unison.

"Long enough to improve his clothing choices," said Ray. "You should have seen him before he met me."

"I keep flushing, but this one doesn't go away," muttered Mason.

"Oh, dear Lord." Ava rolled her eyes. "Focus, people. He's cutting his victims now. We'll figure out the why of it later. What else does anyone notice?"

The men examined the corpse. Soon tired of staring at a large dead body, Mason looked at Ava and felt a calm sweep through him. There was a subtle magic between them he hadn't experienced with another woman, which made him want to rush home to be with her in the evenings. She'd acknowledged feeling the same chemistry. Before they met, the two of them had been content to be alone, but now they'd stumbled on something addictive that'd changed their perspective.

It was a treasured gift.

She looked up and met his gaze. Her brows narrowed in question at first, but then she caught his intensity and fascination. She smiled, her face lighting up. *Stunning.*

Exchanging heated looks with Ava over a decaying corpse, Mason felt like the luckiest man in the world.

• • •

Later that afternoon Ava sat in the office of a women's shelter. Across from her, the director leaned her arms on her desk and told Ava again, "We don't discuss the identities of the women in our shelter. It could mean the difference between life and death for one of them." Cindy Birkholz had dark eyes that were kind and welcoming, but as Ava was discovering, she also had a spine of steel and wouldn't be bowled over by her FBI identification. The woman's hand-knitted sweater and gray hair had misled Ava.

Ava took a deep breath, stress creeping up her spine as she tried not to think about the half hour she'd just borrowed from her murder cases to search for her sister. Even if she'd been the president of the United States, the director of the women's shelter wouldn't have told her if Jayne had stayed there or not. She admired Cindy for sticking to her guns and providing a haven of safety. Some of the residents had left abusive relationships. They had the right to privacy.

But this is my twin.

"I respect what you're telling me and I understand why," Ava said. "I'd like to leave my card. If you see someone who *looks like me*, but perhaps with blond hair, would you please ask her to reach out to me?"

Cindy gave her a sad smile, and Ava suspected she had the patience of a saint. No doubt people constantly contacted her, searching for loved ones or hoping to find someone they were angry with. The director had drawn a line and stuck to it. "Ms. McLane, does your sister know your phone number?"

"I assume she does."

"Has she called you on that number before?"

"Yes."

"Has she ever been to your home?" Cindy asked kindly.

Ava thought of the break-in at Mason's. "Yes."

"Then she knows how to find you if she wants to speak with you," the director finished.

"But . . . but what if she's lost my number? Her phone's been disconnected. People don't memorize phone numbers anymore; they just keep them in their contacts."

"Does she know where you work?"

"She's never been to the building, but I assume she could figure it out. But they'd never—"

"Ms. McLane, it sounds to me like your sister prefers to not be in contact at this time."

Ava caught her breath.

Of course she doesn't . . . she's stolen from me and is probably high.

"I'm worried about her health," Ava said slowly, holding Cindy's gaze. "I'm concerned she's not taking care of herself and may be hurting herself."

Sympathy crossed the director's face. "I understand you are worried about her. Has she ever been declared mentally incompetent?"

"No, but she's been in rehab several times. She doesn't think like normal—"

"Your sister is an adult, Ms. McLane. Neither you nor I can make her do something she's not interested in doing." She paused. "Something tells me you already know this and have encountered it in the past?"

Ava deflated. It was time to admit defeat. She was dealing with a woman who'd heard every story in the book—some probably a hundred times—and was skilled at gently discrediting them all. "You're very good," Ava admitted.

Cindy Birkholz flashed white teeth. "I get a lot of practice. I don't want you to think I'm not sympathetic. I am. But my first priority is my women. We watch for health issues, both mental and physical, in our residents. We make the help available, but we can't make them drink the water. Do you understand?"

Ava sat back in her chair and stared at the worn tile floor, tired from trying to find a crack in the director's walls. "I do. And you're absolutely right that Jayne knows how to find me when she decides to. I guess I'm more afraid of believing that she doesn't want to have anything to do with me." She lifted her gaze to Cindy's. "I know that it's nothing I did. She's avoiding me because she's ashamed and afraid to face me. I don't want her to deepen the hole she is in. I'm afraid she'll never find her way out."

"Are you seeking her for your mental well-being or for her benefit?" Cindy asked kindly.

Ava considered the question. "Both. I'm crazy with guilt and terrified she'll be beyond saving if I wait too long."

The director nodded. "I see."

Ava believed her. Her eyes spoke of a history that'd seen it all, including women who were beyond saving. Ava gathered her bag and stood, holding out a hand to the kind woman. She hoped Jayne was here. Cindy could help her. If Jayne allowed herself to be helped.

The director stood and shook her hand. "You do realize the waiting lists to get into the shelters are months long. If she's only been on the street for a short while, she may not have an established place to go."

"Yes, I wondered if that could be the case. What do people do when there's no beds for the night?"

The director sighed. "There are a lot of options. If she has some money, she could be in a cheap hotel. The problem starts when the money runs out. Does she have a vehicle?"

"I don't know," Ava admitted. "Last I heard it wasn't running." Should she have offered to pay to fix Jayne's car?

"Some sleep in their cars, but they have to keep moving. People don't tolerate seeing the same cars parked in the same place day after day, and they utilize whatever bathroom facilities they can find."

Ava wanted to vomit. The thought of Jayne using the sink to clean up in a rundown gas station bathroom made her heart crack.

"I know some homeless break into empty homes to sleep, or if they're lucky, they can crash on a friend's couch," added Cindy.

Does Jayne have any friends?

Cindy looked at her with knowing eyes. "Does she get along with the opposite sex very well?"

"Too well."

"Ah. Well, sometimes that at least puts a temporary roof over their head. But it can open up a whole new can of worms."

"She's very good at figuring out how to get what she wants out of people," said Ava. "She's a manipulative and skilled liar."

Cindy nodded. "I hate to say it, but those are the ones that survive on the streets. They develop thick skins and often have no remorse. But they survive. The hard part is easing them back into normal society."

Ava abruptly had a craving for vodka with a sugary mixer. A fruity drink to relax her brain and make her believe she was on an island. A mental vacation in a large, colored glass. Or in a coconut. She needed a break from worrying about her sister.

"There's also Dignity Village. They have a waiting list, too, but she might have met someone who has a place there. They can only take sixty people, but I don't know how closely they keep an eye on visitors."

Ava shook her head, praying Jayne hadn't been in a position where she'd made that choice. Dignity Village was a tent city on the city's property. It'd started as an illegal campsite, but had somehow managed to gain the favor of some of the city council as a place for the homeless to go. It'd been in place over a decade and some viewed it as a success in improving the homeless situation. The police saw it as a frequent source of calls.

Cindy handed her a sheet of paper. "Here's a list of other shelters in the city. But I'll warn you that most of them have policies similar to ours. You may not find the information you want."

Ava reluctantly took the sheet. She'd made her own printout of shelters. Cindy's had been her first stop and now she didn't want to visit any others.

Should she bury her head in the sand and wait for Jayne to contact her? Or keep looking?

What I need to do is get back to the bridge murders.

"Good luck to you," Cindy said.

Ava thanked her and stepped out of the woman's office. In the hallway four other women sat on folding chairs, waiting for a chance to speak with the director. Three stared at the floor, but one met Ava's gaze, shooting belligerence at the FBI agent. The anger from the woman caught Ava off guard, and she did a double take, wondering if she knew her.

She saw it wasn't anger; the woman simply had all her defenses on full alert. She sat straight in the chair, her worn clothes and ripped shoes screaming her status, but there was pride in her stiff posture and raised chin. Ava lowered her gaze and walked away.

Ava could see Jayne in that chair. Jayne wouldn't roll over and be beaten by her circumstances. She'd stand up and fight.

Or was that wishful thinking? Jayne didn't think for herself anymore. Her reasoning was controlled by drugs or possibly through someone's manipulation.

Ava needed to keep searching for her sister. But her murder cases had to come first.

13

Mason stood at the back of the room with Ava as Zander Wells and Ben Duncan led the press conference. He felt bad for Zander, who'd been elected from their group to read a statement to the media, because the Portland FBI office's usual spokesperson was home with the flu. Mason hated public speaking and avoided it at all costs, but Zander had stepped up to the microphone like it was his best friend.

Zander was currently taking questions from the small audience and most of the journalists seemed focused on Carson Scott.

"Is there any evidence that Scott's death was politically motivated?" asked a male reporter. Mason recognized him from one of the local news stations.

Zander kept a calm facial expression but indicated with a shallow quirk of an eyebrow that he found the question rather sensational. "No." He didn't expand.

The reporter's hand shot up for another question, but Zander pointed at a woman.

"Obviously this is the work of a serial killer," the reporter started. "Is the Bridge Killer only preying on male victims? Do women not need to be concerned?"

"You're asking questions we don't know the answers to," Zander replied. "We don't know why he's picked men . . . so far. Both women and men should always be conscious of their safety whether Portland has a serial killer or not. Take this as a warning to be aware of your surroundings. There's a lot of nutty people out there, folks."

The audience nodded.

"Do the police believe there was a sexual element to the crimes?" the reporter continued, clearly not satisfied with Zander's non-answer. "After all, the three men were all found nude, correct?"

Mason tried not to sigh. Part of him understood. These people had papers to sell and advertising space to fill, but did they need to focus solely on the scandalous aspects of the crimes? Thank God the presence of the ball gags hadn't made it to the media. They would never have stopped speculating.

"Evening, Detective," said a familiar voice to his left.

Mason turned to see the slightly mocking eyes of investigative reporter Michael Brody from *The Oregonian*. The reporter was a straight shooter, but he was also a rebellious pain in the ass who'd earned Mason's reluctant respect. The reporter held out a hand and Mason shook it. Brody looked past Mason to Ava and waited expectantly for an introduction.

"This is Special Agent Ava McLane," he reluctantly told Brody. "Be nice to her," he ordered.

Brody grinned at him. "Why?" he asked bluntly. "I don't think you've ever asked me to be nice to anyone since I've known you. Why her?" Brody winked at Ava, taking the sting out of his question.

Ava smiled back at him, her attention clearly piqued by the reporter who had no filter between his brain and his mouth. Brody had the sharp instincts of a hawk, but resembled a surfer who never left the beachfront bar.

"Because you have a reputation for ignoring or harassing authority."

"Only when it suits me, or when someone doesn't behave as I think they should," answered Brody.

"Exactly," muttered Mason.

"Have you identified the third body you found this morning?" asked Brody.

"If you'd been paying attention, you would have heard Special Agent Wells say we haven't," said Mason.

"I listened. I didn't like his answer. I think you're holding something back."

"Of course we hold back," answered Ava. "It's how we separate the nut jobs from the real tips."

"But you truly don't know who he is?" asked Brody.

Mason sighed. Brody had a way of asking the same question over and over until he got the answer he wanted. But this time they didn't have a name.

"We don't know," said Mason. "We've released a general description and we're hoping someone will report a missing coworker or brother."

"Age approximately thirty-five, black hair, blue eyes, three hundred fifty pounds," Michael recited without looking at his notes. "That's a big man." His green eyes turned speculative. "That's a very big man for one person to single-handedly hang off a bridge. So you're looking for more than one killer?"

Mason glanced at Ava, who was looking at the reporter with a touch of respect. "Don't let his brain fool you," Mason warned Ava. "He can put random facts together faster than a computer, but his manners and tact are seriously lacking."

"It's possible we're looking for more than one person," agreed Ava. "We haven't ruled that out yet."

"And you haven't found a connection between the three men yet," Brody stated, not questioning.

Ava glanced at Mason and gave Brody a small shake of her head. "An identity on the third will help."

"I'll see what I can do through the paper," Brody offered. "But I'm surprised no one has come forward yet with a solid identification.

Maybe he's not from around here and the story needs to circulate wider."

Mason pointed at a camera. "That's CNN. How much wider do you want it to go? I hate to say this, but we're almost fortunate the first victim was a public figure. It's given us the needed publicity . . ." He trailed off, his brain jumping ahead.

Brody was nodding. "Scott was chosen first on purpose. It wasn't 'fortunate.' Your killer may have had several men on his list to take care of, but he chose Scott first because of who he was and what he knew it'd bring to the case. If you'd found the tire store employee first, would the FBI be involved?"

Ava shook her head. "You know as well as I do that Scott being a congressman pulled the FBI into this case. Our radar would have skipped over the death of Aaron King until more bodies started showing up."

"No doubt your BAU agent already noticed this fact," muttered Mason to Ava. The briefing with Special Agent Euzent from Behavioral Analysis was scheduled to start in an hour. He'd met the brainy young agent when he'd been called in to consult on Mason's ex's stepdaughter's kidnapping. He prayed the agent had some helpful insights on their serial killer.

"Have Samantha Givens and her husband been questioned in Carson Scott's murder?" a reporter shouted at Zander from the back of the room.

Mason glared at the reporter who'd highlighted the sensationalism of the congressman's death by bringing up last fall's affair investigation. Brody rolled his eyes.

Up front, Zander managed to project his annoyance at the reporter without uttering a word, and politely replied, "Samantha and Russ Givens have given statements. We do not consider them to be suspects."

"But you questioned them," argued the reporter.

Zander gave a half smile and scanned the rest of the audience. "I didn't say that. I said they gave a statement." He zeroed in on the reporter and repeated firmly, "We do not consider them to be suspects."

"Why not?" came the ridiculous question. "Why haven't you questioned them? They should be at the top of your list."

Mason wanted to give the pushy reporter a kick in the ass. There was a code of conduct to press conferences. Heck, there was a code of conduct to prove that you weren't stupid, but this young reporter had clearly skipped both classes.

Zander gave the audience an apologetic smile, and then he looked straight at the young man, all pretense of kindness gone. "I'm not going to describe every step that's been taken by the dozens of officers working these three deaths. I'd be standing here for the next twenty-four hours to recap all their work."

Brody snorted and said quietly, "Samantha Givens is undergoing an aggressive cancer treatment back East. Neither she nor her husband has been anywhere near Portland in two months."

"How did you find that out?" asked Ava, not mentioning that the FBI had discovered that fact the day Carson Scott was found.

Brody shrugged. "It's what I do." He gave Ava a winning smile. "Think you could sneak me into your briefing with the BAU agent tonight?"

Mason didn't ask how Brody knew about the meeting. His past attempts to figure out Brody's sources had been fruitless. The reporter never told him anything he didn't want Mason to know. But the sight of the man flirting with Ava was making his spine itch.

"When are you getting married?" Mason asked Brody.

The reporter's grin widened. "No date yet. Soon, I believe. Probably late this summer. I'm trying to break Jamie's habit of planning every step of her life. I think we'll take off on a whim and get married on a beach somewhere."

"You're not letting her plan her wedding?" Ava asked, disbelief on her face. Her admiration for the reporter had clearly dimmed, making Mason very happy.

"It's a long story," Brody said. "But trust me, she's onboard."

"Every woman wants to plan her wedding," she argued. "Why would you stop her? Some women have been dreaming about that white dress since they watched *Cinderella* when they were five years old."

Mason cocked a brow at her. Was Ava one of those women? His ex-wife had planned an elaborate event for their wedding, but he'd always felt it'd been more about her being showcased than about the fact that they were committing to each other. Did every woman want that day at the center of attention?

"It's not like that," Brody stated. "Jamie has plenty of ideas about how she wants to celebrate, but I get to choose the date and location as long as it doesn't affect her job. She's already bought a dress." He grinned at the wary look on Ava's face. "Don't worry. We came to an agreement on how to move forward."

She nodded and settled back into her chair, but looked as though she didn't quite trust the reporter.

Good. Keep that attitude around Brody.

"You'll let me know when you have an ID on the latest victim?" Brody said quietly to Mason.

Mason sighed. "Don't you have someone at the medical examiner's office who can leak you that information?"

"Of course. But I'd rather hear it from you. You don't think I'd print something without triple-checking it first, do you?"

"Tell you what. If you get a name, give me a call, and I'll let you know if it's accurate," Mason offered.

"You'll answer the phone if you see my number?" Brody asked.

"I'll think about it."

"Deal." Brody looked as satisfied as a dog with a big steak. "Last chance to get me into that BAU briefing."

"Now you're pushing your luck. Go away."

Brody leaned closer to Mason. "Good luck to you. I like her."

Brody nodded at Ava and vanished, leaving Mason speechless at the reporter's perception.

· · ·

Ava fought to keep her eyes open. The day had started early on a bridge far outside the city and felt like it would never end. She and Mason waited for Special Agent Bryan Euzent to start his briefing on his analysis of their unsub. Glancing around the room, she saw that the other agents looked as tired as she. Discreet yawns, peeks at watches, scanning of phones. The team was running on empty.

Zander slid into the chair next to her.

"Nice job at the press conference," she told him. "You handled that idiot at the back of the room with a lot more tact than I would have."

He shrugged. "You couldn't see the widespread eye rolling from the other reporters. The lack of professionalism was annoying them, too." He pinched the front of his shirt and shook it. "You also couldn't see how I was sweating under my shirt."

"Seriously? You seemed completely in control."

"Public speaking isn't my thing."

"Careful, if Duncan hears you say that, he'll throw you up front as much as he can to help you work through it."

Zander shuddered. "No, thanks."

On her other side, Mason leaned forward to speak to Zander. "What do you think about Carson Scott being chosen as the first victim to pull the FBI and early publicity to the cases?"

Ava's mind had been spinning with the theory since Michael Brody had mentioned it.

"Are you saying that might be the only motive behind Scott's murder?" Zander looked stunned.

Mason was grim. "No, but that's a possibility. Maybe out of this group of men, he was chosen to make certain all eyes were on the case early on. Both the public's eyes and the FBI."

Zander nodded slowly. "I can see that." He glanced at the agent opening his laptop on a table at the front of the small room. "We need to run that by Euzent."

Special Agent Euzent didn't look old enough to be one of the nation's experts on criminal profiling, or old enough to have graduated from college, but his looks were deceiving. A trim man with glasses, he looked like he could kick anyone's ass at chess. He'd flown out from Quantico, where he worked in the Behavioral Analysis Unit. He cleared his throat and the murmurs in the room quieted.

"So, your lucky city has hatched one of the odd ones, I'd say." Euzent grinned at the choked laughter he sparked in the room. "But in my book, the weirder they are, the more interesting they are, and they provide another opportunity for us to learn." He rubbed his hands together, and Ava could see the excited interest in his eyes. He had a specimen to dissect.

Ava understood the agent's humor. Some might find it disrespectful to joke about the deaths, but when you dived into the minds of killers every day, you learned to remove yourself from their twistedness to protect your mental health. Sometimes humor was the best way. A bit of detachment and a view of the deaths as an important puzzle to solve were how she stayed sane. She'd learned the mental skill while working in the Crimes Against Children division.

Euzent seemed pumped to share his observations with the group. "First let's look at whether or not you actually have a serial killer here. A serial killer hunts humans for the sexual type thrill and believes he can do it over and over, never expecting to be caught. Clearly your man is confident in his skills . . . yes, I'm going to say it's a man instead of a woman. The odds are with us, and there've been a few other signs that tell me we're dealing with a man.

"Our unsub does not expect to be caught. He's orchestrated three elaborate scenes without being noticed during the staging. I know you're still analyzing trace evidence, but for the most part, he hasn't left obvious clues to his identity. He has to be feeling pretty proud about that. He's going to want to do it again."

Moans sounded from the group.

I don't want another early morning on a bridge tomorrow.

Euzent gave a sympathetic smile. "I know. But from what I've seen, most unsubs enjoy their power to keep you hopping. They're addicted to that feeling, and can't keep up their standard of discreetness. They get sloppy as they focus on achieving satisfaction. This is what separates the serial killer from the mass killer. Typically the mass killer has an endgame strategy. He has a statement to make and doesn't expect to come out alive. These are your school and mall shooters."

Ava saw heads nodding all around the room. Clearly this didn't describe their unsub.

"He's also not a spree killer. Although three bodies in three days can indicate a spree, I see too much thought and planning in these deaths."

More nods.

"But how can you say he's getting a sexual thrill from these deaths? There's no sexual abuse of the bodies. I can't believe every serial killer is sexually motivated," stated Mason.

"Correct. He hasn't sexually abused the bodies. The thrill he's receiving is *comparable* to a sexual thrill. It's the manipulation, domination, and control of the crime that feeds the same pleasure center. He's not 'getting off' at the scene or with the victims; he's experiencing an identical high. Often they'll use fantasy to later remember the deaths and staging the scene to achieve a sexual release. This can be when the serial killer will start speeding up his game. His memories and fantasies of the deaths are insufficient, so he goes hunting again to satisfy his need for the thrill. But our unsub has set an amazing pace already. I don't think the sexual thrill is his driving factor. I think it's the control and domination of these particular men and the need for the world to witness it."

Ava raised a hand. "We've been debating a theory that Carson Scott was chosen as the first victim to shine the brightest spotlight on the deaths from the very beginning."

"I completely agree," Euzent stated, nodding emphatically. "Especially since the third victim has yet to be identified. He's clearly a quiet man whose death wouldn't command a lot of attention. Scott's death would. And did."

"But is that the only reason he was chosen?" asked Ava.

"Good question. I don't think we have enough information yet, but we'll keep that in mind as a possibility. It raises a question about the motive. Was there a different motive altogether for Carson Scott? As soon as we understand the motive, we'll figure out the who. We need to analyze the why, aided by the analysis of the how."

That's why we're sitting here. Ava took a deep breath, impatient for Euzent to give them some juicy meat to chew on. BAU agents had a tendency to microanalyze everything, but that was the process that made them the experts.

"Sometimes you have to look at what's not present at the scenes," Euzent went on. "Here's what I don't see in these cases. Our victims aren't wrapped in a sheet or covered in some way. A killer will often take that extra step when he has a bit of remorse or is demonstrating some tender feelings."

Mason and Zander snorted in unison. Ava had to smile. Yes, thinking of their unsub having tender feelings was a stretch.

"There's been no attempt to give the victims some dignity or possibly hide them from sight of other people. Someone who does this would be a person who doesn't feel good about what he's just done. Our unsub proudly displays the victims for all to see. He doesn't give a rat's ass about the victims and has no remorse."

"Clearly," muttered Mason.

"But what about the bandaged wrists and clean bodies?" asked Ava. "Do you see that as an indication of feelings for the victims? He's apparently taken some care to make them presentable."

"Excellent point. I've taken that into consideration, but I feel that he's bandaged them and cleaned them for his own requirements in preparing his scenes, not out of any sympathy. The cleaning is most likely to remove some evidence and the bandaged wrists are to make the victim easier to work with."

Ava leaned back in her chair, mulling over the agent's words.

"I think the unsub is getting back at people he believes hurt or slighted him."

The atmosphere in the room perked up and Ava nodded. They'd all felt the controlled anger expressed by the public display of nudity and violence.

"Now, why is our subject taking this path to express his displeasure?" Euzent paused and looked around the room. "Let's consider what brings a man to this action. Obviously, when most people are pissed off, they don't hang their naked neighbors from the closest bridge, so why did our guy take that step? And repeat it two more times so far?"

So far. Ava cringed. Euzent clearly believed their subject wasn't finished.

"In our research we've found that the subject's history has a great influence on his actions of today. Typically this unsub comes from a background where he felt powerless and out of control. Most abused or neglected children develop coping skills, like sports or hobbies. Others soothe hurt feelings by making others hurt. Who hasn't picked on their younger sibling in an attempt to make themselves feel better? This is part of the mind-set of bullies. They feel better by making others miserable. Some children or teens move on to small animals." Euzent's tone was staid and collected, his jokes gone.

"But everyone who's kicked their dog or picked on a sibling doesn't grow up to kill," an agent commented from behind Ava. "Are some just crazy?"

"'Crazy' is a subjective term, but we all know what you're trying to say. We want a label we can slap on people to explain what they do, but we've found that most people *choose* to act as they do. Someone who is crazy, or maybe I should use the term 'insane,' is compelled to act, but there are very few true insanity cases out there. I believe most people are responsible for their actions."

"They make a conscious choice," said the agent in a stunned voice behind Ava.

"I think so," agreed Euzent. "A lot of them learned early on that manipulating others gave them a sense of control that was missing in their lives."

"A sense of supreme power," added Ava.

"Exactly," said Euzent.

"And you think he's striking out at these particular men because of how they've wronged him in his past?" Ava asked.

"Or how he has *perceived* he's been wronged. Maybe they did truly hurt him in some way, but often the real story has been distorted in the unsub's mind. Either way, he's extremely organized. He's thought through every step of his scenes and considered every possibility of what to do if something goes wrong. I believe he's from the Portland metropolitan area. He knows the area very well and is comfortable with the rural outer areas all the way into the heart of the city. I suspect he's lived here most of his life to develop that comfort.

"His vehicle and home will reflect a very clean person. Maybe to the point of obsessiveness. The way he bandaged the cuts in the wrists and cleaned the victims after letting them bleed out speaks of someone who is a bit of a neat freak. The bodies were incredibly clean, according to the medical examiner's report. Death is a messy business and our unsub took pains to mask that fact.

"He has to have a place to hold the victims, kill them, and deal with the cleaning of the bodies. The timeline shows he's possibly held more than one person at a time. He's not going to have an apartment or condo with close neighbors. We're looking for a single-family home with room for him to breathe and not worry about being discovered. I have a hard time believing a neat freak would let someone bleed out inside his home, so I suspect the house will have a basement where he does his work, or a substantial outbuilding on the property to contain these men. I believe urban areas are too populated. He won't risk someone stumbling on his secret. Most likely a home on a large lot in the suburbs or in the outer rural areas. The missing vehicles are probably stored at his place. This would lend itself to the theory of additional outbuildings on the property. Usually vehicles turn up within a few days and we haven't found them. People complain when vehicles are parked where they shouldn't be."

Ava knew the police had been scouring the giant lots at the airport and malls, checking the usual places vehicles are hidden in plain sight. But wouldn't that require two people—someone to drive the vehicle there and someone to give a ride home? Or would it? At the airport he could enter the lot, park, catch the shuttle to the terminal, and then take a cab home. No additional help needed. But he'd be risking several chances to turn up on cameras. If he was as particular as Euzent believed him to be, would he take that risk?

"Do you think he's working alone?" Ava asked.

Euzent took a deep breath. "Everything tells me he is working alone. His preciseness speaks of someone who believes he needs to do something himself to get it right. I'm a little stumped that he managed to hang such a heavy victim, but he could be incredibly strong, or smart enough to figure out a system to make it happen."

"What do you think of the increase in abuse of the bodies?" Zander questioned. "Each one has been hanged. Then he added the ball gag and then the third one had the shaved head and cuts in the skin."

Special Agent Euzent nodded and paced back and forth, frowning as Zander recited his list. "He's definitely escalating. But it's in a very controlled way. I feel like he has a deliberate plan that he is exposing to us a step at a time. There's a reason for the ball gag and cuts and shaved head. Just as there's a reason they weren't all done to the earlier victims." He stopped pacing and looked at the group of agents, a muscle clenching in his jaw. "He has a story to tell and these are his particular components. I know these elements have been run through NCIC, but we've received no hits."

Ava nodded; she'd run multiple searches.

What will he add to the next victim?

"Age?" asked Mason.

"Close to the age of the victims. Statistics suggest he's Caucasian. The first two men are the same age and the third looks pretty close. I strongly believe we're looking for a member of their peer group who feels wronged by these particular men. Another fact that makes me wonder if these victims know each other is the speed of these killings. Are they being rapidly killed so the others don't have time to hear about their acquaintances' deaths?"

"So keep searching for where their circles intersect," said Zander.

Euzent nodded. "Think of it as a Venn diagram. Your killer will be in the very center."

14

Mason watched as Ava shook her umbrella outside before entering the medical examiner's office the next morning. He'd been spying on her from the waiting room since he saw her vehicle pull into the lot. She leaped over a wide puddle, missed, and soaked the hem of her slacks. He couldn't hear her swear, but he read it clearly on her lips. And then she turned her face up to the rain and laughed.

He smiled. She'd be embarrassed if she knew he was watching her. He watched her all the time, whether she was cooking, playing with Bingo, or frowning at her laptop. Her exhilaration made him happy. He'd been living a dull, dry life, and she was a burst of color in his black-and-white world. When he was around her, the air felt cleaner, more energized, and he sucked it in like a drowning man.

How long could his luck last?

She pushed through the doors, wiping her feet on the mats, and her face lit up when she spotted him.

He grinned and prayed his luck would last a lifetime.

She did a quick glance around the empty room and gave him a peck on the lips, grinning at the stolen kiss.

"Let's go. Dr. Rutledge is ready for us. Ray and Zander already went in," Mason said, taking her elbow and guiding her toward the inner doors. "How was your interview with the manager at Universe of Tires?"

This morning her alarm's music had surprised both of them. Mason had assumed they'd be awakened by a phone call summoning them to another death. They'd looked at each other and grabbed their phones to check for missed calls, believing they'd slept through a discovery. Even now Mason was on edge, waiting for the call to convene on a bridge.

"The interview was fine," Ava said. "Even though Aaron King was an assistant manager, he struggled to be on time. Which jibes with what his ex-wife said about him being unreliable. For the most part he got along with everyone and his boss claimed his work was impeccable. He was one of those guys that was fascinated with vehicles and loved getting his hands dirty with them."

"For the most part?" Mason asked as they moved down the hallway toward the autopsy suites.

Ava shrugged. "His boss said a couple of employees struggled with his ego, and he'd talked with him a few times about toning it down. But the guy knows tires and wasn't afraid to assert his knowledge."

"Sounds more like some personalities clashed. Was he a bully?" Special Agent Euzent's comments about bullying were fresh in Mason's mind.

Ava crinkled her forehead. "I don't know. I didn't get that impression from his boss or from his ex-wife. But I guess he could have been when he was younger. Is that what you're getting at?"

"Yes. If someone feels they've been wronged by Aaron King and Carson Scott, I want to know how it happened."

"I asked the boss if Aaron had an escalated incident with a customer. He said if it'd happened, he didn't know about it. He'd quizzed his staff over the last few days, trying to find out if something had occurred with a customer, but no one had any stories."

"Dr. Rutledge completed the autopsy on our third victim last night while we were at the briefing," Mason told her. "He has some details he wanted to show us in person."

"Great," said Ava, interest lighting up her face.

Mason preferred a written report, but Ava liked the hands-on demonstrations from the ME. He guided her to the office where he'd left the other men minutes before. Dr. Rutledge had pulled up a series of photos on two large computer monitors. Mason silently exhaled in relief, and wondered if Ava was disappointed.

She nodded at the other men and stepped closer, studying the photos before Seth Rutledge began talking.

"I was pretty close on estimating his weight," began Dr. Rutledge. "He was three hundred sixty-three pounds."

"How the heck did our unsub hang him?" muttered Ray, shaking his head.

"I have a theory on that," answered the ME. "If you look here," he clicked his mouse and pulled up a block of six photos that showed the victim's armpits, "you can see some deep abrasions that were made postmortem. They're two inches wide and dig into the flesh under his arms. *And* they line up with that white band across his back."

Ava frowned. "So the stripe across his back was from something tied around his chest? And it was tied while he was on his back long enough to have that daisy pattern? Do you think this was from a strap for a pulley?"

Dr. Rutledge nodded.

Mason pictured a wide band looped under the victim's armpits that was attached to something to lift it. "But if he tries to lift him, won't his arms simply go upward and he'd slip out of the band?"

"My first thought, too." Dr. Rutledge changed the photos to views of the victim's forearms. "There are lighter abrasions across his forearms, just above the bandaging for the slits in the wrists, and it left a thick tape residue. I excised some samples for evidence, but my theory is that he ran duct tape around the victim's belly and arms, pinning down his arms while he was lifted. This was in addition to the light scatter of tape residue I found on all three victims, where I believe he taped their arms down to hold them still as they bled out."

Mason lifted a brow. "To me, duct tape says 'quick fix.' Our perfect-planning suspect may have been surprised that his original plan didn't work quite right, so he improvised."

There were nods from all the investigators.

"I bet that ticked him off," Mason speculated with a grimace.

"So he designed and rigged a system to lift the victim on his own," Zander stated. "Just like we'd thought. Euzent was right that he isn't the type to work with a helper. I assume there's some sort of pulley system he could install in his van?"

"I think so," answered Ray. "Anyone who has a bit of mechanical handiness and has time to do a little research could figure out a way. We already know this unsub is extremely meticulous and prepared."

"Except when it came to doing the actual lifting," added Mason.

"But he had duct tape handy," answered Ray. "So he's the type who's prepared for emergencies."

"A regular Boy Scout," quipped Mason.

"Could he hire someone to install the pulley in his van?" Ava asked.

"That depends." Ray shrugged. "He's got a utility-type van. If he didn't care about drilling holes in it or some other cosmetic damage, I'll bet he spent some time on Google and figured out how to install a system himself. Give me ten minutes on the Internet, and I can find several solutions for his problem."

"It also points to how deliberate his choice of the victim is," Zander added. "He wanted *this guy*. He went to a lot of extra work to hang this particular victim off a bridge. He wasn't grabbing men at random; his list is precise."

"I bet he was hating every moment of extra work this victim created," Mason said, enjoying the image of their frustrated unsub. "He probably wished he had to hang any other guy but this one. You're right, Zander, he has certain people on his list, just like Euzent said."

"Three very different victims," murmured Ava. "We need to find out what ties them together. What else can you tell us about him?" she asked Dr. Rutledge.

"That his weight would have eventually killed him. His organs were covered in fat and his diaphragm was pushed up into his chest cavity, pressing on his heart and lungs. His liver was storing fat instead of dealing with it, making the liver hard instead of a healthy, spongy tissue. And he had the remains of a burger, fries, and a shake in his stomach. So he was killed within a few hours of a meal, which lines up with my time-of-death estimate of noon to three on Wednesday."

Mason swore he felt last night's takeout burger swirl in his gut.

"His hands were extremely calloused, and he had several old scars and healing injuries to his forearms that make me think he does some sort of manual labor. His hands were pretty clear, so possibly he wears gloves when he works." A few clicks of the mouse brought up photos that corresponded to the ME's descriptions.

Mason eyed the healing scrapes and old scars. "It does look like manual labor. Maybe scrapes from wood." He pointed at a rough-looking scrape on the screen. "I used to get marked like that when I worked in the plywood mill during college summers and pulled a board wrong. Or maybe he works in construction. Did he have slivers in some of those abrasions?"

"I was just about to mention that," answered Dr. Rutledge. "I pulled out several old slivers of wood. So maybe he works at a lumber mill or for a builder."

"So he's blue-collar. A far cry from a politician like Carson Scott. Maybe he runs in the same circles as Aaron King?" Zander suggested.

"I gave a general description of our John Doe when I spoke to Aaron's manager this morning," Ava said. "I had him run it by the guys who knew Aaron best, but none of them had seen Aaron with a man who looked like this. I emailed a description to his ex-wife yesterday, but she had the same answer. Aaron didn't have any friends or acquaintances of this size that she knew of."

"Somebody will notice he's missing," Ray asserted. "Obviously he's a working man. His boss will speak up at some point and then we'll have a better trail to follow."

"I wish we could tell the media we don't have a serial killer running loose in the city," Ava commented. "The press is fostering fear. The public are getting nervous to the point where they're going to start shooting at shadows."

"There is one running loose," said Mason. "But I know what you mean. He's got a list. He's probably not interested in Joe Blow who's making a late run to the grocery store. But I don't think that's something we can share with confidence. With our luck, our killer would change tactics because we state we believe he has a plan."

Zander nodded. "I talked to Euzent a little more about motivation after his briefing last night. He pointed out that the approach our unsub is taking says a lot about his motive. Everyone's heard the old saying 'Killers don't call and callers don't kill,' right? Did our killer warn these guys? No, because their friends weren't aware of it, and at least one of the victims would have reported a death threat to the police. Right?

"Did the killer warn the city that deaths were about to take place? No. If he had, Euzent says his motive could have been financial and not to cause death. But because this killer has started out silently and methodically, it shows the mission is very personal to him. I don't think he would target other victims just to be contrary if he thought we had insight into his actions. He's not a *crazy killer.* He's a hunter with a very specific prey."

"Let's get this third victim identified," said Ava. "It'll bring us a giant step closer to stopping that hunter and figuring out why these deaths are personal to him."

• • •

Ava was still in her car, about to get out and head to her office, when her personal phone rang. She studied the unfamiliar number and went against her better judgment, answering the call.

Jayne sobbed at her voice.

After a few moments of Jayne's unintelligible ranting and tears, Ava drew some coherent words out of her twin.

"He thinks they're going to kill him," Jayne blurted.

Ava's bullshit meter shot up, but she managed to calmly ask, "Who? Who are you talking about?"

"Derrick. Derrick says they're going to kill him."

The name rang a faint bell. The other set of fingerprints in Mason's home had belonged to a Derrick. "The guy you're with?" she asked.

"Yes! You've got to do something! Is there a safe house you can hide us in? I know we can't come stay with you!"

Damn right.

"Jayne, why are you hanging around with this man? It sounds like it's dangerous." She spoke with a measured cadence, trying to get her sister to slow down her own words.

"I love him! And he needs someone to help him!"

Ava closed her eyes. Jayne was either high or drunk. Ava was wasting time trying to have a logical conversation. "Jayne, you need to find a place where *you're* safe. He doesn't need your help."

"Oh, Ava. You don't understand. Someone followed him last night, and he only got away because he knew where to hide. He says the guy had a gun."

"Jayne," Ava said firmly. "Tell him to go to the police."

"He can't."

"Why not?" *Because of his long record?*

"The police won't help him. They never help him. He doesn't know what to do."

"Is it because he's wanted by the police? For break-ins? *Like stealing a TV and our mother's necklace?*"

Jayne sucked in a ragged breath.

"Where's Mom's ring on the chain, Jayne? If you sold it for a measly five dollars so you could buy something to drink, I'm never speaking to you again." Ava's voice cracked and tears burned at the corners of her eyes. "You two broke into Mason's home and *stole*! And we know it was you. There are fingerprints everywhere."

"I didn't—"

"Don't lie to me!"

"You don't under—"

"What makes theft okay for you? What has dragged you so low that you would steal from me and my friends?"

"I didn't know you were living with him." Jayne fumbled for words.

"Of course you did. You followed me to see where I was going. You knew full well I was living there, because you took Mom's necklace out of the drawer! Where is it?"

"I still have it," she whispered. "I couldn't sell it."

Relief swept over Ava. *She could be lying.* "If I find out you're lying—"

"I'm not," Jayne cried. "I'm wearing it right now. It's all I have left. I had to move out of my apartment because you wouldn't help me and all my stuff is gone!"

"Where are you living?"

"I can't tell you. Derrick says—"

"*Jayne.* Derrick is bad news. You need to get away from him. I can help you find a place, but first you have to let him go," Ava pleaded, feeling a strong sense of déjà vu. How many times had she had this conversation where she begged Jayne to change her behavior?

It never worked.

"I can't leave him. He needs me."

"He needs you for what? Sex? To whore yourself for money for both of you?"

Jayne was silent, and Ava wanted to scream.

"I've always said I'll help people I see trying to help themselves. What you're doing doesn't remotely resemble helping yourself, Jayne. You're digging your hole deeper and deeper."

"He's afraid they're going to kill him and hang him off a bridge. Like those other guys," Jayne whispered.

A drug user's paranoia. Ava wanted to bang her head on the steering wheel. "Why does he think that, Jayne?"

"He won't tell me. He's terrified and says we have to hide."

"Jayne, I don't know what kinds of drugs you've been doing with Derrick, but you know that no one thinks clearly when their brain is messed up. I know you've heard this a thousand times. And the two of you *are* using, right?"

She didn't answer.

"What are you on, Jayne?"

"It's just a little pot."

Right. "Derrick is paranoid. Even a *little* pot causes that. Do you know there are warrants out for his arrest? No wonder he's paranoid, Jayne. He's constantly looking over his shoulder for the police."

"He says he didn't—"

"Jayne, I don't care what he says. He lies. You lie. Nothing ever changes." Ava's head throbbed with the pain radiating from her clenched jaw. "Maybe I can find you a spot in a women's shelter. Do you have a safe place right now?" In the background Ava heard the sounds of cars, people, and what she suspected was the MAX light rail line. It sounded like Jayne was in downtown Portland.

"We're staying with some friends of Derrick's . . . but I don't like it there," she whispered. "The people aren't fun anymore."

Ava burned with the need to shake some common sense into her sister. *Fun.* Her sister's world revolved around the pursuit of fun at the cost of everyone around her.

Just get her away from that man.

"I just wish it could go back to the way it was," her twin begged. "I don't like living with these people."

"Go back to when, Jayne?" Ava asked, swallowing the lump in her throat.

"To when I was happy."

"When were you happy?"

"Oh, you know. When we were in school, and all we had to worry about was what we'd wear the next day."

Ava was silent. Back then Ava had worried about homework, her part-time job, and pulling her weight, since their mother was a single mom. Worrying about what to wear meant avoiding the exact same outfit as her sister. Apparently Jayne remembered those days differently. Their mother had dressed them alike until they were five, when Ava had started asserting that she no longer wanted to look the same as Jayne.

As a child, had she known that she needed to separate herself from her twin?

"I can't help you," Ava said quietly. "Call me when you're serious about changing your life. That means no man, no drugs, and rehab. Again."

Jayne started crying. "But what about Derrick? How do I protect him?"

"Tell him to turn himself in. He'll be safe from the Bridge Killer in jail."

"You don't under—"

"Good-bye, Jayne." Ava ended the call and turned off the ringer. She wiped her eyes and tucked her phone in her purse. She sat in her car, taking deep breaths and waiting for her heartbeat to slow down.

I won't second-guess my decision.

The color had been sucked out of her day. When she ended the call, the world inside her car had abruptly gone quiet and gray from the rain. The plinking tones on her roof were sounds of loneliness.

No. They're sounds of peace.

When Jayne burst into Ava's world, either in person or by phone, everything lit up and zinged with crazy energy. The void left by her absence was one of peace and quiet.

Not loneliness.

She closed her eyes for a moment and imagined the water was the sound of an ocean. Her first therapist had taught her to view the quiet of Jayne's absence as healthy tranquility.

It was all about perspective. The change she felt each time Jayne stepped away was a good change.

Then why does it hurt so bad?

15

Mason stared at the blood-drenched carpet in Joe Upton's home and wondered why the killer had changed his tactics, leaving a clear view of his killing ground. Their third victim now had a name. Joe Upton's boss had knocked on his front door when Joe didn't show up for work at the lumberyard. He'd glanced through a front window, let himself in, walked through the murder scene, and then called the police.

Joe Upton lived out in the boondocks. Grandview, Washington, was in the middle of nowhere, about halfway between Kennewick and Yakima. A logical route would take a person to the Bridge of the Gods in about two hours during a drive toward Portland. The house was a small ranch-style home on a five-acre lot. County records had revealed the home belonged to Joe Upton's parents, who currently lived in Arizona.

Mason had shared a ride with Zander and Ava, leaving Ray back in Portland. It'd taken over three hours to reach the small town, stretching out a long day that'd begun at the medical examiner's. They'd been met by Grandview's chief of police, who'd made the connection between the unidentified murder in the Columbia Gorge and the bloodstains in the Upton home.

"I'd heard about the murders on the bridges," the chief had said when he'd called the FBI. "Most folks in town don't pay much attention to what's going on outside of Grandview. But when I realized someone had lost a lot of blood in Joe's home, and he was missing, I checked online, and, sure enough, the latest description fit."

The chief was about Mason's age, with a sharp eye and a direct glare that must have made the teenagers in Grandview turn down their car stereos when he looked their way. The chief listened as Mason, Ava, and Zander questioned Joe's boss, Samuel, who sat on the bumper of Zander's sedan in his stockinged feet.

"I tried to call Joe three times yesterday. I kept getting his voicemail," said Samuel, who reminded Mason of a stocky Kevin Costner with a lot less hair. "When he didn't show up for work again today, I decided to drive out. I got a little worried when I saw his truck was in the driveway. He's a big guy. I was half expecting to find him dead from a heart attack."

"Joe worked for you full time?" Ava asked.

"Nah, only three days a week. He works construction the other days when they have work for him. He does framing and drywall for the Carter outfit, but that's mainly during the summer. Right now it's slow all around."

"He have any enemies that you're aware of? He get in any fights with anyone?" Mason asked.

"Who, Joe? Are you kidding me? He's a big teddy bear."

The police chief nodded at Samuel's statement. "Joe's a big guy, but his heart is bigger. He'd give you the shirt off his back."

Mason exchanged a glance with Ava and Zander. *So why murder this guy?* At least Carson Scott and Aaron King had given reasons for people not to like them.

"I assume Joe didn't talk to you about the bridge deaths in the Portland area," Mason said. Both men shook their heads.

"He know anyone from that area? Maybe I should be asking whoever he hangs out with the most," Mason said.

"That'd be me," said Samuel. "Joe wasn't one for socializing. He kept to himself. If he knew anyone from Portland, I wasn't aware of it. He watched movies for entertainment. You'll see he has a huge DVD collection. I told him he could store a lot more movies in digital format than those plastic boxes, but he didn't want anything to do with it. He likes to own the physical movie."

"Surely he has other people he talks with," contended Ava. "Are you saying he's like a hermit?"

"He talks a bit to the people he works with. I wouldn't call him a hermit, but he doesn't go out of his way to get together with people. I can give you the number for the construction company, but they haven't had any projects for the last few months." Samuel frowned. "He really does keep to himself. I guess I didn't think about it until now."

"How long ago did his parents move to Arizona?" asked Zander.

Samuel raised a brow at the police chief, who shrugged and replied, "I'd say at least ten years. They used to come back every now and then, but I haven't seen them for about three years. Nice folks. Your medical examiner told me he'd notify them when he had a concrete identification."

"Good," said Mason. He had no doubts their third victim was Joe Upton; he'd seen his driver's license photo and it matched the man he'd seen on the bridge. Dr. Rutledge's ID shouldn't take long.

"Records show the house was purchased fifteen years ago; do you know where they lived before that?" asked Zander.

The men looked at each other and shook their heads. Mason knew Ava had already set the wheels in motion to find out where the Uptons had previously lived.

Find where the victims' circles intersect.

"You're the only one that went in the house, right?" Ava asked Samuel.

"Yeah, I'm sorry about that. I knew I might have messed up some evidence once I saw Joe wasn't there," said Samuel, looking sheepish. "When I saw the blood, I grabbed the backup key from the fence post and checked the rest of the house to make certain he wasn't hurt somewhere. I really didn't touch anything except to push open some doors inside. I stepped around the blood the best I could, but I got some on my boots." He pointed at the house. "I left them on the front porch when I came out."

The group from the task force, and the police chief, made their way up the steps to the front porch. They gloved and bootied up, and Ava pulled out her camera. They'd requested an FBI forensics team when they'd reached the home, but the team wouldn't arrive for a few more hours. Mason figured Grandview's forensics unit would be a fishing tackle box in the trunk of the chief's car. Ava would take the pictures the group immediately wanted.

Zander carefully opened the door. The group and the police chief stepped through the entry. The odor of iron and excrement assaulted Mason's nose. To their right, a slaughter had occurred in the living room, its tan carpet dark with congealed blood. And other bodily substances.

Murder is untidy. The bowels and bladder release. It's not the clean collapse seen in movies and television. When an artery is sliced, the heart pumps the blood out of the body with strong strokes until it lacks the oxygen to keep working. Mason swallowed hard and studied the carpet. *How much blood does a body hold?* Somewhere from the depths of his mind, he recalled it could hold over a gallon . . . for a normal-size person. It seemed like Joe Upton had held more than twice that. Beside him, Ava started breathing through her mouth.

The four stopped just inside the door, studying the scene.

"He's left us some evidence," Ava said softly. "Finally."

Or did he leave what he wanted us to find?

"Why this time?" asked Zander. "What's changed?"

The house was silent as the group stood still, each memorizing the pieces of the puzzle that'd been left behind. Ava lifted her camera and started to shoot, the clicking of the shutter the sole noise in the silence.

The home's furniture was from an earlier decade and displayed the wear of heavy use. The once overstuffed sofa and recliner had permanent impressions in their cushions. The decor was nonexistent, exactly what Mason had expected in the home of a bachelor. A lack of interior design had been apparent in his own home until Ava moved in. A predictable large-screen TV hung on the closest wall, framed by two ceiling-high bookcases packed with DVDs and Blu-rays. Empty Diet Dr Pepper cans and microwave meal trays cluttered the end tables.

A blue tarp, two utility buckets containing discolored water, two two-by-fours, at least six blood-crusted bath towels, and one utility knife lay scattered about the floor.

"Jesus Christ," muttered Zander. "So this is the remains of someone's obsession."

Mason silently agreed with the term "obsession." Their killer had traveled to Grandview for the sole purpose of murdering Joe Upton and assembling his death scene down to the minute details. But this time their killer had left an open window into his world. "We'll find him. He's left too much behind. Our answer is in this mess."

Zander took a step closer, avoiding the blood, and squatted down to get a look at the three-foot-long two-by-fours. Balls of wadded-up bloody tape lay next to the boards. He glanced behind him at the blood streaks on the walls. "There's the arterial spray Dr. Rutledge told us would show up." Zander traced in the air the different heights of the wild arcs of dried brown blood. "As the blood emptied, the arcs got weaker." He studied the floor in front of the marked wall. "And the pattern isn't broken between where the body lay and the walls. Nothing blocked the spray. Our killer knew where to position himself to not get hit by the blood. I wonder if he learned that from the first two deaths or researched it first?"

Ava pointed her camera at the streaks. "Something tells me he knew exactly what to expect."

Mason tilted his head at her. "You think he's in the medical field? Dr. Rutledge did comment how perfect the cuts were on the wrists." He eyed the bloody tarp. "And it takes a strong stomach to create a scene like this three times."

"I think the medical field is an option," she replied.

"Or he had a rural upbringing," added the police chief. "I could gut and skin a deer without blinking by the time I was sixteen."

Mason semi-agreed. It'd been a long time since he'd hunted, but there'd been a time when he could do the same. "But we're talking about people here," he said, looking at the chief.

The chief shrugged. "Maybe he views these men as less than human." He scowled at the wrinkled tarp lying in a jumbled, bloody heap. "What was he doing with the tarp? He clearly wasn't protecting the carpet."

"He used it to help clean up the body." Mason pointed at the buckets next to the tarp. "I bet he cleaned up the front of the body and then rolled it onto its stomach on the tarp to clean the back. That's what the towels are for. And he rinsed them in the buckets. I think he had to have at least one more tarp he wrapped around the body for transport. There wasn't a spot of blood on any of the bodies at the scenes."

"But how'd he get a guy that size out of the house?" Ava asked.

"He had to have help," stated the chief.

Zander shook his head and pointed toward the back of the home. "Look at these faint smears that go toward the back door. He dragged the body. Probably wrapped up in the tarp Mason mentioned. If our killer had a piece of plywood in the back of his van, he could have used it as a ramp to drag the body up. It'd be heavy, but I think one man could do it. Hang on a minute." Zander carefully hugged the edge of the room as he walked toward the sliding back door. He opened the door with a finger and stepped out onto a small deck. He returned moments later. "I can see a drag trail across the boards of the deck and tire marks in the grass below. The deck height is pretty close to the height of a van. I bet he backed his van up to the deck, used a board, and slid him right in."

Mason couldn't see any errors in Zander's observation. If it was true, it cemented Special Agent Euzent's theory that they had a perfectionist killer who planned well in advance. Mason looked at the scene again. "If our killer is such a neat freak, why'd he leave this mess for us to find? Murder weapon included. Looks like Dr. Rutledge was right that a utility knife had made the cuts."

"I think the utility knife is probably the least important piece of evidence left behind," added Ava. "It was a simple tool for him to use, and we all know there won't be any prints on it."

Everyone nodded.

"But this will be a treasure trove for Euzent to study," she continued. "There are so many questions raised in this room, my mind is boggled."

Mason took a careful step and lifted a corner of the bloody tarp to get a closer look at a black piece of plastic he'd spotted. "Cell phone." He looked up at the chief. "Would you go ask Samuel to call Joe's number? I don't want to touch the screen." The man nodded and vanished.

"There're too many differences here." Zander scowled. "We've got the victim's vehicle out front, his cell phone, *and* the crime scene. This doesn't match up with our first two men."

Mason disagreed. "No, the only difference is that we haven't found the first two crime scenes. I bet they look just like this one. What's different is that he used the victim's home, and I suspect that was because it fit his needs. It's already isolated. The first two vics lived in dense housing that wasn't convenient for murder. Plus it was a long-ass drive out here. I bet he picked the Bridge of the Gods because it was between the victim's home and his own."

"Not to mention it's flashy," pointed out Ava. "Our killer likes to shock and make a point."

"Agreed," said Mason. The cell phone on the floor rang, playing "The Imperial March" from *Star Wars*. Mason stood and studied the shelves of movies. Alphabetized. Scanning, he saw a large section of *Star Wars* boxes including the *Clone Wars* television seasons.

"That music will be stuck in my head all day," said Ava, sticking a finger in an ear as if she could block the sound.

Mason continued scanning the titles, learning that Joe Upton was a huge sci-fi and horror fan. Mason enjoyed a good action flick no matter the genre, but Joe's collection indicated a different level of enjoyment. It resembled a teenager's.

Or a man who'd never grown up and who clung to the behaviors of his youth.

Zander's comment from that morning echoed in Mason's head. *He's a hunter with a very specific prey.*

Why had he chosen this seemingly placid and introverted man?

• • •

Mason rolled his eyes as he saw Michael Brody's name flash on his phone late that evening. The reporter had remembered their deal. Had Mason really thought the near-genius would forget? He answered.

"You know, Callahan, you could have just called me and told me the name as soon as you found out to save me from making a phone call," Brody replied.

"The deal was I'd tell you yes or no on a name. You have a name to run by me?"

Ava glanced at Mason as she added more wine to his glass. "Brody," he whispered, and she nodded. She'd quizzed him about the pushy reporter after their meeting, trying to get a perspective on Mason's relationship with Michael Brody.

"He's the gum on my shoe," Mason had told her.

"But you obviously respect him," she'd pointed out.

"What tells you that?"

"The way you interacted with him."

"You picked that up from a five-minute conversation?" he asked.

"I could tell the minute you started talking to him. It takes a lot to earn your respect. Most people spend a lot of time on your list, waiting for a chance to prove if they're worth your time or not. Brody already earned it."

Mason had stared. She'd perfectly summed up his attitude toward the human race.

She gets me.

Who'd tapped him with the lucky stick?

He watched her move about his living room, patting the dog, straightening a book, and setting her laptop near her bag to grab in the morning. He couldn't take his gaze off her.

"Callahan?" Brody said in his ear.

"What?" he snapped into his cell phone, realizing Ava had completely distracted him by doing . . . nothing.

"I asked if it's Joe Upton. From Grandview, Washington."

"Yes, that's right. And it's Junior, not the senior Joe Upton."

"Noted," said Brody. "Have you found any connections between him and the two other victims?"

Mason sighed. "No. He's the same age. Thirty-five. That's all we've got so far. And I'd appreciate it if you didn't say that we're a bunch of idiots with no leads, please."

"Since you said please," said Brody. "Having a woman around must soften you up. I don't think I've ever heard you say please except to order a cup of coffee."

"We're done talking, Brody. Go bug someone else." He ended the call.

He picked up his glass of wine and sipped. He hadn't been a wine fan. He'd avoided it, not caring for the acidic, fruity flavor he'd always encountered, but Ava had introduced him to something dark and bloody red. He never remembered the name, but it had hints of smoke and coffee and earth. It was a manly wine, he'd told her the first time he tasted it. She'd found his description amusing but agreed. Now they always kept a bottle on hand.

The wine was a reflection of her. That smoke in her low voice and the down-to-earth rationality that shone in her eyes. He identified the scent of the wine with how he felt when he was around her.

She made him relax. A glass of wine, a quiet conversation, maybe some music.

It was a stark contrast to his previous rigid life of work, work, and more work.

He still worked a lot, but now he worked beside someone: The opportunity to partner with her on the same case had proved how well they meshed. He patted the sofa cushion next to him, and she sank into it with a sigh. She scooted close and leaned her head on his shoulder. The scent of the dark wine on her breath drifted to his nose, and he felt his muscles relax.

"A long day," he said as he brushed her hair behind an ear.

"They're all long right now. Not that I expect that to change until we find the Bridge Killer."

"How is your arm?"

She gingerly rotated her left shoulder. "The same."

"You missed your appointment this week, didn't you?"

"I did." She grimaced. "And I caught hell for it. I've been doing my exercises, though. It'll eventually come around."

"Any more out of Jayne?" Ava had told him about her most recent phone call.

"No," Ava said quietly. "Are the doors locked?"

"Yep. And the alarm is set." He'd had an alarm installed immediately, calling in a favor from an ex-cop who ran a reputable alarm business. When it'd just been him living in the house, he'd sort of hoped to encounter a burglar one day. He'd been prepared to make a punk's life miserable if one dared enter his home. Now with Ava in the home, his mind-set had shifted to prevention.

He didn't want anyone getting in. Again.

"I've been thinking about your place," he said slowly, not knowing where the words had come from. They'd delicately touched on the topic of her selling her place a time or two, but both had immediately shied away from discussing it in depth. "You know I love you. I think we've proved we get along pretty well."

Her body shook with silent laughter, making him smile. She'd once said they got along like peas and carrots.

"We mesh perfectly," she said. "None of this 'pretty well' bullshit."

"Good. Sell your place and move in here. Or we could rent it out, I guess, but I don't really want to be a landlord."

She took a sip of wine and her silence filled the room.

"Ava?"

"I don't know. I've been asking myself why I don't put it on the market. I don't think I'm ready to yet," she finished slowly.

He touched her chin to turn her to meet his gaze. Dark-blue eyes looked back at him as he studied her face, loving the small scattering of freckles along the tops of her cheeks. She looked sincere. She didn't look scared. "Are you uncertain?" he asked.

Her lips curved slightly. "I'm uncertain about what to do with the condo. I'm very certain about us."

"I don't want to pressure you." *Yes, I do.* Some odd part of him wanted to beat his chest and command her to do as he said. Instead he smiled.

"Wow." Her face lit up, and she grinned. "That's a fake smile. You're clearly not saying what you want to say."

"Fine." *She wants to hear what I really think?* "I want you moved in here permanently. I want to trip over your dozens of shoes in my closet and complain that you hog all the hangers. If you don't want to live here, we can start looking for another house. I'm fine with that.

I'm not attached to this place. In fact, I'd love to start somewhere fresh and call it ours. Maybe we should be selling two places, not just yours."

She tilted her head at him, surprise parting her lips. "I think you're absolutely right. I love the thought of finding our own home." Her eyebrows narrowed. "The more I think about it, the more I like the idea, and I suddenly feel comfortable letting that condo go. Ohhh. House shopping together." Her eyes lit up as she teased him.

Surprisingly, he didn't have his usual gut-churning reaction to the idea of shopping.

"It's a big step," he said cautiously.

Dark-blue eyes smiled at him. "I'm ready. Hell, I can't wait. Where would you like to live?"

Mason scratched at his head. He hadn't thought that far ahead. "I'm not sure. I like bigger lots and established neighborhoods, but I don't want a longer commute. Do we have to talk about this right now?"

"Nope. We've got all the time in the world. Just as long as you know I want a dream kitchen. Custom cabinets, imported glass tiles, expensive appliances." She leaned closer and kissed him, blending her wine-flavored lips with his.

"You barely cook."

"So? Don't I deserve something gorgeous?" Her lips smiled against his.

"Absolutely." All thoughts of houses left his brain. The sensation of Ava pressing against him sent his mind racing in a different direction. He couldn't help it. When she was near, he wanted more. Hell, he wanted all of her. Being near her in an office environment kept him under control, but with her so close in his home and the comfortable sofa and her natural female scent mixed with the smoky wine . . .

He stood and pulled her up from the sofa, a knowing grin on her face.

"Sleepy?" she asked.

"No." He buried his hands in her hair, tugging the loose band out of her ponytail. It fell silently to the area rug as he started on the buttons of her blouse. She tipped her head back, exposing her neck, and he took the invitation to explore the soft skin with his mouth.

She sighed.

"I need to shower," she whispered. "I need to wash away the grime and memories of that scene today."

"We'll do it together."

• • •

Ava leaned her back against the wet tile and let Mason take over. He'd turned up the water as hot as she could stand it, creating steam clouds in his spacious shower. He pointed the spray at her chest and stepped close, letting the water pool between them. He took hold of her and tipped her face up, meeting her gaze as the water pounded both of them.

He looked so serious, this cowboy cop of hers. He wasn't one to throw caution to the wind and plunge head on into whatever life had to offer. He studied it first, weighed his options, and then grabbed with both hands. Once his mind was made up, he was as stubborn and willful as a hound. But he'd never back down, and whomever he'd committed to would never be alone.

She had his commitment. He'd taken his time before he'd told her he loved her, but she'd known when he did it that he truly believed it. She wouldn't have had it any other way. Mason didn't say things he didn't mean; he didn't try to please other people; he did what he thought was right.

At this moment the sensation of his wet skin against hers was right. Completely right.

He kissed her, and she opened her mouth to him, loving the mental, emotional, and physical feeling of being dominated by a male.

Dammit, sometimes she needed to let someone else take the reins. Mason knew exactly when that was. Right now she wanted to forget the blood on the floor at Joe Upton's, forget she had a needy twin, and forget she had a cell phone that might ring at four A.M., demanding she get out of bed.

He moved his thigh between hers, and she parted her legs. His chest pressed against her breasts and she pushed back, creating tiny sparks of pain that alternated with pleasure.

Greed pulsed through her, and she ached for him to touch her everywhere at once.

He chuckled under his breath, and she realized she was panting.

"Need something?" he asked next to her ear.

"Damn right. Time to prove your worth, cowboy." Her eyes stayed closed, and she relished the spray of the shower on her shoulder and face.

"Challenge accepted." His rough cheek brushed hers as he pressed closer, increasing the pressure with his leg between her thighs.

She laid her left arm across his shoulders, ignoring the sharp twinges near her joint. Her right hand ran up and down his side, gliding across wet skin, and then tracing the muscle around to his spine.

His leg between her thighs vanished and he deftly bent and hooked his arm under her right leg, lifting it up and raising her to her toes. She felt exposed. His mouth crushed against hers and the gliding sensation of his tongue captured her attention. Until she felt him stroke gently between her legs.

"Wet everywhere," he muttered against her mouth.

She didn't respond. Instead she tilted her hips toward him and his shoulders quivered under her arm. He moved against her entrance and gave an upward thrust, sinking himself fully in one move.

Ava sighed and clenched him.

"Better?" he asked, holding completely still.

She moved against him, needing him to get in motion. "No. More."

"More?"

She shoved her hips at him. "Yes. Now."

He held still. "Open your eyes, Agent McLane."

Her eyes flew open and she glared at him.

A slow smile crossed his face. "I just wanted to be sure I had your attention. Didn't want you to forget who was in control here."

Her hips pressed against him again. "You are. Now go!"

His brown eyes narrowed. "Are you just saying that?"

"Dammit, Mason!" She thumped him on the chest.

"You're ready to move in with me? For good?"

"Yes!"

"We'll find our own place and let our old places go?"

"Yes! You don't need to get me into this position to ask me that! I love you. Everything's good. Now *please*, move!"

He threw back his head and laughed, making her heart leap to see him so happy. Her man letting go was a rare sight indeed.

"Love you, too, Agent McLane." He kissed her deeply and got to work.

16

Troy was so tired, he couldn't see straight.

He *consistently* couldn't see straight, he amended. He was used to his vision doing wacky things, but it usually rectified itself within a few moments.

He'd overdone it last night. He'd made every preparation he could and thought through every possible outcome, but it still hadn't prepared him for dealing with Joe Upton's dead weight.

Maybe it would have been easier to kill Joe by hanging. Then he could have walked where I needed him to go.

But setting the right scene was important.

His back had seized up, and he'd taken some leftover prescription pain pills. They'd put him to sleep and given him odd dreams. He'd dreamed he couldn't get Joe out of his house. He'd pulled and pushed and tried everything he could, but the big man wouldn't budge as he lay naked on the tarp. Upon waking, he'd been in a minor panic, his heart racing as he believed he'd left the man in his home.

Now he stared at himself in the mirror in his bathroom, blinking, trying to get a clear image. The clippers lay on the counter and he picked them up, testing the weight. Some of Joe's hair fell out of the blades and into his sink. Short black reminders of yesterday's events. He tapped the clippers on the sink's edge, ridding it of the rest of the hair and rinsing it down the drain.

Evidence in his home.

He didn't care. By the time the police pulled their heads out of their asses, and searched his house, it wouldn't matter. It'd be too late.

Bridge Killer.

Troy snorted. People didn't kill bridges. He didn't know whether to be honored or amused. He lifted the clippers to his hair and ran them straight down his part. Brown hair floated around him. He brushed at his head and studied the strip of scalp in the mirror. Crooked. And uneven.

He'd done a half-assed job on Joe. The man had refused to hold his head still and had twisted and turned at every cut. He'd thought about doing it after he slit the wrists, but he wanted Joe to experience the shame and panic over what was about to happen. The head shaving spoke volumes between the two men.

His own shaved head needed to be even, not raggedy and half-done like Joe's. If he went out in public, he didn't want to give people a reason to stare.

He buzzed another strip on his head and then spent the next fifteen minutes trying to get every bit off. His clippers weren't the greatest, and reaching the back of his head turned out to be an exercise in patience and agility.

At last he was bald. He ran a hand over the short stubble, wondering how fast it'd start to grow back. He neatly cleaned up the hair with a tiny broom and tray.

You're not done, said the female voice in his head.

Swearing under his breath, he strode to his kitchen and removed a utility knife from the multipack he'd bought at Home Depot. Would the police try to trace the one he'd left at Joe Upton's home? Probably. Where would it lead? To every Home Depot in the Portland metropolitan area? He squinted at the silver tool in his hand, looking for serial numbers or some sort of identifying mark. If there was one, he couldn't see it.

It doesn't matter.

Troy unbuttoned his shirt, holding his own gaze in the bathroom mirror. His head looked pale and too small. He'd never realized how much color he had in his face and neck. Now he looked ill. He gave a grimace. Wasn't that ironic?

His shirt dropped to the floor, and he popped the blade out of its hidden slot by sliding the lever on the handle with his thumb. He eyed the sharp silver triangle. This was going to fucking hurt.

Six strokes. Go quickly. No flinching. Her words encouraged him.

Exhaustion poked at him, suggesting he do it later. Perhaps another nap. He shook his head and gritted his teeth. He flattened his pec with his left first finger and thumb and drew the blade down his flesh in a smooth pass.

His brain screamed and tears flooded his eyes. He blinked them away. Blood flowed from the cut, and he pressed a towel against it to slow the blood.

Joe Upton hadn't bled.

Don't stop! she begged.

The towel fell onto the counter as he swiftly made the rest of his cuts. Fire burned on his chest, and he dropped the open blade into the sink. Pain. Pain. Pain. He mashed the towel against his chest with both hands. He wanted to fall to the floor and curl up in a ball.

This is how she felt.

Troy stumbled to the kitchen, his vision spinning in circles, and fumbled to open the freezer, intending to grab an ice pack.

No! You don't deserve any relief, she said.

He slammed the door shut and leaned his back against the door, slowly sliding down until he was on the floor. The pain ebbed. Slightly. He focused on his breathing. He'd slept in the ball gag for the last two nights. That'd been easy. His jaw had hurt like hell but nothing like the current pain on his chest. He relaxed, leaning his head backward against the door, and the pain eased another degree. He blew out a loud breath and listened to his heartbeat.

Her voice was quiet.

He felt cleansed and restored. Looking around the kitchen, he noticed his vision was back to normal and he was struck by a sudden thought. *What if my years of guilt and stress created my medical issues?* Had he created and nourished the tumor in his brain? The one that was stealing his sight and mixing up his words?

Laughter bubbled out of him. Troy laughed and cried until he couldn't breathe. His tears stung his new wounds, making him gasp. With the fresh pain came another wave of revitalization. He stood and pulled a knife out of the block on the counter. He pressed the blade against a rib and his vision tunneled. Blood welled around the knife and he watched the rivulets run down his stomach. Adrenaline flowed through his limbs the same way it had when he'd sliced open the wrists of the men.

He felt the power.

In those moments he'd known he'd found his purpose, and he'd had no doubts about his actions. Just now he'd felt the same moment of clarity; he was right to suffer as the other men had.

In the suffering, maybe he'd find some lasting peace.

17

Another morning without a dead body. Ava had showered and gotten ready for work, waiting for her phone to ring with news of another hanging, but it never did. Around ten A.M. she finally relaxed. Surely everyone who crossed a bridge in the Portland area now kept an eye out for any morning surprises.

Her only phone call had been from Zander.

"We've had a breakthrough," he'd said the moment she'd answered.

She perked up. "Let's hear it."

"Joe Upton spent the first twenty years of his life in Newberg before moving to Grandview."

Her mind had shot into overdrive. Newberg was on the outskirts of the Portland metropolitan area. "He grew up in the same large general area as Carson Scott and Aaron King," she stated. "They all lived here; they were all the same age. They could have connected back then. That's a damned good connection."

Three creates a pattern.

It was a good reason to focus on an earlier time in the men's lives. All their research into the victims' recent years was turning up nothing. It was time to dig deeper in the past. First on her personal list was talking with Joe Upton's parents.

Mason had balked yesterday when Upton's parents had suggested doing their interview via Skype this morning. They said they often communicated with their son using the video chat software.

"I've seen you Skype with Jake," Ava had said. "Don't you think this is a good way to get a feel for the parents? They can't get to Oregon for a few days."

Mason had made a face. "I know. It just seems odd. What's wrong with a phone call?"

"Nothing." She studied him for a few seconds. "Too new for you?"

"Phone calls have worked just fine for me in the past."

She bit her lip to hold in a laugh. "And eight-tracks deliver music just as well as that iPod you wear to run." She'd bought him the iPod when she noticed he cranked his country music while working in his garage. Now he wore it every time he ran.

"That's different."

"Try something new. I like to see the faces of the people I'm talking to. If you hate it, you can go back to phone calls."

He'd reluctantly agreed and now sat with an ultra-straight back in front of a computer screen as Ava and Zander shared the Skype call at the FBI building.

The news of their only son's death had crushed Joe Senior and Evelyn Upton. They wanted to help the investigators in any way they could, but Joe Senior's poor health kept him from traveling. They were waiting for clearance from his doctor before flying to Portland to arrange Joe Junior's funeral. Ava assumed the thin clear tube looped over Joe's ears led off their screen's view to an oxygen tank. Both parents looked exhausted, but Evelyn held up her chin and clung tightly to her husband's hand as she answered their questions.

"We hadn't talked to Joe since Saturday," said Evelyn. "We have a standing appointment for a Skype session every Saturday. He acted like normal. We mostly talked about the latest installment in the *Avengers* movies. My husband and I go to the movies a few times a month. It gives us better topics to talk to Joe about than discussing our health. Joe Junior doesn't like to hear all that."

Ava smiled, appreciating parents who put effort into finding common ground with their grown kid. "Do you like the same movies as Joe?"

Evelyn and Joe Senior exchanged a glance. "Some of them," said Joe Senior in a rough voice. "Don't care for the horror garbage he likes, but even Evelyn likes a good *Star Trek* or Bruce Willis flick."

"Did Joe ever tell you that he felt threatened by someone? Or that he was worried about his safety for some reason?" Ava asked.

Both parents shook their heads. "Never," said Evelyn. "I worried about him being alone in the house and tried to get him to move down here, but he didn't mind living alone and said he didn't like the heat. His weight, you know," she added, nodding emphatically.

"It made him uncomfortable?" Mason asked.

"Oh, he sweated nonstop. Even in the air conditioning. I thought maybe it'd inspire him to lose some weight, but it just made him miserable."

"So Joe didn't feel like he had any enemies." Ava guided the conversation back on track.

"None. Or at least he didn't feel the need to talk to us about them. But who could hate Joe?" Evelyn asked. "He wouldn't harm a fly."

"That's what his boss said, too," stated Ava. "Has he always been the sort of easygoing guy everyone gets along with?" Mentally she started a personality list, comparing him to Aaron King and Carson Scott.

"Oh, yes. Ever since he was a teenager. He's not much of a social sort. Well, he was in high school. He did sports and debate team, but he settled down and became more of a homebody after he graduated."

"No." Joe Senior poked at Evelyn. "He was a homebody his senior year, remember? He didn't play any sports even though the football team wanted him back. He told us he was tired of competing all the time. We let him quit."

"That's right," agreed Evelyn. "He focused on his schoolwork during his senior year. His classes were really hard, and he was afraid sports would eat into his study time."

"But he didn't go to college? Did he apply?" Why would someone work hard at his studies if he didn't plan to utilize those good grades?

"He applied to a few. His grades weren't as good as he'd hoped, and he went to the community college for a few courses. A neighbor hired him to help with his construction business, and he decided he liked that better than sitting in a classroom."

"When he played sports, did the other players like him? Did he have a big circle of friends or a few close ones?" Zander asked.

"I'd say he had a few close friends. He was a sensitive boy. He didn't need to be the center of attention."

Ava watched Joe Senior roll his eyes.

"He wasn't sensitive," corrected Joe Senior. "He was just quiet. He may have been more outgoing when he was younger, but he grew into a reserved young man."

Ava studied the brief written summary of Joe Junior's history in her hand. "He was born in Newberg and lived there long enough to graduate from Newberg High School." Her instincts were pushing her to investigate his time in Newberg. Fifteen years ago, all three men had lived within an hour of each other.

How would the paths of three men of the same age have intersected back then?

The ways were countless.

High school sports, high school events, professional sports games, under-twenty-one clubs, private parties, mutual friends, a temporary job, a day at a festival. The possibilities made her head hurt. Glancing at Zander's notes, she saw a list of things to look into in Carson Scott's and Aaron King's backgrounds. What sports teams and clubs had they belonged to? Employment histories were easier; the Social Security Administration had all the official records. At least of the legitimate jobs. What if they'd worked somewhere and been paid under the table?

That's why interviews with families and friends were important. It was like mining for tiny gems, hoping to find the flawless one. There was never a wrong question or too much information to cross-reference.

Ava asked Joe's parents to recount all the activities he'd taken part in during his middle and high school years. Then she asked what sort of jobs he'd had and what kind of activities he'd liked to participate in. As they talked, she noticed a pattern of Joe's social world getting smaller and smaller. The twelve-year-old boy who'd played sports every season of the year and attended summer camps and played outside had abruptly evolved into a young man who stayed close to home and hung out in his room, either doing homework or watching TV.

She didn't know if that was normal.

Mason's son was a freshman in college. Mason should have a good perspective on a male teen's behavior. Maybe. Was he noticing the pattern Joe's parents described?

"Did you ever think your son was depressed?" Ava asked delicately. "You're describing a young man who was very active and then changed."

Joe's parents looked at each other and then at her. Evelyn shook her head, but Joe's father spoke. "He stopped seeing his friends and seemed to only want to watch TV. I asked him one time why he didn't want to do things anymore. He said he'd lost interest in sports, and claimed he wasn't good enough to play at college, so why bother? As for the friends, he said they preferred to hang out with their girlfriends, and he felt like a third wheel all the time."

Mason nodded. "My son went through a phase like that. He was done with sports once high school was over and was a late bloomer when it came to girls. He told me he felt left out when his friends started dating. High school's a rough time for boys."

"Girls, too," Ava added. "So did he have other interests as he got older? What about after-school jobs or clubs?"

"His only job was at the local video store for a while during high school. I know he loved getting first look at all the new video releases. Once he was done with sports, he seemed to find interest in more sedentary things that he did by himself. His computer, and movies, and building models from the movies he loved."

"Did Joe mind moving to Washington with you? He was twenty by then, correct?" Ava asked.

"He was happy when we told him we'd decided to move," Evelyn said. "I'd assumed he'd want to stay in Newberg, but he said he was ready for a change of scenery. He was very content in Grandview."

"Did some of his interest in activities come back?"

"Not really," answered Evelyn. "By then he'd started to put on some weight and didn't even enjoy watching sports. The cooler weather up there makes you want to stay home. It's hard to be active when you don't want to go out in the cold or wet. He was happy to work and watch his movies. He was a good son." Tears slowly tracked down her cheeks, and Joe Senior patted her hand.

Ava wrapped up her questions and thanked the Uptons. After they were gone, she turned to the two men. "Is that really how it is for teen boys? They can change that much? I would think that if a boy loved sports, he'd always love sports."

Zander lifted a shoulder. "Maybe he was disappointed to learn he didn't have as much talent as he'd hoped. But yes, no one is the same person at eighteen as they are at twelve. Especially if they had a rough time in high school. Some kids are sensitive and their peers can be cruel."

Ava leaned forward. "See, that's what I think. I think something happened to Joe in high school that depressed him. I'd guess right before his senior year. The kid turned into a hermit, happy to live with Mom and Dad and watch movies for the rest of his life in Hicksville."

"Maybe he got dumped by a girl, maybe he got bullied, maybe he had a fight with a close friend. I think you're reading too much into it," Mason said. "We need to set up interviews with others from Carson Scott's and Aaron King's pasts. Can we get some more man-power to help?"

Zander nodded. "That shouldn't be a problem."

"I also want yearbooks from their middle and high schools. Maybe there will be a possible link in there that we haven't thought of," said Mason.

"Good idea," agreed Ava. She couldn't get the image of an over-weight man hiding in his parents' home out of her mind. That life seemed very different from the painfully public one of Carson Scott and the average one of Aaron King.

Three very different men. What had tied them together?

· · ·

Ava pulled into the parking lot of the Starbucks by her office. She needed her afternoon hit of caffeine if she was going to stay awake the rest of the day. She dashed through the rain and smiled at the man holding the door open for her, and then nearly tripped as she recognized Michael Brody, the reporter.

He gave her a venti-size grin.

Coincidence?

"Afternoon, Special Agent McLane." He tipped his paper cup toward her in salute with his greeting.

"You were expecting me," she stated.

"You're rather predictable. You're here most afternoons when you're working out of the office, right? You could save a lot of money if you drank the office coffee." He took a sip of his drink.

"The office coffeepot gets rinsed about every six months. I like to think they do it more often here."

"Get your drink, and I'll grab a table." He smiled and turned toward the seating area.

Ava wanted to fume but was amused instead. *No wonder he gets under Mason's skin.*

Minutes later she joined him at a table near the window. Brody had a relaxed appearance, but she noticed his gaze assessed every person in the room. "Deceptively casual" was the phrase that popped into her head. He tried to give the impression that he was laid-back. And she bet most people bought it, but he put out a high-alert vibe that triggered her radar immediately.

He didn't fool her one bit.

Well, he didn't fool her now that Mason had clued her in.

"What can I do for you?" she asked as she sat. "I only have a few minutes."

"I'm sure Callahan has filled you in on our somewhat odd relationship."

"Relationship?" She raised a brow.

"I consider him a friend."

She studied the serious look on his face, getting the impression Michael didn't call many men "friends." "I think he feels the same in some sort of twisted, John Wayne–masculine definition of friendship."

His eyes lit up. "I knew it."

"So why are you here?"

"I have two things I'd like to discuss with you. The first is about your case. Carson Scott wasn't a friend of mine, but I did know him. My father is in politics and Carson's a little younger than me. Our paths crossed quite a bit in the last few years."

Ava blinked, making a mental connection. "Your father is Senator Brody?"

"Yes."

"So your uncle was—"

Michael cut her off with a wave of his hand. "I know. Yes, my uncle was the governor. It's not something I like to discuss."

Ava nodded. Former Governor Brody was sitting in prison. She tried to remember the details from the scandal last summer. Attempted murder . . . or had he been charged with actual murder? "What was Carson Scott like? How well did you know him?" she asked.

Michael scratched his chin. "The first time we met was at a party at the governor's mansion. Carson represents Washington, but the Vancouver officials were usually included in any invitations. We try to keep them on our good side since their city is tied so close to Portland."

"We?" Ava asked.

He gave a half smile. "Sorry. Habit. Speaking of my father. He always uses the term 'we' when talking about other politicians."

"You're not a politician."

"Hell no. But I spent eighteen years in the household of one and too many years rubbing shoulders with the rest of them. They never looked down on me and treated me as their equal. Looking back, they were probably trying to butter up my father and uncle, but I took it as my due. I knew how to talk with them and operate in their world."

"Carson Scott," Ava reminded him, fascinated in spite of herself.

"He was born to be a politician."

"Is that a good thing?" Ava cut in.

"Depends what you want to achieve in life. He knew how to talk to people and show a genuine interest in their concerns. It felt like you had one hundred percent of his attention when you spoke with him. A lot of people can't do that."

Ava nodded. She hated it when the person she was talking with seemed distracted.

"Anyway, we're of an age. We discovered we both liked kiteboarding. The first time I met him, we spent a good hour exchanging stories about the best places to board."

"Did you like him?"

Michael paused. "I did. But I didn't trust him. There was something about his personality that made me keep my distance. I've been with him when he's had a bit too much to drink. You can learn a lot about a person when he's buzzed. This was a guy who wanted to be the center of attention wherever he went. He liked the ladies' eyes on him, and he liked the men to listen to what he had to say. He was the type that knew how to get what he wanted, you know?"

Ava knew the type all too well. "Would you call him a bully? Did he always have to get his way?"

"No." Michael thought hard. "But yes."

"What?"

"Physically, no. He knew how to take the lead and get everyone to follow. But he had a way with words and gestures that gently turned people to want to do as he said."

"You make him sound like a cult leader."

"Oh, Lord. I've met those types. Carson wasn't like that. If you didn't buy into his philosophy, he respected that. But he could still make you feel a bit sheepish if you didn't share his ideals."

"His chief of staff idolized him," Ava pointed out. "She thought Carson was a great supporter for his community. Did you know he wasn't running for reelection?"

"I'd heard a rumor about that. After his scandal last fall, who could blame him? And I'm sure he did lots to help his district. That's his job, and he's the type to succeed at what he attempts."

"We're searching for a past connection among the three victims. They all grew up in the Portland-wide metro area, and you did, too, right?"

He nodded.

"We've torn apart their history of the last five years, and they don't seem to have anything in common. So we're using the years that Joe Upton lived in the area as a general guide for when these men might have crossed paths. That would be fifteen years ago and earlier. As a high school student living around here, what did you do that brought you into contact with students from other schools?"

"I'm sure you're looking at school sports, but there's sports outside of school. I loved to ski on Mt. Hood in high school. I got up there every moment I could. There were teenagers from all over." His forehead wrinkled as he stared off in thought. "One year I was a volunteer at the zoo. My mom tried to get me to volunteer at the library. That was a bust. I picked berries in the summer when I was a bit younger. Christ, there's a million places they might have met." His green eyes narrowed at her. "I don't envy you, trying to find that connection."

"Yes, it's a bit intimidating. I'm hoping something will turn up in one of their homes to point us in the right direction."

"When I saw you were part of the FBI team assigned to the Carson Scott investigation, I wanted to know your reputation," Michael said. "So I asked some questions. But that's not the only reason I've been digging around; when someone shows up with a friend of mine, I check them out."

Ava raised a brow.

"Don't be offended. I caught Callahan's jealous vibe when I spoke to you. That's enough to make me curious. Callahan doesn't like anyone, but he clearly likes you a lot."

"You were looking out for him? By snooping about me?"

"Exactly."

"What'd you find?" She tamped down her annoyance, curiosity taking over.

"Your work record is impeccable and your reputation stellar. I read about your assignment last Christmas with that missing child, and I knew Callahan had a personal connection in that case. I assume that's how you met?"

She could only nod. *Where does he get his information?*

"You're pretty squeaky-clean. A good girl, I'd say."

"Damn right. I worked hard to be that way."

"But your twin sister is not."

His words stabbed like an icicle to her heart. She couldn't move. Of course he'd found out about Jayne. Why was she surprised? She took a deep breath. "No, Jayne is not like me."

"Her history is pretty volatile. It's almost like you don't even have the same DNA. You got the law-abiding genes and she did not." Michael appeared to see directly into her brain and hear every thought.

We've always been two different sides of the same person. "Sometimes that happens with twins," she said with a weak smile.

"How close are you?"

"Is there a point to your questions?" Annoyance flowed into her words. She didn't owe him any answers.

"There is," he said simply. He looked at her and waited, honesty in his gaze.

He's smooth. Part of her wanted to dump her entire history with Jayne in his lap.

"Tell me your point first."

"Your sister is running around with some bad company."

"That sounds like a song lyric."

He snorted. "Derrick Snyder isn't an ideal boyfriend."

"No kidding. This is the second subject you wanted to talk to me about?"

He nodded.

"I suppose you know the two of them broke into Mason's home?"

"Yes, I saw that. Snyder has a half dozen warrants out for his arrest. The marshal's office has tried to pick him up a number of times but can never find him."

"That's exactly the type that attracts my sister. The bad boy. The badder they are, the more she wants them."

"I assume you've taken steps to prevent identity theft?" he asked with a lecturing tone. "You are ripe for the picking with a twin like that."

Ava choked back a laugh. "The first time she stole my identity, I was sixteen. You bet I've done everything I can."

"Sixteen?" he asked, disbelief on his face.

"Yep, I passed my driver's license test and she didn't. She stole my license out of my purse all the time. In her mind it was hers. Over the years she's opened credit cards in my name, taken out loans, and even used my college transcripts."

Ava enjoyed the disbelief on Brody's face. He'd seemed like the unshockable type.

Gotcha.

"So anything you have to tell me about my twin probably isn't going to surprise me."

"Christ. I guess not." He shook his head.

"I'm lucky I have connections to keep tight tabs on my personal records and get my credit quickly fixed when Jayne does try. Did you find where she and Derrick Snyder are living right now?"

Michael shrugged. "Who knows? That sort of guy slimes his way around the city, leaving a messy trail behind him. It takes luck to catch him." His expression narrowed. "Did you know a few of the charges are for rape? And some physical abuse counts? He's more than just a 'bad boy' that attracts women. I wouldn't want any woman to meet him in the dark."

Oh, Jayne. Ava couldn't breathe.

"You don't keep in contact with her?"

"Our relationship has ups and downs. Right now we're in a down. Although she did call me yesterday." The relief on Michael's face alarmed Ava. "He's that bad?" she whispered.

"Bad enough that I'd get my enemy's girlfriend away from him."

"I'll see what I can do." Her mind raced. She still had the phone number Jayne had called her from in her cell phone.

"Do you want me to try to locate Derrick Snyder? And your sister?" Michael asked.

KENDRA ELLIOT 161

Ava eyed him warily. "I'd rather you used your *connections* to look at the history of my victims."

"But you've got an army of agents and detectives to do that. Who's searching for your sister?"

She gave a sharp laugh. "That would be me. Even though Jayne throws everything I've ever done for her in the trash. She's mentally ill." Ava pressed her lips together, stunned that she'd revealed something so private.

He nodded slowly. "I gathered that from the history I saw."

"I've done everything. She may be in danger, but she put herself there, and anything I do will probably endanger me as well. That's the pattern with her, but I can't give up," she said softly.

"I understand. I'll poke around a bit more for Derrick Snyder, and I'll see what I can come up with for the Bridge Killer victims. I'll let you know what I find."

"Thank you." Ava stood and held out her hand.

She needed to call Jayne.

18

Troy was glad he'd saved Rick for last. All his research on him had been worthless. The man had moved. Three weeks had passed between Troy's reconnaissance and the evening he'd gone to take down Rick. Two women now occupied the apartment where he'd watched Rick talk on the phone and watch TV all day.

It'd destroyed his perfect schedule.

One man left.

If he didn't grab Rick soon, there was a chance he would go to the police. Rick wasn't the type to watch the local news or glance at a newspaper headline. He was more concerned with finding his next high and getting laid. The chances were good that Rick hadn't realized three of his past acquaintances had recently died. But once he heard, he'd be on high alert.

The killings were supposed to be over within four days. Troy had planned it down to the hour. And Rick had screwed with the plan. *What if he moved because he knew what was happening?* He shook his head. He'd left Rick for last because he deserved the highest level of torture.

So much for plans.

Troy steered his sedan into a just-vacated curb spot on the crowded suburban Portland street, accepting that he would have to walk a few blocks. This was what he hated about this section of the city. The closest public lot was blocks away and finding street parking was like scratching a lottery ticket.

Sometimes you got lucky. But when you did, it usually wasn't that great.

Casual questioning of the two women at Rick's previous apartment had revealed Rick hadn't lived there to begin with. The women had let him crash there temporarily while he looked for a job. After much discussion and opinionating, they'd agreed that the most likely place to find Rick was at another friend's place.

Troy shoved his hands in his pockets, tugged his cap down lower, and started to walk, gaze on the sidewalk, ignoring the sporadic foot traffic. Coffee aromas came and went. He passed two coffee shops and dozens of people with paper cups.

He stopped across the street from a painted lady Victorian home. At one time the house had probably been something to admire, but its glory days were long behind it. Faded paint and plywood nailed over two of the windows spoke of its neglect. Weeds filled the small yard behind the chain-link fence. The home had been divided into five rental units. Two on each level and another in the attic space.

The women believed Rick's friend lived in the attic. As Troy watched, a man and a woman came out, arguing loudly about her footwear. The man stated that she wouldn't be able to walk a half block let alone the mile that they needed to go. Her vocal disagreement made Troy's ears burn.

The man's familiar carriage made Troy continue moving down the sidewalk. He stopped to tie his shoe, subtly observing the bickering couple. Troy couldn't get a good look at the man, but the woman was dark-haired and petite. She gestured, punctuating her words. They moved through the gate and headed west.

Across the street Troy followed, strolling slowly through the mixed neighborhood of residences and small businesses. At one time it'd been all single-family homes. Now it appeared 70 percent of the old homes had been converted into business or multifamily housing.

The man was definitely Rick. Troy's mind shifted the puzzle pieces involved in catching the man, searching for a new plan. He preferred to encounter his targets near their vehicles. It was simpler to take control and drive off in their vehicle with the unconscious body. A target on foot was harder. Joe Upton's isolation had made his turn very simple, but Rick was presenting issues. The man was in constant motion and always with people.

Troy's research had shown that Rick didn't have a car. Or a license. The man moved from loser job to loser job. He seemed to survive by bumming rides and housing off his "friends."

The couple stopped at the window of an old bookstore. Troy tried to get a clearer look at Rick's profile in the reflection. He'd aged along with the rest of the group, but in Troy's opinion he'd aged the most. Rick's lined face wasn't that of a thirty-five-year-old. It belonged on a much older man.

It isn't the years; it's the mileage.

Rick had had many years of hard living. He was the opposite of Joe, who'd spent most of the past decade living off his parents, and another opposite of Carson Scott, who'd moved into the public's eye and charmed them. Rick could have lived a good life, but he had a screw loose. Their group had been aware of it in the past, but none of them had known how dangerous he was.

Back then he'd seemed like a leader, the type of person people wanted to hang out with, hoping that some of his coolness would rub off. Troy had stood back and laughed while Rick called other teens pussies and fags. If he wasn't the one saying the words, then he hadn't endorsed it or hurt anyone, right?

Wrong.

They should have stood up to Rick, but instead they let him fly unchecked. Carson and Aaron joined in sometimes. Joe usually stood by and watched but kept his mouth shut. Troy had seen the desire to do the right thing in his eyes, but Joe had never spoken up. Guilty by association.

They were all guilty.

Two months ago Troy had weighed his options before gathering the old group. He could have gone to the police and turned himself in, giving evidence to implicate the other four, but he'd wanted them to do it themselves. They should have seen it was the right thing to do. He'd tried to find Rick, but the man had been living under the radar for too long. He'd settled for confronting Carson, Aaron, and Joe together, believing he could convince them that they had to do the right thing.

He'd seen the truth; surely they would, too.

They'd met late in the evening in a parking lot outside a 7-Eleven. With a little digging on the Internet, Troy had figured out where they lived and worked. The three men had responded to his request to meet once he'd threatened to go to the police and tell all. They'd been visibly nervous as they waited for everyone to show.

Then he'd dropped the bomb.

Carson had reacted in shock, stating he had a career to think of. He claimed he'd paid back society through his community service as a government employee.

"Isn't that a paid position?" Troy had asked. A paid job didn't have an element of sacrifice.

Their group sin called for atonement.

"It doesn't matter. I've willingly taken on one of the hardest jobs in the country. Our salary doesn't begin to compensate for the hours. And I'm trying to better this world." Carson had looked at Aaron. "What have you done with your life besides change tires and fuck up a marriage?"

"I've lived a good life!" Aaron had shot back. "I didn't steal or do drugs or beat on my wife. I learned my lesson. Just because you think you're King Shit of Turd Island doesn't give you the right to look down on me."

Carson had visibly steamed.

Troy had thought Aaron had nailed the description of Carson, but wasn't about to say so. His goal was to get the men to confess to the heartache that'd plagued them for fifteen years.

"You guys won't do this?" he'd asked in disbelief. "What do you think her family has gone through all these years? We have the chance to bring peace to a lot of people."

"Are you fucking nuts?" Aaron had asked. "I'm not going to prison so your conscience can feel better. I've gotten over it and you need to *do the same.*" He'd poked Troy in the chest with a finger, emphasizing his words. Carson had nodded in agreement, his arms crossed. Wide-eyed, Joe had stared at the other three, fear radiating from his gaze, his wide face tight with apprehension.

"We were just kids, Troy," Carson had stated. "We fucked up. That doesn't mean we sacrifice the rest of our lives. I'm not the same person I was back then. I'm not going to give up my future for what my stupid high school self did."

Troy had suddenly understood. These men weren't going to do anything. They were going to let the wound fester for the rest of their lives.

Could he live with that?

No.

They'd left him no choice. If they wouldn't man up and set the past to rights, then he'd do it for all of them.

You have to pay, said the soft voice in his head. *All of you.*

He'd decided to go to the police and tell his story.

But first his "friends" had hired someone to kill him.

After that, Troy's plans had changed. His time left on earth was too short for him to wait for the police and the legal system to bring the group to justice. He would take steps to see the men pay for what they'd done. He'd prioritized his subjects. Carson went first. His high-profile job was used to draw the media's attention to the cases. When he'd taken care of Carson, he'd been stunned at his overwhelming sense of relief and conviction that he'd done the right thing.

It was proof that he'd made the right decision. The voice in his head had wept in relief and expressed thanks. She'd been powerless for so long, and he'd given back her dignity.

It'd felt intoxicating.

He'd hung Carson out so everyone would see the error of his ways. The message wasn't clear to the public yet, but by the time Troy was finished, they would understand.

No one gets away with murder.

Troy watched Rick and the woman step inside the bookstore.

One left.

Does Rick know what happened to the other three men? Does he know why?

He'd never been able to contact Rick to give him the chance to turn himself in. It'd taken him weeks longer to find Rick than the other men. Perhaps he should offer Rick the same chance he'd offered the other three. He shook his head.

Who am I fooling?

Rick was the worst of the group. He'd lied, cheated, stolen, and bullied. And that was just as a teen. Men don't grow out of that. Any chance he offered Rick today would be met with lies and denials.

He glanced at his watch. It wasn't even noon yet. He lifted his cap and ran a hand over his bare scalp. The odd sensation on his fingers was a reminder of his purpose. He had plenty of time to follow the couple and watch for a prime time when Rick was alone. *No witnesses.* It was one of his personal rules. It'd worked well for the other three men. He wasn't going to break the rule for Rick.

A witness would force his hand.

19

Mason found the printouts under a stack of Ava's papers about the Bridge Killer. Confused, he glanced across the conference table at Zander, whose focus was on the computer screen in front of him. Ava had stepped out of the room. They'd met at the FBI building to review the results of the manpower the agency had thrown at the Bridge Killer. The media, the public, and Congress were demanding answers to the death of one of their public servants. They managed to ask about the two regular guys, too, but Carson Scott's death was the question on everyone's lips.

But according to the printouts buried next to her computer, Ava was focused on finding Derrick Snyder.

She's searching for Jayne.

Mason wanted to bang his head on the table. Ava had a job. And that job was to find the Bridge Killer. Why was she looking for her wild sister? She'd told him several times that she was happier and saner when Jayne stayed away. But now she was deliberately trying to bring the woman back into her life?

Maybe she's just curious.

Of course she's curious. It's her sister. He slid the Bridge Killer papers back over the Derrick Snyder information. Why hadn't she told him what she was doing? Was she embarrassed to tell him? Knowing he wouldn't approve?

He got up and paced to the window, staring out at the traffic on the busy road behind the FBI building. The majority of the traffic was from the airport. Vehicles of thousands of people who'd been traveling passed by, or friends and family doing the kind thing by offering the travelers rides. All those people going about their daily lives while he sat alone and looked for a killer.

You're not alone anymore.

Ava had stepped into a gaping hole in his life he hadn't realized existed. He knew she was a hell of an agent, but what did he know of her personally? Her coworkers liked her. That was a plus. They'd spent tons of hours in conversations since they'd met. They'd bared their souls to each other. He'd thought he knew what was going on in her head, but did he really?

So you found something she didn't tell you. Big deal.

But this wasn't small. It might seem small to a casual observer and even normal that she was looking for her sister. But they'd talked about Jayne. They'd hammered the subject to death, and he'd tried to be supportive about her decision. She'd agreed to let it go. And now he could see that she hadn't.

It worried him.

God fucking damn it.

Ava was happier when she didn't think about Jayne. Why was she doing this to herself? And why did she feel the need to hide it? Mason realized he was hurt by the discovery. *Doesn't she trust me?* He'd opened his trust to her unconditionally. He trusted her and understood her drive to look out for her sister, so why didn't she feel that she could talk to him about Jayne? Maybe she had more doubts about their relationship. Maybe she struggled with his age . . .

"Jesus Christ."

"What?" asked Zander behind him.

"Aw, nothing. Just talking to myself." Mason turned and looked at the agent. "You're not married, right?"

Zander paused and glanced down at his keyboard. "Not anymore."

"Girlfriend?"

He gave a half smile, looking back at Mason. "Not now. Problems with Ava?"

No way would Mason dump his insecurities on the table. "Only in my head."

Zander nodded knowingly. "That'll eat at you every time." He went back to his computer screen, leaving Mason to deal with his annoying doubts.

"I'm an idiot," Mason mumbled to no one.

"Do you need a beer?" Zander asked.

Mason snorted. "Yes. Or something stronger. Any of that around here?"

"I wish. Maybe later."

"I might hold you to that."

Ava stepped back into the room. "I've got Joe Upton's cell phone records cross-referenced with the other two victims. Again, nothing matched up. If someone called them, he didn't call from the same phone number. Or he didn't call their cells."

"Upton's email came up clean, too," added Zander. "Going on the chance these guys were contacted by our killer, what are we missing?"

"Euzent seemed pretty certain he would have communicated with them somehow," Mason said. "Email, cell phone, landline. He could have called them at work. What about a chat room? I know we have agents going through their social media."

"I heard back on their social media," said Ava, digging through the papers next to her laptop where Mason had found her notes on Derrick Snyder. She yanked out a page. "Aaron King had virtually nothing. An old Facebook page that hadn't been touched in six months. Carson Scott had quite a bit of stuff, but the majority of it was handled by one of his staffers. And neither Aaron King nor Joe Upton shows up as a contact. Scott's private accounts don't show any odd activity that caught our investigator's eye."

"What about Joe Upton?" asked Mason.

Ava smiled. "Exactly what you'd expect for a reclusive science fiction fan. All sorts of profiles and discussions on every science fiction site on the web. He has a strong interest in space travel, both real and imaginary. The computer forensics team is still digging through Joe's hard drive, but they haven't found anything resembling a message of the type we're searching for."

"We saw spaceship models in one of the rooms in his house," Mason said, remembering the plastic *Star Wars* and *Star Trek* replicas. "They made it look like a teenager's room. Did we follow up on the yearbooks from their high schools?"

"I have a call in to Laura King, Aaron's ex-wife," Zander said. "She thought she might have yearbooks in her garage. That would be quicker for us to get than sending someone out to Gladstone. I sent an agent to Carson Scott's Vancouver high school to borrow copies, since it wasn't too far. Usually the libraries keep copies of all the yearbooks. Let me go see if he's back." Zander pushed out of his chair and left the room.

Ava tapped on her keyboard and frowned at the screen. Mason took a breath, reached out, and slid the paperwork off the notes about Derrick Snyder. She glanced at the pages and did a double take. Blue eyes looked up at him.

"What's this?" he asked.

"Derrick Snyder. The guy who stole your TV."

"I know that. But why are you looking into him?"

"I want to know where he is. I don't think Jayne is safe with him."

Mason sat down in his chair and rolled over beside her. He took her hand and looked her in the eyes. "Why now? Why are you worrying about your sister now?"

She set a finger on one of the pages. "Look at this. This guy is dangerous. He's been accused twice of rape and abuse. This isn't someone I want Jayne hanging around with."

Mason glanced at the sheet. He already knew what it said. "You're trying to find him so you can get Jayne to leave him. What will you do then? Where will you send her?"

Ava stuttered. "I don't know. I just need to know she's safe. That reporter we met the other night, Brody, told me Snyder is worse than we'd first realized."

"When did you see Brody?" Mason's nerves vibrated.

"He hunted me down," Ava said ruefully. "I guess my routine is a bit predictable. He put himself in my path after our interview with the Uptons."

"He has a way of turning up when you least expect it. Like I said. Gum and shoe."

"Anyway, he had some interesting information on Snyder, who is a man no woman should be near. With the panicked call from Jayne yesterday, it was a double hit within two days. I'm wondering if she was asking for help to get away from Snyder but wouldn't admit it."

"You said she was worried for Snyder."

"That was what she said. But now I'm questioning if she didn't want to tell me the truth. That she was the one who needed help." Stress wrinkled her forehead. "I've learned I can't take what she says literally. I have to read between the lines on everything."

"Then you never know what to believe." Mason's brain throbbed at the thought. He always listened for subtext in conversations, but what was it like to talk to someone who *never* said what she meant? He stood and pulled Ava into his arms, breathing in the scent of her hair and skin. *Instant relaxation.* He felt his headache flee and his muscles relax. Ava softened in his arms and a small breath escaped from her. Did touching him do the same thing for her?

"You should have told me. I would have helped," he whispered.

He was there to help her, be a rock for her. She needed to learn she could lean on him. But he knew she hadn't done a lot of leaning in her past. Part of her baggage was the instinct to do everything herself. He'd brought his own baggage to the relationship. It wasn't a lot, mainly a detective's sense of distrust. And the damned insecurity about their age difference.

Zander cleared his throat. Ava jumped, but Mason slowly let go. Hell if he was going to act like he'd done anything wrong.

"Look what was dropped off for us." He held up four yearbooks. "Carson Scott's."

"Sweet," said Ava. "Let's take a look." She took two books and handed one to Mason. "See if there's an index in the back."

Mason took the heavy book and flipped some pages. "No index."

"Mine has one," said Ava.

"I've got one with an index and one without," said Zander. "I wonder why they weren't consistent."

"Student council his junior year. Along with debate club. Carson Scott also played baseball," announced Ava. "That opens up a lot of possibilities for meeting someone from another school. We need to check the other victims' past interests."

"I feel like we're chasing ghosts," stated Mason. "I don't know if we should be looking this far in the past."

"Well, we've got a team picking apart the last five to ten years," said Zander. "That's easier since there are so many digital footprints, and it's simpler to cross-reference. It's the years before that that are blurry. The years when people didn't enter every step they took into statuses in cyberspace."

"What about vacations?" asked Ava. "What you just said made me think of airlines and their extensive reservation systems. Maybe they all traveled somewhere at the same time. I swear our list of things to investigate grows by leaps and bounds every time we talk."

Zander nodded. "I'd start looking with Joe Upton. He didn't appear to go that many places. Unlike Carson, who probably flew fifty times a year. I'll put some wheels in motion."

"Do we have reports on the evidence from the Upton home?" Mason asked. He turned the pages in the yearbook, feeling out of touch as he eyed the dated hairstyles and fashion. Jake would have been an infant when Carson Scott was a senior. With no index, he was scanning the names under each group and club photo to find Scott.

"The obvious stuff. The trace evidence will take longer. The blood was Joe Upton's. The tire treads haven't been ruled out as belonging to the type of van we saw in the Fremont Bridge video. There's no sign of forced entry."

Mason looked up. "None? So Joe opened the door. Either he knew him or wasn't nervous about who was at his door."

"Or the door was unlocked and the guy walked right in," added Ava. "Maybe it's the type of community where no one locks their doors."

"Do those still exist?" Mason didn't think so.

"I'm calling Laura King to ask about Aaron's yearbooks," Zander said, touching his phone's screen.

"Anything?" Ava looked at the yearbook in Mason's hand with a curious gaze.

"This one is from his senior year, and I have to read all the names with the photos. So far I've found him in baseball and tennis, and here's his senior photo." He twisted the book so she could see.

She smiled. "He didn't change much over the years. Look at that wide smile. They should have known he'd be a politician."

Mason agreed.

"I'm going to pull up the photos from his condo," Ava stated, scrolling on her laptop. "Seems like he had a lot of sports trophies. More than just baseball and tennis."

"Laura, I'm putting you on speaker," Zander said. "Special Agent Ava McLane and Detective Mason Callahan are in the room with me. Can you repeat what you just told me?"

"Well, all I said was that I'd found Aaron's high school yearbooks in the garage," came the scratchy female voice through Zander's phone speaker. "And I mentioned that he'd kept a lot of stuff from high school, like his models."

"What sort of models?" Zander prompted.

"His rockets. He belonged to the rocket club all through high school. Is that what you wanted to know?"

Mason flipped through the yearbook in his hands, looking for the clubs. "Was there a rocket club in yours, Ava? I don't see one."

"I don't have one listed in the index," said Zander. "But what if it wasn't a school thing? It could be outside of school. I think my high school had an unofficial rocket club. Something run by one of the science teachers after school. This sounds like something Joe Upton would have done in high school, right? He was a space travel fan."

"I think that's what Aaron did," said Laura. "The after-school thing. I don't quite remember."

"Wait. How long were you two married?" Ava asked.

"Fourteen years. We started dating in high school."

Ava exchanged a knowing grin with Mason and Zander. "Perfect," she whispered. Mason agreed—someone who had known Aaron back then.

"What was Aaron like in high school?" Zander asked. "Was he one of the smart ones? Or a jock? How do you remember him?"

"Umm. None of the above?" Laura said through the speakers. "I'd always thought he was a bit of a wild guy through school—the type I tried to avoid. But we had one class together our senior year, and I discovered he wasn't really like that."

"Maybe he changed," Mason suggested. "Maybe he matured a bit and realized life wasn't party, party, party." *Joe Upton changed during high school. Did Aaron do the same?*

"I guess. It's hard to say. I didn't pay much attention to him before then."

"Can I come by to pick up the yearbooks tonight?" Zander asked. "I wouldn't mind seeing what else is in that box from his high school days."

Laura agreed, and Zander wrapped up the call.

"Good. She might remember something that happened to him in school," Ava said. "Joe's parents said he changed. Maybe something affected all three men."

"I'm still wondering if our killer is done. We haven't had a new body in two days. Will there be more?" Zander questioned. "Or were we supposed to figure out what was going on from just these three?"

Mason's ears perked up. "You think he wants us to solve the murders? You think he wants us to expose him?"

Zander shrugged. "I don't know about exposing him, but he wanted these men publicly punished for something. I assume he wants us to crack that code and reveal it."

"We're not stopping until we take him down," promised Mason.

· · ·

Ava's phone buzzed on her nightstand, and she didn't recognize the number. *Jayne?*

"Ava, it's Michael Brody."

She exhaled, disappointment and relief simultaneously rushing through her. She'd left her personal number with the reporter. "You found something already?"

"I have a convenience store employee who knows Derrick and says he was in his store this afternoon. He claims Derrick sometimes pops in twice a day, usually buying cigarettes or alcohol. And he's had the same woman with him several times."

"Jayne always swears she's quit smoking." Ava shook her head. Why was she pissed at her sister for smoking when she was taking drugs and clinging to a guy who was known for beating women? Jayne had been sneaking cigarettes since middle school. "Where's the store?" She tapped the address into her computer as he spoke and studied the location on a map. "Southeast Portland?"

"Yes. Not the greatest neighborhood. And I'll tell you my source says he's lost track of the number of women Derrick comes in with. He seems to enjoy showing off the new faces."

"Lovely. Sounds like a true romantic. But we already knew that, right?"

"She needs to get away from this guy," Michael said. "Do you need some help?"

"I work for the FBI and I'm dating an OSP detective. I'd like to think I have some resources," Ava said. She wrapped up the call and pressed her palms to her temples.

Who am I fooling? The Marines couldn't convince Jayne to change her path.

"Problem?" Mason asked, stepping into the bedroom.

She lowered her hands and smiled at him. "One guess."

He sat on the bed next to her, gently pulling her computer off her lap and setting it on the floor. She'd been going over the trace evidence reports from Carson Scott's home. Her work was never finished and thank goodness Mason had a job that followed the same guidelines. Working in bed wasn't uncommon. The sudden loss of her laptop startled her, but then she relaxed. She needed to set it aside more often.

"What's happened?" he asked.

She explained her call from Brody.

"Nothing to do about it tonight. Maybe you can swing by that store sometime tomorrow."

"I know. But the need to rush over there right this instant has clouded my brain. It's almost like a reflex. Jayne does something; I react. At least it's not like it used to be. When we were kids, I swear eighty percent of my life was spent reacting to something she'd stirred up. Part of me has always believed that if I could just set her on the right path, she'd handle the rest herself."

"How's that worked out for you in the past?"

"A zero percent success rate."

"But you still hope."

"I have to hope. But that's all I allow myself to do. I can't let it influence my daily life." Her smile felt artificial. *How many times have I stated that sentence?*

Will Mason get tired of watching me struggle?

"What's the worst thing Jayne has done to your life?" Mason settled back against the headboard and wrapped an arm around her shoulders, guiding her to nestle against him. She moved into his solid chest and felt his warmth spread through her. His desire to hear about her sister made her throat swell with gratitude. She rarely shared her past with her coworkers or acquaintances. A small part of her was terrified to talk about the black hole that ate away at her heart. Mason didn't seem to mind.

"By the time we were in high school, I had the reputation of the good student. I focused on school and my job. I liked student council and clubs that carried a bit of a geek reputation with them. Jayne was an average student and didn't get involved with any school activities. She was all about her circle of friends and chasing guys."

"Did you have the same circle of friends?"

"Jayne didn't like to share her friends. Which was fine with me. She was drawn to drama, which I saw attracted a different breed of girl. There was usually a cruel streak in them. I selected my friends carefully. They had to be strong enough to see through Jayne's manipulation."

"I bet she hated that," Mason observed.

Ava laughed. "Oh, yes. And a girl who didn't fall for it became a victim of scorn from Jayne. 'You don't like me? Well, you must be stupid' was the gist of her reasoning."

"I know a few adults who still think like that," stated Mason. "If you don't fall for their bullshit, then you're screwed up and not worth associating with."

"One time during our freshman year, I started getting some odd attention from two senior guys. Freaky stuff. Like long stares and suggestive movements with their tongues as they passed me in the hallway."

"Oh, shit. I don't want to know where this is going," muttered Mason.

Ava didn't stop. "One day one of them stopped behind me as I was at my locker. He braced his hand on the wall and leaned close, whispering some nasty sexual crap in my ear about what he'd like me to do to him."

"Did you elbow him in the gut?" Mason shifted on the bed, her story agitating him.

Ava could hear the boy's voice and smell his breath like it'd just happened. The cafeteria had served tacos for lunch that day. "I turned around and shoved him away. He called me a slut and whore and stomped off. I remember shaking, watching him walk away with anger radiating around him."

"He thought you were Jayne?"

"No." Ava paused, her mouth feeling dry. She took a sip from the cup of long-cold decaf on her nightstand. "When it happened again that same day with a different guy, I flat-out demanded why he would ask me to give him a blow job. He told me that some friend of his claimed I would do it. Just like I'd done for the friend, because I enjoyed it.

"I told him I'd never given that guy a blow job. He asked if I was Ava McLane." She shuddered. "That's when it hit me. Jayne was in an 'embrace the glory of being a twin' cycle. She was wearing her hair like mine and dressing like me. Apparently she'd decided to use my name when it came to sucking off guys after school."

"Holy Christ. She admitted it?"

Ava nodded.

"What did you say to her?"

"I blew up and made her cry."

"Did it do any good?"

She smiled, knowing he was attempting to lighten the moment. "About as well as you think it did."

"Where was your mother during these times?"

"She worked full time and she didn't have the energy to deal with Jayne. I usually hid most of Jayne's behaviors from her. I rarely ratted her out."

"She was already flirting with danger," Mason pointed out. "Who knows what some of those older guys were capable of?"

"I couldn't see that back then. Twenty-twenty hindsight, you know."

He tightened his arm around her shoulders and didn't say anything more. Ava was grateful for his restraint in his analysis of Jayne. Her ex in LA had frequently lectured her on Jayne even though Jayne had lived almost a thousand miles away and rarely stuck her nose in Ava's business. Part of her wished for those days when there had been a greater physical distance between the two of them. Moving to Portland had been a bit of a crazy idea five years ago. As usual she'd hoped Jayne had changed, but her expectations had been ground to dust.

"I'm glad you moved to Portland, Special Agent McLane," he said close to her ear.

Ava closed her eyes and let all thoughts flow out of her brain except her feelings toward the man beside her. His touch instantly settled her jarred nerves.

"Me, too. Want me to show you how glad I am?" She ran inquisitive fingers down his chest.

"More than you know."

20

Troy stopped to ponder his dilemma. Had her voice fed the mass in his brain? Or had the mass come first? He'd first heard her voice that violent day when everything changed. Had the tumor already been present? Had it been a small seed, waiting for the right nutrition to grow? Her voice had gotten louder and more distinct over the years. But it'd escalated in the last twelve months, along with his eyesight problems and headaches.

Had she fostered his tumor?

He tried to focus on the sidewalk under his feet. It was nearly eight A.M., and he'd been walking for an hour, combing the neighborhood where he'd lost track of Rick yesterday. He'd been patiently waiting for Rick to come out of a deli when he realized too much time had gone by. He'd finally gone in.

No Rick.

Was I spotted?

The clerk behind the counter had pointed out the delivery entrance near the bathrooms. He'd claimed he hadn't noticed if Rick had left through that entrance. The woman in Troy's head had cried in frustration.

We're so close, she'd sobbed.

Troy had repeated his promise to fulfill her goals. *I haven't let you down yet.*

He felt her silently slide away to the corner of his mind where he couldn't hear her, leaving him empty and alone. She didn't do it to punish him; she vanished when she was crushed and upset. He ached to make her happy. When he'd first thought of his plan to avenge her death, she'd wept with joy, and he'd realized her happiness meant everything to him. When she was happy, he felt powerful and at peace.

Too many years of his life had slid by in a blurry haze. He'd gone from job to job and woman to woman, searching for something to destroy the stain on his conscience. One night he'd stared in shock at Carson Scott on the news. His old buddy had made something of himself. Troy had followed Carson's career, watching covertly from a distance, wondering if the man was as satisfied with his life as he appeared. Carson had started in a city council position and steadily climbed a political ladder, making news headlines when he ran for Congress. At first Troy hadn't been able to believe that a person with rot in his soul like Carson could attain such lofty heights.

Carson had won his election to Congress, and Troy had heard her sob all night, an echo of his own confusion over Carson's reward for his rancid past. It'd been the first time he'd heard her so clearly. Before, he'd heard gentle, indecipherable whispers, but he'd known instantly who'd been speaking them.

That night Troy had decided to search and find the rest of their group. He'd witnessed Aaron slogging along in a backbreaking job as his marriage slowly crumbled. One evening Troy had followed Aaron as he hooked up with a female coworker; rage had rushed through Troy as he watched the two of them alone. He'd had several moments of intense fear as he worried Aaron would harm the woman. Instead Aaron had taken his pleasure and gone home in a happy daze, walking right past Troy as he knelt behind a hedge.

Aaron's ex-wife, Laura, seemed like a good woman. Troy had studied her closely to see if she'd physically suffered in the relationship, but most of the pain seemed to be mental and emotional. Troy had been pleased to see her come to her senses and demand that Aaron leave.

Joe Upton had hidden in his home since that night. Life had dealt the man a difficult hand and Joe had suffered appropriately, unlike Carson and Aaron. Joe had grown fat and reclusive, his world not much larger than his house and his TV.

Rick had been the toughest to locate. He'd been the ringleader from the start. The one who'd tipped over the domino that had started the rapid chain reaction in which they had all taken part. But Rick was the essence of the incident. Without his primary actions, none of that day would have happened. He was the key.

Now the sight of him made Troy's anger burn. Rick had been the spark and then had fanned the flames to involve the rest of their group. If anyone deserved to suffer for what had happened to Colleen, it was Rick. It was fitting that he would be the last victim.

They would have continued on as five normal teenage boys if Rick hadn't pushed so hard. Acne, school, sports, and girls. A normal teen's life that would have led to a normal man's world.

He wouldn't have a mass of cancer growing in his head if Rick had kept his temper.

He was certain of that fact.

Troy had found a dozen articles that preached the same message. A healthy life and healthy mental state created a healthy body. His brain had festered from the guilt and visions of the day Colleen died. If he could only go back in time and stop the other boys.

It's too late.

He'd accepted that he couldn't change what had happened. But he still wished and often dreamed that he had. In his dreams he stepped forward, unafraid of the other boys, and told them to stop.

He grabbed Colleen and pulled her out of Rick's grasp before the evil began. In this alternate reality she cried and thanked him.

In his dreams he did the right thing.

Why didn't I save her back then?

At first he'd thought she was haunting his house. When he started to clearly hear her voice, he'd wander around the rooms, calling out to her to show herself. In public he'd watch for people's reactions, assuming they could hear her, too. But no one flinched. No one asked, "Who is crying?"

Only he could hear her.

The one good thing he'd done in his life was implement his plan to avenge her.

One man left.

He froze, a woman catching his eye. She appeared to have on the same coat he'd noticed Rick's friend wearing yesterday. Her dark hair seemed the right length and the same style. He walked faster, trying to get a closer look. She paused at a street and looked both ways, flashing a glimpse of her profile, and started to cross.

It's her.

His stomach churned. Something about her was eerily familiar outside of his glimpses of her yesterday. Yesterday his focus had been on Rick. He'd barely glanced at the woman. He stopped at the same street, the traffic making it impossible to cross. He watched her arms swing at her sides and her hips sway with confidence. A cold flash of dread touched his heart.

Colleen?

Rick stepped from a doorway and into the woman's path, grabbing her arm and yanking her to a stop. The woman took a step back, trying to jerk her arm out of the man's grip. Rick leaned close to her face, his mouth moving with angry words that Troy couldn't hear.

The woman's scared face turned Troy's way for an instant.

It is Colleen.

Rick moved down the sidewalk, hauling the woman along, her feet tripping to keep up with his fast strides. Troy followed, determined not to lose Rick again. He moved into a slow jog to close the long distance between him and the arguing couple.

He can't hurt her again.

21

"I tried calling Ava, but her phone went to voicemail," Zander said.

Zander's phone call was the second occurrence to wake Mason Sunday morning. The first time, Ava had woken him by getting up early and dressing, promising to be back in time for a late Sunday brunch at their favorite riverfront restaurant.

Mason glanced at the clock on his nightstand. "She's probably in her car. She was going to put in a few hours at the office this morning and then run an errand. What's up?" He yawned silently and rubbed the sleep out of his eyes. Beside him Bingo had claimed Ava's side of the bed, even placing his head on her pillow.

"I picked up Aaron King's yearbooks last night. His ex-wife was right. He'd kept all sorts of high school memorabilia in a box. Made me feel sorta sorry for the guy as I rummaged through it."

"Sorry? How so?"

"He seemed like a guy who was going places back then, but his dreams never came true. Looks like he had hopes for a professional baseball career."

"Didn't we all," muttered Mason. "But most of us know better and move on."

"His ex-wife said he was bitter about it. Sounds like he had some depression issues."

"Over a lost dream of pro ball?"

"She said that was part of it. He seemed to have good months and bad. She said she married him because she'd seen a good guy. And when he wasn't that good guy, she believed she had enough strength to help bring him back. I guess some of the time it worked, but she got tired of the ups and downs."

"Who can blame her? Did she have a need to justify to you why she filed for divorce?"

"A bit. Still fresh, I guess," said Zander.

"Give it time. There was a point when I felt I had to explain to everyone why Robin and I split. After a while I realized people didn't want a long explanation."

Zander was silent for a moment, and Mason thought back to their brief conversation about his marital status yesterday. "Not anymore," the man had said. *What's Zander's story?*

"Did you find anything in the yearbooks?" Mason asked, filling the silence.

"Not in the yearbooks, but Aaron kept a bunch of mementoes from his interest in rockets. Looks like he belonged to an informal rocket club and attended camps and conventions. There were old flyers and photos from a half dozen different events. He must have been pretty passionate about it. When I asked Laura what she remembered about those days, she said he'd given it up before they started dating and that she'd been surprised to see he had so many keepsakes because he never talked about it."

A small bell started to chime in the back of Mason's brain. *We're getting close.* "If you're calling me early Sunday morning, you must think it's important." He sat up and swung his feet out of bed in an attempt to think more clearly. Bingo scooted into the warm spot he'd vacated, his furry head burrowing under the covers.

Zander paused. "I do. After visiting Laura King, I dug through the evidence we recovered from Joe Upton's place. There were three dozen small rockets in a storage box."

"Do you think it's a coincidence they shared that interest?"

"I don't know," Zander said slowly. "But it's the only coincidence so far. It caught my attention."

Mason heard him cover a yawn. "How late were you up last night?"

"You mean this morning? I think I got three hours of sleep. Didn't feel like I missed any sleep until an hour ago. You know how it is at this point."

Mason did know. Sleep didn't matter when he was closing in on an answer during an investigation. When he started feeling the pieces falling into place and making connections. The desire to find answers drove him to keep searching, and rest seemed unimportant.

"I know." Mason was wide-awake, his brain speeding down different avenues. What did they need to take a closer look at? "I think we should go back to Carson Scott's place. Or else talk to his parents. Maybe they have his high school stuff, and we can see if there are any common threads with the other guys. You did their initial interview, right?"

"Yes, I went to their home twice after we found him, but I didn't talk to them about Carson's high school days. I'll contact them this morning and try to see them today."

"Good. Did I miss anything else while I was sleeping?" Mason asked.

"There's some trace evidence reports from Aaron King's apartment in your email. I scanned them but haven't taken a close look. Maybe you'll spot something. I think our theory that our killer never stepped foot in that apartment or in Carson Scott's is still correct. I bet evidence from Joe Upton's home will be how we find him."

"Agreed. That's why we've got three times the manpower on that one."

"Is there any news on Ava's sister?"

Mason wondered how much Ava had shared with Zander. "The errand she's running is following up on a lead. You know her sister broke into our place, right?"

"Yeah, she told me that. Personally I don't know why she keeps trying to help her twin. The woman clearly doesn't want help."

"You're preaching to the choir. But it's her twin. There's a bond there that we can't begin to fathom. For Ava's sanity, she has to walk a thin line that offers help but doesn't enable Jayne's dangerous habits and addictions. It's a crazy balancing act."

"What's she think her sister will do next?"

Mason sighed. "Hell if I know. In a perfect world, Jayne will check into rehab, get ongoing mental health counseling, and walk the straight and narrow. But in the real world, I suspect none of the above."

But he knew Ava could never completely give up on her sister, and his job was to be there for her.

. . .

Ava waved the picture of Jayne at the cashier again. "You've never seen her? One of you said you did."

"Well, it wasn't me," the female clerk snapped. "There's two other people who do this job. Why the fuck didn't you ask for the name of the person who said it?" She cracked her gum, not intimidated by Ava's questions. The fiftyish woman had to be a tough character if she was willing to work the cash register in this neighborhood by herself. Her ancient, worn-down nametag read Dot.

"Do you work your shifts alone?" Ava asked, scanning the empty store. "Doesn't that make you nervous?"

Dot fixed angry eyes on her. "Usually people who ask me that are scoping the place out to rob it." She moved her right hand to a shelf under the counter. "Do I need to call the police?"

Ava raised her hands and backed away. "I suppose you wouldn't believe me if I said I was law enforcement." Her badge, ID, and weapon were in her purse over her shoulder. Not the most convenient place for them, but it was Sunday and she wasn't on official duty. She never used her position to influence personal situations. Usually.

Dot cocked her head and gave her an I-don't-give-a-shit look. "You know how many times I've heard that? Do I look stupid?"

Ava thought Dot looked very shrewd. And perfectly capable of pulling out a shotgun from under the counter. She kept her hands in plain sight. "No, actually I admire a woman who dares to take on a job like this. I'm glad to see you don't take crap from people."

Dot didn't melt into effusive thanks. She raised one eyebrow at Ava. "Are you buyin' something?"

"Ah, sure." Ava glanced around and spotted the coffee counter. "I'll grab a cup of coffee." She lowered her hands and headed to the counter, keeping one eye on the clerk.

"A cup of coffee," Dot mimicked. "That's all anyone wants these days. Then they fill it up with a half dozen creamers. The damned cup and lid costs more than the coffee. Add in the cream, and I'm paying you to drink it."

Ava stopped. "I like it black. And I'll buy a . . ." She glanced at the case of tough-looking donuts. *Ugh.* "I'll buy the banana," she said, pointing at a sad-looking banana.

Dot scowled.

I'm not going to win here. Ava grabbed a cup and held it under the spout of the coffee carafe and pushed down on the pump. Coffee sprayed and splattered her white shirt. "Shit!" She pulled her purse off her shoulder and set it on the counter, digging in it for the emergency detergent wipes she kept handy for this exact situation. She pulled her shirt away from her chest, dabbing at the brown spots.

Now Dot smiled.

The wipe failed to remove all the color. Giving up, Ava removed the excess coffee from her hands and threw the wipe in the garbage. She held her cup under the other carafe and carefully pushed the button. A steady stream of coffee filled her cup. *Sheesh.*

"Stop it!"

Ava turned mid-pour to see a woman trip through the entrance. A man had held the door open for her, then had pushed her as she walked past him. Ava's heart stopped.

Jayne?

Her sister had cut and dyed her hair. Ava hadn't seen Jayne as a brunette since Ava had moved to Portland. She had dark circles under her eyes and sores on her face that she'd attempted to cover with cheap makeup. Her collarbones highlighted the deep fossa below her neck. Ava had never seen her sister so thin. "Jayne?" She set down her cup and took a step in her sister's direction.

In unison, Jayne and the man turned toward her. Ava looked at the man. *This must be Derrick Snyder.* She'd seen his various mug shots, but she wouldn't have recognized the man. His hair was long and shaggy, with a new beard and mustache that she assumed had been grown to hide his identity. Or he'd simply not had the facilities to shave them. He was tall and thin, his dark eyes angry, and he loomed over Jayne like he owned her.

Jayne spotted her sister. "Ava!"

Derrick grabbed her arm as Jayne stepped her way, and jerked her back. Fear flashed across Jayne's face. Jayne glanced back at Derrick and wilted; her chin dropped to her chest, and her shoulders drooped.

Ava steamed. No one manhandled her sister.

"Jayne," she said again. "Are you okay?" She took a cautious step closer, meeting Derrick's gaze. She saw understanding register on his face.

"Is that your sister?" he said to Jayne, his gaze still holding Ava's. "Did you used to look that good?" A sneer curled his lips.

Jayne met Ava's gaze. Derrick had speared Jayne directly in the heart. It'd always been a source of pride for Jayne to outdo her sister in the looks department. Ava had let the competition roll off her back, knowing that any attempt she made to one-up her sister in style would be taken as a challenge. Ava preferred not to feed the constant competition that seemed to exist in Jayne's head.

But the pain in her sister's eyes stabbed at her. Hard living had taken its toll on Jayne's skin, hair, and weight. Pain ripped through Ava's chest, and she wanted to grab her sister and tuck her in bed for a month while force-feeding her a healthy diet.

Jayne dropped Ava's gaze. *She knows how bad she looks.*

Jayne never admitted defeat. But defeat shone clearly on her face. Ava wanted to kill Derrick Snyder for dragging Jayne down to his low level. He'd destroyed all of her spine and determination. Ava stepped backward, reaching for her purse on the coffee counter.

"Don't move, Fibbee!"

Ava froze at the sight of a knife that appeared in his hand at her sister's neck. He grabbed Jayne's hair, pulling her head high against his shoulder, exposing the long white expanse of skin.

Bruises dotted her neck. Fingertip-size bruises.

Jayne's gaze stayed on the floor.

She knows I can see what he's done to her.

"That's right," said Derrick. "I know what you do for a living. Jayne doesn't shut up about her big-shot sister in the effing-bee-eye. Don't touch your bag and keep your hands where I can see them, unless you want to watch the pretty red blood run down your twin's neck." He looked at Dot behind the counter. "Same goes for you. Let me see your hands."

Ava watched Dot slowly raise her hands, gazing from Ava to Jayne, grasping the situation. *Did she hit an alarm first?* Ava listened for sirens as she shifted into her hostage-negotiator mode.

"You haven't done anything illegal yet, Derrick. Let's not start with hurting Jayne." She didn't mention his outstanding warrants. *Make him think it's not too late.*

"Shut up." He started dragging Jayne backward toward the door, clearly planning to leave with her sister.

Ava stood still, not wanting to antagonize the angry man. If he wanted Jayne to leave with him, he probably wasn't going to hurt her any more than he'd already done. A shadow appeared outside the glass door and a man in a baseball cap pushed his way in.

"Rick!" he roared, lunging at Derrick.

Derrick spun, terror on his face, and he shoved Jayne at the man. Jayne slammed into the man's chest, tripping over her own feet. With agility Ava hadn't expected, Derrick spun and dashed toward the back of the store, slamming through a door labeled EMPLOYEES ONLY.

Ava ran five steps and grabbed Jayne's waist from the back to help her balance. Jayne slapped at her hands, screaming for her to let go and kicking backward with her feet. She didn't look over her shoulder at Ava; all her focus was on the large man in front of her. Jayne's sharp heel caught Ava's shin, making her see stars, and she let go. Jayne scrambled after Derrick, shrieking for him to stop and leaving Ava in her wake.

Ava watched her sister stumble and crash into the back door. She made it through and vanished, her screams of Derrick's name echoing in the store.

She couldn't move. Jayne had abandoned her again in pursuit of a man and the drugs. Tears smarted in Ava's eyes. She turned to look at the big man who'd burst through the front door and rescued her sister from Derrick's knife.

"Thank you," she said. "I don't think you realize . . ." She trailed off. The man was staring at her, his mouth open in shock. She could see the whites of his shadowed eyes.

He appeared to be about her age, but the stunned look on his face resembled a twelve-year-old's. *Is he simple?* "Are you all right?"

she asked slowly. She took a step backward, remembering that her purse with her weapon was still by the coffee.

Comprehension flashed on his face and joy filled his eyes. "Colleen," he said with a smile. He moved toward her as if to give her a hug.

His fist crashed into her jaw and the lights in the room exploded. As the darkness claimed her, Ava knew she was in trouble.

22

Mason felt sick to his stomach and clenched his teeth at the taste of bile in the back of his throat. The flash of the lights from the Portland police cars in front of the shitty convenience store pulsated into his brain. He put one foot in front of the other as he numbly crossed the blocked-off street toward the store. He flashed his badge at the cop at the police tape and signed the crime scene log.

This isn't happening.

Ava is fine.

But the gnawing, aching, empty hole in his chest told him something was very wrong. It'd started an hour ago when he'd tried to call her, wondering how long she planned to be gone that morning. The call had gone to voicemail. He'd waited twenty minutes and tried again. Voicemail. He'd stepped into the backyard to throw the slimy tennis ball for Bingo a few dozen times. And called again. Then he'd opened the app on his phone to trace her location.

Well, the app traced her cell phone's location.

It showed her phone was in Southeast Portland. He'd ignored the warning signs in his brain, knowing that the store Ava had

planned to visit was in Southeast. He'd been in the process of pulling up what existed at the address when Zander had called.

Portland police had responded to an incident in Southeast Portland, and Ava's purse with her identification, firearm, and cell phone
had been found at the scene. A witness said Ava had been hit in the
head and kidnapped.

Mason's brain had slowed to a crawl to process the facts as
Zander talked in his ear. Mentally he rounded up all his emotions
and shoved them into a closet, barking questions at Zander as he
grabbed his keys and got in his vehicle. He needed to focus.

The drive across town had taken forever.

Mason stepped through the convenience store door and spotted Ray and Zander talking with several Portland police officers
and an older woman in jeans. The group turned and stared as he
approached. Ray slapped him on the shoulder as he joined the
group, and Zander nodded at him. Ray lived closer to the location.
He'd been Mason's first call when he got off the phone with Zander.

"What the fuck happened?" Mason asked the group.

The older woman sniffed. "You must be the boyfriend. Thought
you'd be younger."

Mason saw red. His vision zoomed in on her nametag. "Dot," he
said through clenched teeth. "Kindly repeat for me what you've told
these gentlemen."

She glanced at the other cops. "The woman said she was law
enforcement, but I didn't believe her. Customers tell me that all
the time, and after that I was watching her like a hawk. Makes me
uncomfortable when people ask if I'm the only one working in the
store."

Mason nodded. *Get on with it.*

"Like I told these guys. I didn't recognize the picture of a
woman she showed me. And she was getting a cup of coffee, and
I assume was about to leave when that couple came in the door.

I've helped him before. He's an ass. Buys cigarettes. Always wants four books of matches. How many matches does it take to smoke a pack?" She shook her head in disgust. "Anyway, he pulled a knife on the woman who'd come in with him and was telling the FBI agent to stay away when another guy came hollerin' through the door. The first guy split and his woman went screeching after him, leaving your agent and the second guy staring at each other. I'm thinking it's all over, but then he socks her in the face and she goes down like a brick. He slings her over his shoulder and leaves. That's when I called you guys."

"You see him drive away?"

Dot shook her head. "I didn't step out of the store after he left. I was shakin' like a leaf."

"Video?" Mason asked Zander.

Zander nodded. "Yep. We were just about to take a look."

"No one in the neighborhood saw him leave? He had a body slung over his shoulder. Didn't that stand out to anyone?" Mason asked, scanning faces.

"We've got guys doing a canvass," said one of the Portland police sergeants. "But if he ducked around the side of the store to the back, there are alleyways and shortcuts between all the homes and businesses. He could have avoided most eyes. We're still searching the area and knocking on doors."

"Jesus Christ." Mason wiped at his forehead.

"We'll find her, Mase," Ray stated. "She's tough. He'll have to be on his toes to get away from Ava unscathed."

"I've got the video running," said a plainclothes detective from the door at the back of the room. "There's only room for a few back here."

Zander pointed at Mason, Ray, Dot, and the sergeant. "Us first."

One of the uniforms started to speak, but Zander cut him off. "That's our agent missing." He led the group to the back and Mason followed, his gaze momentarily caught by the sight of a familiar bag in the hands of an evidence technician. "Wait." He stopped and reached for the bag. The woman backed up, keeping the bag away from his touch.

"Evidence, sir," she said politely.

Mason froze, staring at Ava's black bag. Ray put a hand on his shoulder and propelled him forward. "Later. There's nothing there you need."

He followed the group. *Nothing I need?* His fingers needed to touch Ava; if they couldn't touch his woman, then they needed to touch something of hers. It felt like she was just beyond his grasp, and he needed to grab hold of *something* to keep her safe.

Like touching her bag will keep him from harming her?

If that man did anything more to hurt her. . .

Stabbing pains ripped through his stomach, and he wanted to strangle someone. Instead he quietly followed in line while his brain screamed for Ava's return. He felt Ray's gaze on him. He glanced at his partner, hating the pity in his eyes. "I'm all right," he muttered.

"It looked like you were going to knock down that poor tech and steal the bag," Ray said. "I don't blame you. I'd be out of my head if something happened to Jill. I'd be ready to murder someone."

"Not promising I won't," said Mason. They squeezed into a microscopic office in the stockroom. "Office" was a generous word. There was a desk, a chair, a million unorganized sheets of paper, and an ancient computer. Mason stared at the screen.

A silent, grainy black-and-white movie played out. Mason watched as Ava walked in, spoke with the clerk, splattered coffee on her shirt, and tried to clean it up. In his mind he could hear her swearing at the mess. Jayne and Derrick Snyder entered. The camera angle showed the back of Ava's head as she looked at the two, but Mason could read her shock in the tilt of her head and stiff shoulders. Jayne had colored her hair, he noted. No more platinum blond.

Jayne had started to rush toward Ava when Derrick yanked her back and put the knife at her neck.

Snyder must have been worried Ava would arrest him. Mason watched stone-faced as Snyder used Jayne as a shield to start to back out of the store. *Coward.* A large man moved in and Mason noticed Snyder nearly wet his pants at the sight of the big guy. Both Snyder and Jayne took off like they'd seen the devil himself.

Mason's mouth dried up as he watched Ava collapse as if her bones had suddenly dissolved. Watching someone hit her . . .

"Can you freeze it on the frame of the second guy as he comes in the door?" Mason asked. The outdoor light had been the best, briefly showing the man's face under his cap. The detective backed up the video, and Mason watched Ava return to standing from her collapsed position on the floor. The detective stopped the feed.

Mason stepped forward, looking closely. The image was too grainy for him to make out any features. The store system must have been installed in the eighties or nineties and still used actual videotapes for surveillance. No doubt the tape they were watching had been recorded on over and over. "Back up a few frames," Mason requested.

The man on the screen took a step backward out the door and looked to the side, giving the viewers a grainy view of his profile.

"Stop." His heartbeat thumping in his ears, Mason stared at the screen, wondering if he was seeing things. He glanced at Ray and Zander. "Look familiar?"

Zander appeared ill. "He's the guy from the Fremont Bridge video." He turned and shoved his way out of the room.

"The one hanging over the edge," Ray whispered.

Hello, Bridge Killer.

Mason couldn't breathe as his anxiety for Ava shot off the charts.

. . .

Troy pounded the pavement. He'd done it. Colleen was safe.

He'd been given a second chance. He'd been standing in the right place at the right time and all his good karma had suddenly been redeemed. His original plan to seek redemption for his part in Colleen's death had been the right one. Today had proved that.

Why else would Colleen be brought back for him to save? For decades he'd wished he could go back in time. Someone had listened.

But he still had one last loose end to tie up. Rick needed to be punished for his role. They all had to make the sacrifice for what they'd done. Rick wouldn't be allowed to escape.

He'd carried Colleen to his van in the alley and spirited her back to his home. He'd hated to lock her up in *that* room, but she was still unconscious and he knew she'd be safe. With Rick still on the street, Troy wasn't taking any chances.

Why were there two Colleens?

He put the thought out of his mind—one had to be a fake. He'd seen the fake Colleen go screaming after Rick toward the back of the room, and when he'd looked at the other woman standing in front of him, her face had been illuminated like an angel's. As if a giant spotlight were shining on her, highlighting her as his reward. Colleen smiled at him, and he'd heard her low voice in his head, asking if he was all right. But then something on his face had scared her. She must have remembered he'd been present when she died the first time.

Punching her had hurt him as much as her. But it'd stopped her a split second before she would have run off. He couldn't let her get away. He had to protect her, show her all he'd done for her. It was important that she know he hadn't abandoned her as the others had done. He'd put a lot of effort into making everything right. Just for her.

Would saving her save him? Could she reverse the murderous mass in his brain?

No. That is your punishment.

Everyone had his own price to pay. He wouldn't be so presumptuous as to ask for his sentence to be lightened. He scanned the neighborhood. Somewhere close by, Rick was hiding. He could feel it.

In the past he'd spied on the real Colleen for three days before he got up the nerve to speak to her beyond "More potatoes, please." Colleen was the dream girl who worked in the kitchen and had all the guys drooling. She was rumored to be twenty-two. A woman to a seventeen-year-old like him, but not so much older that she was unattainable.

"I heard she slept with three different guys from the camp last year," whispered Rick when he caught Troy staring a little too long at the spot of gravy Colleen had spilled on her T-shirt. "She doesn't mind doing it with younger guys as long as the equipment is right."

"Bullshit," Troy muttered, looking away from the expanse of fresh skin below her neck. Rick was making shit up. He always did. Now that he'd caught Troy ogling her chest, he'd never let up.

"Swear to God," said Rick solemnly. "I don't joke around about getting laid."

No, you just lie through your teeth.

Rick's front teeth severely overlapped and it looked like he simply had one huge tooth in front. It stuck out between his lips even when his mouth was closed. Troy found it rather disturbing, and he imagined girls did, too. Rick claimed he was getting braces that summer, but most kids Troy knew had had braces on in middle school. He figured Rick was the type who simply lied about most things. Especially the things he believed made him look better.

"She goes and swims at the river after dinner most evenings. I've seen it. She has this tiny bikini that I swear will pop off if she turns too fast," Rick said next to Troy's ear.

Troy stole a look at Colleen's chest. Not huge, but the shape was sweet. What would she look like with her shirt off? "At the river?" *Is Rick lying again?*

"On Monday I was avoiding Old Man Thornton's stupid physics lecture and saw her heading off through the woods. I followed. And man, it was worth it."

Rick made a slurping sound that made Troy gag.

"On Tuesday she did the same thing. She swims and then lies in the sun and reads for a while. No one else goes with her. You should come with me tonight."

Troy wanted to see. In his mind he could already see her long, smooth legs and her rounded ass. She had to be hot in a bathing suit. Or out of a bathing suit. "We'll see. We're supposed to be in the lecture hall after dinner tonight."

"It's not like they take roll. What will they do to us? Flunk us out of camp? It's not school. It doesn't go on our permanent record. You need to loosen up."

Rick had a point.

Sometimes Troy took things too seriously. What harm could come from watching Colleen swim? "Okay. It better be as good as you say it is."

"Oh, it's better."

Troy rubbed at his eyes; the memory of that summer before his senior year of high school was permanently branded on his brain. It'd been life-changing. But in a way that no one could know.

Rick had gotten his teeth fixed. It'd been one of the first things Troy had noticed when he'd gotten close enough on the street yesterday. He hadn't lied about the braces. And he hadn't lied about how good Colleen had looked in a swimming suit. But according to Colleen, the stories about her sleeping with teenage guys weren't true. She'd claimed to be a virgin. Rick had called her a liar.

Troy had stared at the new Colleen as she lay unconscious at his home. She'd aged. Hadn't they all? There were small lines near her eyes and her hair was shorter. But she still had that luster to her skin. The one that had made him want to simply touch her over fifteen years ago. He'd touched her cheek today, drawing a finger along her cheekbone. Her lashes had fluttered and he'd jerked his hand back. She hadn't woken. He'd waited a while, hoping she would, but he didn't want to let too much time elapse for Rick and the fake Colleen to hide.

He turned down an alley, quickening his stride as his gaze studied the shadows. This time he was armed. He'd never used the handgun before. He'd only showed it to his three victims, and he hoped that was all he'd need to do for Rick. But Rick had a sense of desperation about him. He seemed like the type to fight back or run. He smelled scared and had the shadowed look of a man being hunted.

He *was* being hunted. Rick must have known Troy was looking for him. The other three men's names had been in the news along with a weak description of the Bridge Killer. Unless Rick had been living under a rock, he had to know he was next on the list. Troy stopped, smirking at his thought. From the looks of things, Rick *had* been living under a rock. He was unwashed and stank of drugs. He'd looked feral.

Good. Rick deserved to suffer for the agony he'd caused Colleen. Just wait until he was in Troy's grasp. He planned to put him through every suffering and indignity that Colleen had endured. And Colleen could watch. The Colleen who'd spoken in his head had gently guided him through the other abductions and stagings. But now she was available in person.

She would love him for making them pay.

He froze, eyeing a small shed inside the chain-link-fenced yard of a house. The shed backed up to the alley, a good fifty feet away from the house. *If I were Rick . . .*

Stepping quietly, Troy moved closer to the shed. Leaning over the low fence he placed one ear on the wall of the shed. Inside he could hear a quiet sobbing. A man hissed a command, too low for Troy to understand, and the sobbing stopped.

He stepped back and smiled. He'd parked his van less than half a block away, and they were a good six blocks from the convenience store. Driving through the area, he'd seen the signs of police activity and kept his distance.

Removing his handgun from his inner coat pocket, he lifted the latch on the gate of the fence and stepped into the yard.

This was going to be easy.

23

Ava's left shoulder and upper arm were on fire. She tried to move her head to look at her arm, believing someone had stuck her with a red-hot poker, but her jaw screamed as she turned her head against the hard floor. Rough carpet scraped her cheek, and she forced her eyes open. A narrow strip of gray lay just beyond her nose.

Duct tape on the carpet.

She was at the academy. Her lids fell shut. She must have gotten hit harder than she realized in her hand-to-hand combat class. She needed to get up. What if one of her instructors found her collapsed on the dormitory floor?

Haul your ass up!

Her arms wouldn't move. She tried again and realized her hands were fastened together behind her back. Her eyes flew open.

Not Quantico.

Yes, there was duct tape covering holes in the carpet near where she lay, but this was not one of the rooms at the dorm. She rolled onto her right side and cried out as her jaw brushed the carpet again.

He hit you.

The tall man in the store who'd frightened away Jayne and her boyfriend. He'd seemed so happy to see Ava at first, but then . . . he'd taken a crack at her jaw that still resonated through her head.

How long have I been out?

She twisted her neck, looking for a window or clock, and found neither. The room she was in had thick insulation, the type you see on a roll that looks like cotton candy, lining the walls. She cranked her head and looked up. It was on the ceiling, too. If there were any windows, they had been covered up. The flooring was rough industrial carpet in an uneven shade of brown. Several places had been repaired with duct tape. She spotted an outline of a door that had also been covered by the pink fluff. Someone hadn't wanted any sound to escape from the room.

Mason. *Does he know I'm gone?* Crap. He would be out of his head with worry. No doubt he'd tried to call her a half dozen times and had alerted the police and the FBI. If anyone was going to push hard to figure out where she was, he was the man. His strong face appeared in her mind, and she drew courage from her no-nonsense better half. He knew how to support her when she was struggling. Like now.

No wimps allowed.

She shuddered, noticing that the floor was slightly damp. A large push broom and three buckets sat by the door. Sniffing, she caught a fading scent of pine cleaner. And blood.

Wide-awake, she jerked her head, scanning the room again, looking for the source of the rusty iron odor. She struggled to focus on the floor in front of her nose, trying to see if there were bloodstains in the dark color. *Someone cleaned up blood. A lot of it.*

The pain from her twisted arm made her lay her head on the cold, damp floor. *Think, McLane. How are you going to get out?*

She fingered the bindings at her wrists. Rope. Bound very tight. But her feet weren't tied. She rolled onto her right side and gave a gentle kick with her legs to lever herself up to a sitting position.

Dizziness swamped her but slowly faded away. She crossed her legs like she was sitting in a kindergarten class and studied her surroundings again.

Why had he brought her here? Hell, why had he grabbed her in the first place? Surely the cranky clerk had called the police. Assuming he hadn't hurt the clerk after he'd hit Ava. And Jayne and Derrick had to know something had happened to her. *Unless they never stopped running.* She wrote them off, preferring to rely on the clerk, who'd hopefully been left standing to sound the alarm.

Damn you, Jayne.

Obviously the tall man had been after Jayne and Derrick. Ava didn't know what they'd done to anger him, but she assumed it had something to do with drugs or money. And she was trapped in the middle.

Just as long as he doesn't think I'm Jayne.

Shoot. Hopefully he hadn't noticed the resemblance between them and decided to hold her hostage to get what he wanted out of Jayne and Derrick. Ava knew Jayne would sell her twin to save her ass. Jayne had said that someone was after Derrick. No doubt the upstanding citizen her sister was living with had people angry with him all the time.

Ava closed her eyes and took deep breaths, seeking calm. A few minutes with her kidnapper and she should be able to talk her way out. She'd been trained in negotiating with kidnappers; surely she could apply some of that knowledge while sitting on the opposite side.

She recounted Jayne's pleading call where she'd begged Ava to find her and Derrick a safe house. No doubt she'd known that this man was angry.

But Jayne said Derrick claimed the Bridge Killer was after him.

Ava opened her eyes, adrenaline pumping through her.

Why would the Bridge Killer want Derrick? Unless he was next . . .

She mentally scanned Derrick Snyder's rap sheet, which she'd studied after his fingerprints had been matched to those found in

Mason's home. *He's a year older than me.* She'd looked, comparing his age to her and Jayne's.

His age matched that of the other victims.

Arrests in McMinnville, Tualatin, Newberg, Yamhill. He had local arrests going back over a decade.

She strained to recall the oldest arrest on his rap sheet.

Twenty years old. Wilsonville Police Department, for theft.

He'd been in the local area for a long time. Like the other victims.

Her breathing sped up. Was Derrick Snyder the next target of the Bridge Killer? But he'd taken Ava instead? Small lights began to flash in her brain. She stared down at the ugly carpet, her fear making bloodstains fade and reappear.

Was she sitting in the killer's lair?

"I suspect the house will have a basement where he does his work, or a substantial outbuilding on the property to contain these men."

She started to shake.

· · ·

Mason stood back and listened as the uniform politely asked a business owner if he had camera surveillance set up that showed a street view. His thoughts rocketed in a dozen different directions as he tried to focus on the conversation in front of him.

Why did the Bridge Killer take Ava? Does he know she's one of the investigators on the case? What will he do to her?

He fought to keep the image of Ava with a noose around her neck and her wrists neatly bandaged out of his brain. He was unsuccessful.

"God damn it!"

The cop and business owner turned to stare at him.

"Never mind," he mumbled, moving away to lean against the brick wall of the business. He put his hands on his knees, bent over, and tried to slow his breathing, staring at the dirty sidewalk. Ray's shoes moved into his line of sight. Mason didn't look up. He bit his lip, willing the nausea in his gut to go away. The copper taste of blood and death filled his mouth. He spat.

"We'll find her," Ray said. "We got twenty more cops from Portland police and every available FBI agent headed this way. They're attacking this head on."

"As they should." *What if we're too late?*

"I don't think he knew she was an agent," Ray said. "Listening to what Dot said about the exchange between Ava and the perp, there was no time for her to tell him who she was."

"But why her? Why would he suddenly grab a woman? I don't get it. And it's been over *two hours*."

"We'll find her," Ray repeated.

"Fuck off," Mason muttered. He wanted to hit someone and if Ray kept getting in his face, even though Mason knew he meant well, he was going to be the victim. Ray took half a step back.

"Sorry," muttered Mason.

"I get it," Ray said. "I'd want to pound on everyone in sight, not caring who it was. I'd just want someone to feel the same pain I'm in and assume it'd make me feel better."

Mason nodded, avoiding Ray's gaze. He straightened his back. He wasn't doing Ava any good by having a pity party. The uniform looked over and shook his head. The business owner didn't have a camera. Few places in the neighborhood did. It was a financial issue. They'd been lucky the convenience store had something.

"Hey, Callahan!" Zander yelled from across the street. He glanced both ways and jogged across, his face hopeful.

"What happened?" Mason asked. Caution kept down his excitement.

"Ava's phone from her purse rang a minute ago. It was her sister, wanting to know if Ava was all right. I took down her number and told her you'd call her right back since the phone was being processed." He handed Mason a scrap of paper and Mason dialed, stress making his fingers shake.

"Hello?" answered a high voice.

"Jayne? This is Mason Callahan, Ava's . . . friend. We met at the hospital."

"Where is she?" Jayne begged. "Why isn't she answering the phone?"

"Who was in the store with you?" Mason asked. "We saw the video of you and Derrick Snyder running away from another guy."

"I don't know! He just took Derrick! We were hiding and he found us. I got away, but he pulled a gun on Derrick and made him go with him!"

Mason's muscles contracted. *He wants Derrick? Is he on the killer's list?* "Where are you?"

Jayne paused. "Why?"

Mason wanted to shake her. "The man who took Derrick also has your sister. He grabbed her after you guys left. We need to find him and you're the last person who saw him. *Where are you?*"

"How can you help me?"

"Ava didn't tell you I'm with the Oregon State Police?"

"No. She never tells me anything."

Mason closed his eyes. "I'm still at the store where he grabbed Ava. We've got dozens of police and FBI agents looking for this man. *You were the last person to see him. Where did he grab Derrick?*"

"No police," Jayne whispered. "We can't trust them. I didn't know you were a cop. Why would she hide that from me? They'll arrest Derrick if they find him."

"They can't arrest him if he's dead!" He was talking to a brick wall. "He's got your sister and we think he's already killed three other guys. You can help us find him."

Wet sobs sounded through the phone. "I don't know what to do."

Mason met Zander's and Ray's worried gazes. He could feel her slipping away. "Jayne," he said in a calmer voice. "You'd be helping us. That has to be a good thing for Derrick's situation. We don't want him killed by this man. Our goal is to prevent any more deaths, not arrest some thief. Can you see the difference?"

She whispered the name of the intersection she was near. Mason passed the information to Zander, who ran back to the police at the convenience store. By Mason's estimate, they were a good six blocks from her location. "Thank you, Jayne. That'll help us find him. Maybe someone got a look at his vehicle or the plates while he was over there. We'll get Derrick and Ava back before they're hurt."

I hope.

She continued to sob on the phone.

"I'll stay on the line until the police get there. Are you hurt?" Mason asked.

"No," she said in a shaky voice. "I'm just scared. And Derrick's going to be angry with me. I wasn't supposed to involve the police. He's going to yell at me."

"Why did Derrick believe the Bridge Killer was searching for him?"

"Derrick said he'd killed everyone else already. That he was the only one left."

Mason blew out a breath. *Derrick was to be the last victim?* "How did Derrick know he was the only one left? Did he know the other victims?"

"That's what I asked him. He said they'd been friends a long time ago but got in a big fight, and no one spoke to each other anymore."

A long time ago. The task force had been on the right track. "Did he tell you this guy's name?"

Jayne was quiet for a moment. "He called him Troy. He never mentioned a last name."

Mason wanted to cheer. It was a good start. He covered the microphone of his phone and whispered to Ray, "She says the Bridge Killer's name is Troy. No last name." Ray gave him a thumbs-up and pulled out his phone to pass on the information.

"Derrick swore he saw Troy following us yesterday."

"Did you see him?"

"No. I never saw anyone. Sometimes Derrick sees things. I just go along with what he wants to do."

Mason bit his tongue. It wasn't an appropriate time for a lecture on her taste in men. "Does he live in that area of town? Do you think he's close by?"

Sirens started to wail through the line.

"They're coming!" Her voice cracked and escalated into a shriek. "I can't let them find me. Derrick will kill me!"

"Jayne!" Mason shouted. "They're there to help you!"

"No! No, I can't!" She ended the call.

"Shit!" Mason hit SEND to call her back, but got a message that the caller wasn't available. *She's turned off her phone.*

"She's running?" Ray asked, worry on his face.

"Like a frightened rabbit."

"They'll find her."

"I don't know. She's pretty good at crawling into a hole when she wants to disappear."

"At least we've got the Bridge Killer's possible last location. That'll help."

Mason nodded. "We need to get over there. Hopefully he hasn't gone far."

Something needs to lead us to Ava.

24

Ava moved into the corner farthest from the door, her back against the wall and her feet ready to kick. She'd worked at the ropes around her wrists but couldn't loosen or untie them, and her hands had grown numb over the last few hours. She wished the numbness would envelop her left upper arm and shoulder. Instead she funneled that pain into anger. Her feet and her teeth were her best available weapons. She could do a lot of damage if she got close enough to her attacker.

Bring it on.

She wasn't afraid to fight back. Her back was against the wall, and she'd do whatever was necessary to escape. She wasn't going to calmly allow the man to slit her wrists and drain her dry. He'd have some painful bruises if he tried. And if he came at her hair with scissors or a razor, *watch out.*

She stared at the door, willing it to open. A motor had approached and stopped outside a few minutes ago. She'd felt the vibration through the floor before she'd registered the noise. It was the first engine she'd heard since she'd been there, and the sound had been very faint. Her location was definitely isolated and soundproofed. Special Agent Euzent had been spot-on with that analysis.

The soundproofing created an odd lack of acoustics that screwed with her perception of space. She'd yelled. A lot. But the lack of echo in the room had made it feel like she was underground several miles. She'd been dozing when she became aware of the vehicle, and she'd screamed for help again. Nothing had happened and she didn't believe the soundproofing could block her voice, so she assumed it was her abductor out there. She'd probably pissed him off with her screams.

A knock sounded at the door.

Ava tilted her head. *He wants permission to come in?* "Come in," she shouted.

The bolt slid to the side, and she heard a key rattle in the second lock. The door slowly opened, and her abductor peered into the room before entering.

He was as she remembered. Tall. Rather gawky-looking for a full-grown adult. He had the physique of a nineteen-year-old who hadn't filled out yet. Wide-shouldered but gangly-limbed. His cheeks were hollow, and gray shadows formed half-moons under his eyes. He took off his baseball cap, exposing a shaved head, as he made eye contact. "Are you okay?"

Ava stared. *Did he forget that he punched me in the jaw?*

"My hands are numb."

He dropped his gaze and shuffled his feet as if embarrassed. "Ah, yeah. I don't think I should take the rope off yet. Maybe I'll loosen it a bit later."

Her plans to kick him in the balls and face took a backseat. Something was not right. He was acting like a shy schoolboy. Could she talk her way out of this? "I'd appreciate that. I can't move my fingers." She watched with curiosity for his reaction to her request for kindness.

He made quick eye contact and dropped it again. "I didn't hurt you."

He has regret? "Umm . . . well, my jaw is a bit sore from something hurting me."

Frustration crossed his face, and he met her gaze. "I meant to say I didn't *mean* to hurt you. Sorry about your leg. I mean your jaw." He mangled the words and anger flashed in his dark eyes.

Ava watched him cautiously. The anger seemed directed at himself, not her. Could she take advantage of some remorse?

"I need to bring in Rick." He looked at her as if asking permission.

"Okay."

His face lit up. "I knew you'd be pleased." He turned and left the room, closing the door behind him.

Her knees weak, Ava slid down the wall into a crouch. *Hurry up, Mason.* She needed out of this situation. Now. She wanted to go back to her warm bed and curl against his solid back and drift off to sleep. Sunday mornings were for being lazy and reading in bed. Why in the hell had she gone looking for Jayne instead of spending a relaxing morning with her man?

Who was Rick, and why would she be pleased? She repeated their conversation in her head. He'd seemed frustrated and eager at the same time.

Was he the Bridge Killer? She'd had a few hours in the empty room to consider it. She'd gone back and forth, convinced one minute and doubtful the second. The man she'd just met didn't act like a killer. Maybe this Rick would shed some light.

Do not let your guard down.

Her gaze fell on the door. She hadn't heard the click of a lock. She pushed to her feet and slowly crossed the room. Was he right outside the door? Had he purposely not locked it to tease her into doing something stupid? She crept within two feet of it. Scuffling sounded outside, and she shot backward to her corner. She waited, prepared to do whatever needed to be done.

The unlocked door flew open. "Move!" the tall man ordered, and

Derrick Snyder stumbled in, falling to his knees from a kick in his back. "Ass!"

Derrick's wide-eyed gaze met Ava's, shock showing on his face. The ball gag in his mouth garbled his words, but she understood her name.

"Do not speak to her!"

Ava held her breath. *Where's Jayne?* The tall man was looking at her, waiting for her reaction. He'd called him Rick. Was that a nickname for Derrick?

Am I supposed to be happy?

"Where did you find him?" she asked, deciding to go with a neutral topic.

"Hiding. Like the coward he's always been. His type slinks through the gutter and hides behind garbage, waiting to take advantage of decent people."

Derrick shook his head and the man kicked him in the ear, knocking him onto his side on the nasty carpet.

"This is what you wanted, right?" he asked Ava. His wide, expectant eyes reminded her of a child's.

"Wasn't there a woman, too?" she asked. Clearly he wanted her praise for bringing the scumbag to her feet, but she wasn't comfortable commending his actions. What did he expect her to do with her twin's boyfriend?

"We don't need her," he stated confidently. "She wasn't real. She was only pretending to be you."

More accurate than you realize.

"You let her go?"

He made a dismissive gesture. "She left. Wait." He darted out the door, leaving it open, and reappeared before Ava could think. He held out a bunch of daisies for her, watching her with hopeful eyes. In his other hand he held a gasoline can—the red plastic type people use to store gasoline for their lawn mowers.

She didn't move, her gaze going from the gas can to the daisies, and then to his face. *Oh shit.* She wanted to ask his name, but he'd spoken like they'd already had several discussions. His emotions had swung from one end of the spectrum to the other, and she didn't want to trigger more anger. "Thank you." *What is the gas can for?*

His face lit up, but Derrick Snyder started to mumble from behind his ball gag.

"Should you take that off of him? I'd hate to see him choke."

The tall man bent at the waist and laughed, setting down the gas can and crushing the daisies against his thigh. Ava blinked and glanced at Derrick, who seemed as stunned as she felt. *I'm missing something big here.*

"Oh," he laughed, wiping at his eyes. "I haven't heard anything that good in a long time."

"You're welcome."

He tossed the daisies beside her, stepped over next to Derrick, and crouched down to look the man in the eye.

Ava caught her breath. *Run! Kick him over!*

But what would she find outside? They could be miles from help.

There has to be a vehicle. She stared at the man's pants pockets, searching for the outline of keys.

"Are you ready?" the man said to Derrick. "You realize you're going to pay today, right? You're going to feel every ounce of pain that Colleen felt back then, you cowardly piece of shit. You know exactly why I have that gas can, don't you?"

Derrick shook his head and protested behind the ball, his feet pushing against the floor and scooting him away from the man.

Colleen? Terror inched up Ava's spine as the scent of the fuel in the can stung her nose.

The man pointed at Ava. "She's too kind. I would have requested that you be burned alive if I were in her position. Instead she asked for you to be made more comfortable. I guess she's blocked the memory of the agony you gave her.

"This time the roles are reversed. She'll get to watch as you suffer." He turned his head toward Ava, his mouth in a dreamy smile, his eyes unfocused. He slid a utility knife out of his coat pocket, and Ava couldn't breathe.

· · ·

Mason stepped out of Ray's car and into a flurry of action. White-and-blue Portland police vehicles lined the streets and driveways near Jayne's last reported location. Cops were knocking on doors and talking to people on the street, searching for Ava's flighty sister and possibly the Bridge Killer. Older, depressed-looking homes lined the neighborhood, along with a few struggling businesses at each intersection. The mist falling from the sky made the area more dreary.

He spotted Zander moving toward a group of cops and men in suits who seemed to be the hub of organization. "Over there." He gestured and Ray nodded.

As he neared the group, he noticed one of the cops holding up a tablet showing an image of Jayne that had to be from an old driver's license. Mason grimaced. The woman in the picture looked happy and healthy. "She doesn't look like that anymore," he announced as he joined the group. "She's a lot thinner and looks like some-one who's been living on the streets with meth. And she's not blond today—she's dark-haired. You'll notice her eyes first. They're a dis-tinctive dark blue."

All faces in the group turned his way. He nodded at them and introduced himself and Ray. "We're part of the Bridge Killer Task Force, and you've probably heard by now that Jayne McLane claims the killer grabbed her boyfriend. We're giving the story quite a bit of weight."

"Why?" asked one of the cops. "From what I've heard, she's a junkie. Why would you believe anything she says?"

Mason wasn't ready to reveal that they were relying on grainy video from the convenience store where Ava'd been kidnapped.

"She's not the only source. Believe me, we *want* the guy who she says took her boyfriend." He held the questioning cop's gaze and the man looked away.

He scanned the group. "Find her. And we're looking for this guy." Ray passed around his phone with the image he'd snapped from the convenience store video. The image wasn't great. The man's face was shadowed by his hat and grainy from the monitor.

"Send those images to central so they can get them out to us," requested one of the officers.

"I did two minutes ago. You should have them soon," answered Ray. "We also requested images of Derrick Snyder be sent out. He's the one who Jayne McLane claimed was grabbed and may be on his way to becoming the next victim of the Bridge Killer."

"We're also looking for FBI Special Agent Ava McLane." Mason tried to keep his voice steady. "She was nabbed an hour ago at the convenience store six blocks from here. Possibly the Bridge Killer is holding her and Derrick Snyder in this area."

The cop with the tablet touched the screen and Ava's image from her federal ID popped up.

The solemn picture made Mason's heart hurt. Ava's dark-blue eyes looked directly at him.

A couple of the cops exchanged glances and low murmurs circulated.

"Yes, she's the twin of the first woman," Mason answered before any of them spoke. "She's on the Bridge Killer Task Force. You've got four people to look for, but Jayne McLane was most recently in the area. She's the one we'll trip over first."

"Okay," said the sergeant. "Let's—"

Thunder boomed and the sidewalk quivered. *Earthquake?*

As one, the group looked to the east, where a plume of smoke appeared. The gray mass rose over the rooftops, a dark, roiling cloud of ash that rapidly spread outward.

"Shit," Ray mumbled. "It's coming from a house."

Everyone ran toward the smoke. Mason heard the sergeant order two men to stay in the area and continue the canvass. Mason's eyes locked on the billowing smoke, dread stabbing in his brain.

Ava?

He ran harder, remembering another explosion, in a forest where a manhunt had ended when a killer blew up his cabin. The two victims inside had nearly died. Mason could still feel that fire's heat on his face.

"Been in this sitch before," Ray said as he ran beside Mason.

Mason nodded. Ray shared the same memory. They ran down the street, passing home after home. A fire engine siren sounded from far away. Panting, Mason turned up a cross street, following the group of police. Ahead, on his left, flames spilled out of the upper-level windows of an old home. Neighbors stood clustered in groups, watching the flames. A few were venturing close but quickly backing away.

"Is anyone inside?" several cops were shouting as the group arrived. Scanning the neighbors' faces, Mason saw heads nodding, but confusion reigned. One younger woman was screaming, trying to run into the home, but was being held back by two men. Mason darted to their group.

"Who's inside?" he asked, raising his voice to be heard over the woman's shouts.

"Jeff!" she screeched, thrashing at her holders. Tears streamed down her thin face and her blowing hair stuck in her mouth. Mason turned to look at the fire. The smoke had become a thick black, hugging the outside of the house as it climbed up the siding and into the sky.

"Is that your son?" Mason asked. The woman shook her head and screamed Jeff's name again. "Is there anyone else in the house?" he shouted. She nodded, hair flying around her face. "Any children?" She shook her head.

One of the men holding her arms said, "Jeff's her boyfriend. They both live here. She came running out after the explosion, but has been trying to get back in ever since."

"What floor is he on?" Mason asked. The amount of black smoke pouring from the upper windows made him cringe. A fire engine arrived and firefighters spread through the scene. No one had entered the house since Mason had arrived. Two of the cops had dashed up the porch to the front door and then quickly backed away, forced to safety by the heat.

The woman collapsed, the men's grip keeping her from falling to the ground. They lowered her into a sitting position, but kept hold of her arms. "No one could live through that," said the man on her left. She wailed at his words.

Three firefighters went through the front door and Mason said a silent prayer. He noticed two of the cops cross themselves as the firefighters vanished. Several of the firefighters went down the driveway and around to the back of the house.

Within the odor of the smoke, Mason smelled burning chemicals. "Was there a lab in there?" he shouted at the woman. She wouldn't look at him. She hunched over and buried her face in her knees, her torso shaking. Mason looked at the two men and raised a brow. The men exchanged glances.

"Probably," said one. "Sometimes the air smells weird over here. Sort of a sweet, sickening, chemical smell. And people are constantly in and out."

"Shit." Mason stood, looking for whoever was in charge of the firefighters to warn them. "Don't let her go," he ordered the two men, and he jogged toward the fire truck. He grabbed the arm of the closest one and flashed his badge. "You guys know there was probably a meth lab in there, right?"

The firefighter nodded. "We smelled it."

Relieved, Mason looked for Ray and Zander. Both men were

helping to move the crowds to the other side of the street. The crying woman Mason had spoken to was moved by the two men. Mason put some more space between himself and the house. Shouts went up from the crowd, and Mason glanced back toward the fire. Coming around the side of the house were two firefighters supporting a stumbling man between them. They helped him to the back of the EMT vehicle and sat him on the edge. He leaned forward, with his hands on his knees, and coughed until he gagged. An EMT slipped an oxygen mask over his nose and mouth.

The shrieking woman tore away from her two helpers and rushed the man, throwing her arms around his neck and smearing tears on his smoke-covered face. Mason moved closer.

"Anyone else in there?" Mason asked, showing his badge.

The man coughed and spit before answering, holding the oxygen mask away. "Stupid bitch. She's still in there. I already told the other guys."

"Who?" Mason asked sharply.

"Jayne. Derrick's girlfriend. She was all freaked out and lit up a cigarette." He spit again and triggered a thirty-second coughing fit. "We have a no-smoking rule for a reason. The place went up instantly."

Anger shot through Mason. Jayne had run here? "She was living here?"

"Off and on. She knew the rules! God damn her! Serves her right!"

Mason wanted to punch him in the face. "You run a meth lab in a suburban neighborhood and you're pissed at someone for smoking? You're the one who was endangering everyone. If she's dead, you'll be looking at murder."

"Get the fuck away from me!" The man turned away, inhaling in his oxygen mask. His girlfriend gave Mason an evil stare, her arms wrapped around her man.

"Yeah, you, too, sweetheart. If you knew what was going on in there and didn't report it."

Ray appeared and pulled Mason away. "What are you doing?"

"Idiots blew up a meth lab. Sounds like Jayne might have burst in with a cigarette."

"Jayne?" Ray halted. "She was in there?"

"I think so." Mason stared at the burning building. A hose sprayed water through the central window on the main floor. "How am I going to tell Ava?"

Ray turned and looked back at the man with the oxygen mask on. "That's not him, right?"

"No," said Mason. "He doesn't look anything like the guy on the video from this morning or like Derrick Snyder. I think this is one of the places the two of them were crashing occasionally."

"Crap. Can you imagine living in a house with a meth lab?"

"Hell no. The places stink and attract all sorts of lowlifes."

Ray watched the smoke. "And you're risking your life."

Two firefighters appeared in the front door, an unconscious woman over the shoulder of one of them. He dumped her in the grass, a good distance away from the house, as the EMTs rushed over with their equipment.

"Aw, shit," muttered Ray, and Mason dashed across the property.

It was Jayne. Mason had known the instant he'd seen her hanging lifeless over the fireman's shoulder. Physically, there was too much similarity between Ava and Jayne for him not to see it. He felt his hat blow off as he ran across the lawn, but he didn't stop. Beside the kneeling EMT, he saw brown hair splayed across the wet grass. More police crowded around the woman and the movement of the EMT's shoulders told Mason he'd started CPR.

Mason stopped at Jayne's feet and knelt as the EMT pressed on her chest. A second EMT had a mask over her mouth and nose and was rhythmically forcing oxygen into her lungs with each squeeze of his hand on the bag. Her eyes were closed, and Mason saw Ava on the grass even though his brain told him it wasn't her. The ash-covered face was too thin. She didn't move.

"Aw, fuck," whispered Ray beside him.

The EMTs kept up their task, one of them counting out loud.

Jayne's shoulders suddenly heaved upward and one arm flew up to bat at the mask and bag over her face. The EMTs rolled her to one side, and she coughed and vomited as they carefully watched.

"Thank God," stated Mason. He went to touch the brim of his hat and realized it was gone. He glanced at the ground behind him, not seeing the hat. Jayne retched. He walked around to her head and knelt beside her, ignoring the EMTs.

"Jayne, was anyone else in the house?" he asked.

Coughing, Jayne shook her head. "I don't know," she wheezed. "I'd just gotten there."

"What about the guy who grabbed Derrick? Have you seen him or Derrick since then?"

She shook her head and pushed to a sitting position, knocking away the hands of the EMTs who tried to support her. "No one," she croaked. She wiped at her nose and eyes as an EMT thrust a towel into her hand. She peered at Mason, recognition flashing in her eyes. A pain shot through him. *Ava's eyes.*

"You're Ava's guy. The cop." Her voice trailed off as she gasped and tears flooded her eyes at the pain. "My throat," she wheezed at the EMTs.

"Don't talk," said one. He offered her a bottle of water.

Mason sat back, spotting the huge blistering burns on her left arm as she took the water. She didn't seem to feel them. He glanced at one of the EMTs and saw the man focus on the burn. As she drank, he swiftly started an IV and injected something into the fluid. Within thirty seconds her eyelids drooped, and they helped her lie back down.

"She's gonna feel those burns later," Mason said in a low voice. The EMT nodded.

"Mason. Ray." Zander's voice sounded behind them.

Mason glanced back and Zander gestured for them to follow him. The three men moved away to a quieter spot.

"She say anything?" Zander asked. He handed Mason his hat.

"Says she hasn't seen Derrick or our guy. She's lucky to be alive," answered Ray.

Mason studied Zander's face. Something was up. "What do you have?"

"I just got the results of another VICAP search," Zander said. "The ones Ava had run had come back without any matches."

"And?" Ray asked.

"I went back two decades this time. We'd been running searches within the last five years and had specified a male victim."

Mason held his breath.

"I got one hit. Seventeen years ago in Yamhill County. A twenty-two-year-old woman was found murdered. Her wrists were slit, she was gagged, and most of her hair had been cut off. She'd also been doused with gasoline and burned. The cause of death wasn't from the wrists; it was from strangulation."

"And?" Bile rose in the back of Mason's throat, and he knew there was more.

"She was found hanging from a small bridge out in the country. The crime was never solved."

25

Troy looked at Colleen. She seemed horrified and shocked, but he'd expected that. She was a good girl, not the type who liked watching others get hurt, even though she'd been urging him on over the last few months. He understood that wanting to see it and actually seeing it were two different things.

He would be strong for her.

He knew what was best; she needed to watch Rick suffer. Then she could be at peace. Colleen huddled in the far corner of his work shed, her dark-blue eyes watching his every move with Rick. Every now and then she looked away, but when he commanded her to watch, she obeyed.

For a long time the work shed had sat empty—one of several unused buildings on the land his parents had left him. Once Colleen began speaking to him in his dreams, he'd started to alter the building for his needs. He'd always dreamed about Colleen. Nearly every night since he was seventeen. But her actual conversations with him had begun a year ago.

His old dreams had been terrors, reliving her death over and over. Sometimes the boys turned on him and he suffered the same fate. Other times he stopped the attack and one of the boys was sac-rificed in Colleen's place.

Layer after layer of insulation covered the inside of his shed. He'd reinforced the door and walls. No one could escape. He'd shut himself in and tried to beat down the door and break through the walls. It'd been impossible. Carson and Aaron had been in the shed at the same time. He'd made Aaron watch as he prepared Carson for his fate. It'd been an extra dig at Aaron. After Rick, Aaron had been the one most guilty of hurting Colleen. Carson had shown some reluctance, but Aaron had eagerly followed Rick's suggestions.

Troy had worried the police would track him if he outright duplicated Colleen's murder scene with Carson Scott's. The idea to increase the torture had come from Colleen. "Start small," she'd suggested in his dreams one night. "Then add more layers. That will confuse the police and protect you until you take care of the last killer. By then it won't matter if they catch you."

"Because I have to pay, too," he'd replied.

"Yes," she'd said sadly. "You do. You did nothing to help me that day."

Rick's noises grated on his nerves. The ball gag stopped him from forming words, but he could still scream behind it. Troy had laid the beautiful daisy form on the floor, rolling Rick's naked bulk on top of it. He'd made the form a decade ago in a welding class, and it'd hung on the wall in his bedroom. It'd reminded him of Colleen and the single daisy she'd always tucked into her dark ponytail at camp.

A sign of innocence and purity.

The boys had taken that away from her.

After he'd killed Carson Scott, he'd stood staring at the white body, wanting some way to permanently mark it for Colleen, to show the world that this sacrifice had been for her. A scene from a cop show had appeared in his mind, along with the explanation of the odd blanching on dead bodies that indicated what they'd lain on for hours after death. The daisy. It'd been simple and perfect.

He closed his eyes and ignored Rick's pleas behind the gag, remembering every second of the day his world had changed. In his mind he saw the daisy left on the ground after Aaron and Rick had taken Colleen's body to the bridge. Joe had accidentally stepped on the daisy that'd fallen out of her hair and crushed it. Troy had kept his gaze on the flower rather than on Colleen's battered body.

"Wuss," Carson snapped at him.

Troy jerked up his head and looked at his circle of friends. *Friends? Are they really my friends?* "Did we just do this?" Troy gasped. "Did we kill her?"

"They did it," Joe whispered. "I didn't do anything."

"You were here!" Rick snapped at him. "You didn't say anything. That makes you an accomplice!"

Troy stared at the four boys. The woods surrounding their camp were dense and they were a mile away from the camp buildings. No one knew where they were. If someone had wanted to commit the perfect crime, this had been the place to do it.

This wasn't supposed to happen.

They'd gone to the river to see if Colleen was in her usual spot relaxing with a book. For a week the boys had ogled and joked about the good-looking cook at the camp. All the attendees had a crush on her, but she simply smiled and ignored them. Rumor had it that she was engaged to a rich guy in medical school, but she didn't wear a ring.

Rick and Aaron were the most enamored. Troy and Joe could see she was plainly out of their league, and why would an older woman be interested in high school boys? But the others seemed to view her as a challenge. Rick bragged about his experience with girls. Claimed to have slept with five and swore they'd all loved it. Troy kept his mouth shut but nodded along like he knew what Rick meant. He was a virgin. Sure, he'd had his share of crushes on girls, but had never had the guts to ask one out.

The camp was for rocket fanatics. There was nothing he loved better than the science behind the toys. Watching something he'd built shoot into the sky was intoxicating. Rick swore sex was better, but rockets were a close second. They all dreamed of building rockets that went higher and faster. Troy knew the other kids at his school thought he was a geek and a nerd, but here he was among peers who understood him.

There were cliques at camp. Guys who emerged as natural leaders and were the type one simply wanted to hang around. Carson was a natural. Good-looking, athletic, and charismatic. Troy had been watching the first time Carson asked Joe about a project. Joe had looked as if God were speaking to him, his eyes wide and worshipful. Their small group had come together. Carson was the speaker. Rick was the driving force who could manipulate Carson's words. Aaron was the angry follower who wanted to feel like he was being heard. Troy and Joe were the listeners and the grunts, happy to go where others led.

It worked. For five days they blended into the natural elements of a team, getting to know one another better, and feeling proud to have established friendships around a common core. But then jealousy about Colleen built up between Rick and Aaron. And Rick felt the need to prove he could win.

At Rick's urging, they'd followed her late one afternoon. She'd found an ancient hammock hung between two firs in the woods, its ropes and material looking as worn as if it'd been there since the sixties. It was a quiet, sunny, and peaceful spot. No interruptions. Until the five of them approached her.

It'd started off fine. Colleen had sat up and chatted with them, but Troy had known she was pacifying them and wanted to be left alone to read. Then Rick had gotten personal. Fear had shown in her eyes as Rick moved close, taunting her and pulling at her bathing suit top, telling her he knew she wanted him, claiming she'd slept with other campers and that she had no right to turn him down.

Troy froze.

Colleen told them to leave and it turned ugly.

Rick ordered Aaron and Carson to hold her down as he raped her. Troy had never seen a rape before, and he couldn't look away. He covered his ears, but her screams tore through his brain.

It'd been brutal and humiliating. But worst of all, *none* of them had stopped it.

Rick had put his hands around her neck as Joe and Troy finally looked away. Aaron and Carson had continued to watch and pin her arms. When Colleen stopped breathing everyone panicked except for Rick. "We'll make it look like she killed herself," he'd said. "That she went into the woods and slit her wrists."

He'd bent down, taken a penknife from his pocket, and sliced across her wrists. Nothing much happened. Troy now knew that her heart had stopped beating and was no longer forcing the blood to move within her veins.

"It's not working," Rick had said, his eyes frantic. "We've got to hide her."

"We've got nothing to dig with," Carson had pointed out. "Did anyone see shovels back at the camp?"

Troy and Joe had shaken their heads. Troy couldn't look away from Colleen's face. To get her to stop screaming, Rick had shoved a big stone in her mouth. It hadn't worked; she'd still screamed. Now her face and lips were limp around the gray piece of rock wedged between her teeth. Troy stared, hoping she'd move an arm or leg.

She's fine. She's just unconscious.

But he knew something was very wrong.

"We've got rope from the hammock," Aaron suggested. "Could we make it look like she hung herself?"

"No, we need to hide who she is. That's a better idea. The police won't know what to do if they can't identify her," said Rick.

"But they can figure it out," said Joe. "There is all sorts of science now to identify people."

"What if we burn her?" said Aaron. "They can't figure it out from a pile of ashes."

Troy wanted to throw up. *Burn her?*

"We can't do that," whispered Joe. His face was pale. "That's wrong."

Rick got in his face. "We've already gone beyond wrong! You want to go to prison for the rest of your life because of this? Or are you going to help?"

"I didn't do anything," shrieked Joe. "It was you! You and Aaron killed her."

"You didn't stop us!" shouted Aaron. "That's just as bad. If I get arrested, you're all going down. So let's take care of this!"

The next hour passed in a daze. Aaron had sneaked back to camp and found an accelerant in one of the labs. It hadn't worked. Bodies aren't easy to burn. It'd charred part of her hair and most of her clothing before extinguishing. Aaron had chopped off the rest of her hair with his knife, hoping to help hide her identity. Both Joe and Troy had vomited in the woods, the smell of burning flesh too much to take.

"It's not working," Carson stated. "We need a different plan."

Troy stared at the battered body. "This is crazy," he whispered. "How did it come to this?"

"That's it!" blurted Rick. "We'll make it look like someone crazy killed her. We'll hang her from that old footpath bridge. It's not far."

"It's blocked off," argued Aaron. "It's a rotting mess."

"Perfect," said Rick. "Only a crazy murderer would kill her and hang her from something like that. It makes no sense. No one would dream that we did it."

Troy helped tow Colleen's body on the hammock fabric through the woods to the bridge. They tied the rope around her neck, tied the other rope end to a semi-stable bridge post, and pushed her over. It held. She dangled, her toes ten feet from the quiet flow of the water.

The boys all stared for a moment.

Colleen was a mess. Her hair was gone, her clothes had burned off, and blood had seeped from the wounds at her wrists. The rock was still in her mouth. The fresh and beautiful girl was long gone.

Joe turned away first.

"Hey," Rick had said. "We need a pact. We need to agree to never talk to anyone about this."

Troy glanced at the other faces. "We need to go to the police," he whispered.

"No! Rick's right," Carson stated. He held his hand, palm down, in the center of the circle of boys. "We all swear *right now* to never speak of this again."

Rick laid his hand over Carson's. "I swear." He met Troy's gaze, his own triumphant.

Of course you swear. You're the one who did this.

Aaron's hand joined the other two. "I swear to never breathe a word of what happened."

Troy glanced at Joe, whose hand slowly covered the rest. "I swear," he said in a small voice.

Troy did the same. His brain screaming for him to run to the police as his mouth proclaimed, "I swear." The other boys looked relieved.

Rick dug out the knife he'd used to cut Colleen's wrists. "This needs blood." He ran the blade across his palm and a thin line of red welled. He let it drip over the other boys' hands. Aaron and Carson immediately presented their palms. Rick looked expectantly at Joe and Troy. They reluctantly turned over their hands.

The blade stung and Troy blinked back tears. Rick rubbed his palm against it, and Troy placed his hand back in the messy pile.

"We've sworn in blood," Rick said in a harsh voice. "No one speaks about it or they face the same punishment that was given to her."

Troy's head jerked up. *Punishment?*

"Wh-what?" asked Joe, his wide eyes rapidly blinking.

"We swear to punish whoever speaks of this. This is a pact we have to take to the grave."

Fingers of fear strangled Troy's spine. *How did this happen?*

"I swear," said Carson and Aaron together. They looked at Troy and Joe.

"I swear," Troy forced out at the same time as Joe. The look in Rick's eyes terrified him. Troy would have sworn to anything at that very moment, because he knew that Rick would use his knife across Troy's neck to protect himself.

"Good. Let's clean up," suggested Carson, taking charge again. "Break off some branches to sweep the ground and get rid of our footprints. Let's work our way back to the site. Look carefully. Let's not leave anything behind."

Aaron shoved a fir branch in Troy's hands, and he started to automatically brush at the footprints. He walked backward, moving farther and farther away from Colleen. The other boys were silent, concentrating on their work.

Colleen's body slowly rotated from the rope in the quiet woods. Troy's last glimpse was of the back of her burned, shorn skull.

• • •

Zander watched Mason pace in the old conference room in the Yamhill County Sheriff's Office. Ray sat next to Zander in one of the rock-hard plastic chairs and cracked his knuckles until Mason shot him a dirty look. Ray sighed and shifted his muscle-bound bulk. Zander felt like a stick next to the former college football player.

The VICAP hit had led them to the sheriff's office that had investigated the young woman's death. Neither he nor Mason nor Ray recalled the case, which was surprising. An attack that violent on a young woman should have received a hell of a lot of publicity, and all three of them had lived in Northwest Oregon at the time of the crime.

Zander's media checks had uncovered only small local stories about the death. The crime hadn't made it to the larger Portland area news stations or newspapers. Instead a bombing of a federal building by American terrorists had dominated the headlines. Yamhill County was relatively small in population, primarily made up of rural towns. It sat southwest of Portland, outside the crowded suburban areas. Farms dominated much of the county.

"Where is he?" Ray muttered.

Zander glanced at his phone. They'd been waiting ten minutes for the county detective who'd handled the case. The man was probably digging the case file out of storage and refreshing his memory, concerned that the FBI and state police were going to look for errors in his investigation.

"Joe Upton grew up in Newberg. That's only a dozen miles from where this young woman was found," said Mason, briefly pausing in his pacing.

"Right," said Zander. "But he moved away about two years after this murder happened. I gave his name to Detective Kenner. We'll see if they had any encounters with Joe or his family."

Mason looked haggard. He hadn't mentioned Ava's name for quite a while, but Zander could tell his stress level was in the danger zone. Mason was the type to internalize his anxiety and focus on the work at hand. Zander was the same way. Logically he knew the best way to get Ava back was to solve the crime at hand. Find the Bridge Killer; find Ava. Quickly.

But he saw it was eating Mason from the inside out. The man was head over cowboy boots in love and to know Ava was in danger and out of reach could push him over the edge. Mason was the type who needed action; he needed to see that progress was being made.

Zander understood perfectly. A silent, invisible killer had taken his wife. She'd fought hard while Zander was powerless to do more than hold her hand and cry with her. He'd wanted to see the assailant and strangle it, destroy it the way it was destroying his wife. Instead she'd wasted away over a matter of months, her doctors admitting she had no way to win.

Nothing compares to that lack of power when a loved one is being hurt. But not knowing what'd happened to Ava McLane was coming in a close second. The tortured bodies of the Bridge Killer's victims kept flashing through Zander's mind.

And Mason had to be experiencing the same.

The pace had rocketed in the Bridge Killer case and no one wanted to pause for sleep or to eat. They grabbed food on the run and kept following leads. Right now this old Yamhill County murder case with the similar elements was their biggest find.

A door swung open. The detective strode in and set a large file box on the table. Detective Jensen Kenner looked ready to retire within the next few years. His hair was white with a matching thick mustache. His florid face spoke of years of stress and poor diet. But his gaze was razor-sharp. Zander was relieved by his first impression; this was a seasoned cop who missed little.

The men shook hands and made introductions. Zander noticed Kenner took a hard look at Mason, as if he could tell the case was personal. Mason wore a face of stone, but his eyes reflected his personal pain. The detective opened the box and dug out a three-ring binder. "There's your book." He handed it to Mason.

Zander mentally raised a brow. Most cops would have handed it to him, assuming the FBI to be the leader on the case, especially when one of its agents was missing. Kenner had been astute enough to observe that Mason needed to see the murder book.

The murder book encapsulates the paper trail of a murder investigation. Photographs, autopsy reports, forensics reports, and all the investigator notes. The file box was packed with supporting material, but the key pieces were in the binder.

"What do you remember?" Zander asked, starting with a broad question. He wanted to know what stuck out most in the detective's mind.

Kenner shoved his hands in his pockets and looked out the window. "I remember a lot that I wish I'd never seen. The first sight of that poor girl hanging from the bridge still haunts most of my nights. I hadn't ever seen anything like that."

Zander nodded, the Bridge Killer's recent victims fresh in his mind. He wouldn't be losing those memories anytime soon.

"Primary suspect?" Mason asked, flipping though some photos.

"We looked real hard at a transient for a while. He'd been camping in the woods a few miles from where we found her. A real nut job. He stole whatever he could get his hands on, but I never saw any murderous tendencies in him. The community was focused on him. An outsider, you know. People never want to believe that one of their own could be a murderer."

"You cleared him?" Mason asked.

"Nothing tied him to the crime other than location. And I looked him up after you called. He's been dead ten years."

"Maybe we should go check that bridge," Mason stated.

"It's gone," Kenner answered. "Whole thing collapsed a few years ago. County was under fire for not replacing it, but they just didn't have the funds."

"Who else did you look at?" asked Ray. "Surely you had more suspects than just one transient."

Kenner slowly shook his head. "I've never had more of a dead-end case. She'd been dead for three days by the time we found her. It'd rained hard all three days, and a lot of trace evidence was lost. She was reported missing by her employer. She'd been working as a cook at one of the local camps in the woods."

"Camps? What kind of camps?" asked Zander.

"You know. Run by ecology nuts. They take kids out into nature for a week or two. Take away their cell phones, TVs, and showers and teach them about the water cycle and forest."

"You mean outdoor schools," commented Ray. "Both my kids spent a few days when they were twelve at outdoor schools. I think one of them was in this area. They loved it. Came home talking about how to protect the environment."

"That's the type. We've got a half dozen in the area. Most of the school districts in the Portland area send their kids out here to attend. The campgrounds are also leased to other groups. Sometimes churches or special interest groups."

"She died in late June," said Mason, studying a page. "Were the outdoor schools happening at that time?"

Kenner held his hand out for the book. Mason passed it over, and Kenner sped through a few pages. "We found her in a location that was within three miles of two different camps." He stopped at a page and ran a finger down to the bottom. "One of them was hosting a church retreat for families and the one she worked at was holding a science camp for teens. A rocket camp."

Alarms went off in Zander's brain, and Ray shot up out of his chair.

"Rocket camp?" Mason whipped his head to meet Zander's and Ray's gazes. "We need to see everything you have on it."

26

Ava breathed through her nose, fighting to stay calm. The duct tape Troy had placed across her lips helped her keep her screams inside, but made it hard to breathe. Derrick was terrified. From behind the ball gag, he'd tried to reason with the killer, his words unintelligible. He'd kept repeating one word that'd sounded like "oy." Was the killer named Roy?

The killer had referred to Derrick as Rick. Did he have the wrong man? Or was the name just shortened?

She tucked away the portion of her brain that wanted to cry and hide. She needed to focus and figure out how to get away. She didn't want to be the next victim.

The killer glanced at her occasionally. He kept saying she'd be at peace soon. Her mind had grabbed that sentence and sprinted full speed ahead. *"At peace" means "dead."* She had to get out.

Derrick had been tied to a table made of boards to keep him from fighting back. The killer had laid a twelve-inch metal circle with a daisy pattern on the table and moved Derrick on top of it. *There's the source of the blanching on the bodies.* She caught her breath. Did that mean Derrick's death was imminent? Did he expect her to watch?

He brought in a few more buckets and positioned them below Derrick's hands. *For the blood.* They'd been right that their killer was obsessively neat. Besides the buckets and boards, he had rope and padding, which she recognized for wrapping the wrists, scissors, and the gasoline can.

She didn't see anything that might aid her escape. She moved to the right an inch, wondering if she could make her way to the opposite side of the room without the killer noticing. *Impossible.*

Could she pretend to faint? Would he stop?

She placed that thought in her "maybe" category.

She could rush at him, throw herself into him in a tackle.

With your arms tied? One blow to your face and you're out cold again.

He was big. Not bulky, but tall. And physically handled Derrick without any problems.

The killer calmly cut off chunks of Derrick's hair. Ava watched it fall to the floor, eerily reminiscent of her hair being cut at her salon. The act seemed to push Derrick over the edge. He flailed against his restraints and jerked his head back and forth. The killer glanced at Ava.

"He knows what will happen. I'm going slowly, step by step, so that he's mentally tortured. It'd be too kind to kill him immediately."

Ava shook her head at him. The killer gave her a condescending look. "*You* wanted this. I'm doing this for you." Anger flashed across his face, and Ava froze.

She didn't want that anger focused on her. It was too easy to see herself tied to his boards, an iron ring under her back.

She ducked her head in submission. *Keep him calm.*

The killer went back to his haircut, scraping Derrick's scalp with his scissors on some of the cuts and making the man cry harder.

The hands holding the scissors jerked in impatience. Sweat beaded on the killer's forehead, and Ava saw drops slide down his temples.

He's not entirely comfortable with the path he's chosen.

How could she use that to her advantage?

Hair drifted down and landed on his shoes. He started to mutter. His speech a jumble of swear words and commands for Derrick to hold still. She heard him mix up his words again. With each vocal mistake, he jerked his head in resentment and his scissors chopped harder.

When Derrick was nearly bald, the man tossed the scissors into one of the buckets. Ava stared at the bucket. *If I could get my hands on the scissors.* The killer took out a utility knife and held it next to Derrick's neck. The man shrieked behind his ball gag as the killer calmly dragged the knife down Derrick's chest, cutting open his T-shirt. Realizing the knife hadn't touched his skin, Derrick went limp in relief. The killer tucked the knife back in his front pants pocket and slowly unbuttoned his own shirt. He held the shirt open, letting Derrick see his chest.

"See the marks? I have them, too. We all have to pay as she did. The marks show our respect for the female form."

What the fuck? Respect?

Ava caught a glimpse of infected slashes on the killer's chest. He'd cut the same symbols they'd seen on Joe Upton. He pulled his knife back out and slashed at Derrick's chest. He screamed. Ava looked away and fought back the bile in her throat.

The hair, the marks on the chest. What was next? She thought back to the last body. That was the extent of the degradation beyond the hanging and wrists. Clearly the killer planned to perform those two steps, but he'd always added something new to each death. What new element would be added to Derrick's?

Her gaze went to the gasoline can, remembering Derrick's reaction to it. *Oh, no.*

The killer stared at the triangles he'd carved into Derrick's chest and started to ramble. Ava listened closely but the words were a tangled mess. He tentatively touched one of the cuts and smeared the blood across Derrick's chest as his lips continued to move in his monologue. Ava caught Carson's, Aaron's, and Joe's names. He seemed to be reliving conversations with the men. Derrick held still, his gaze locked on the ceiling, too terror-stricken to look into the eyes of the man who was about to kill him.

Ava scooted over another foot. One look from the killer and he'd notice she was no longer in the corner, but she hoped he was distracted by the man under his hands. She hadn't seen him lock the door behind him. And when she'd examined the door earlier, there hadn't been an apparent locking mechanism on the inside. It had to be unlocked.

If she could get to the door . . .

Then what? Sprint with her hands tied behind her back? Sprint where?

People. She just needed to get to where there were other people.

The killer turned. "What do you think? Has he suffered enough?"

Ava froze. And nodded.

He smiled. "No, he hasn't. You're getting soft." He frowned as he noticed how she'd moved out of the corner. "Going somewhere?"

She shook her head, and he gave her a patronizing smile.

"I think we'll take a trip." He looked back at Derrick and stroked the man's wrist, his knife in the other hand. Derrick squirmed, his eyes bulging. "No, not yet. I want you conscious for the next part."

The gasoline?

Ava choked back saliva, making a coughing sound behind her tape. He gave her a puzzled look. "Are you all right?"

She ducked her chin again and shook her head. He was at her feet instantly, tearing the tape from her mouth. Tears burned her eyes as her lips felt ripped away.

"Breathe," he ordered.

She took deep breaths, her attention focused on the blood on his fingertips that held the duct tape. He'd touched her skin as he ripped off the tape. Was Derrick's blood on her face?

Nausea rolled through her stomach.

"I've been thinking," he started. "Let's take him to the bridge and let him bleed into the water. He can burn there, too." He grabbed her upper arms and gave her a gentle shake until she looked at him. He seemed to stare right through her, as if he were focused on an object three feet behind her head.

So that's what evil looks like.

"We can do this together and don't need to hide here. This needs to be done where people can see and learn what kind of man he was." Tears ran down his face. "They need to know you were an innocent."

Ava didn't speak. Her lips burned, and she had no words.

This is your chance to reach him.

"Roy?" she whispered.

His face went blank. "I'm Troy." Red started at his neck and swept over his face. "Do you not know *who I am*?" He grabbed a handful of her hair and yanked her head back. Whipping scissors out of a pocket, he hacked at her hair. He threw the handful behind him and shouted again. "Who am I?"

"Troy, yes," she said frantically. "My lips are numb from the tape." She infused her gaze with sincerity as fear narrowed her vision.

His color returned to normal and he stood, staring at the few strands of her hair that stuck to his fingers. He brushed them off his hands.

"I'll get the van ready." He stood, avoiding her gaze, and went over to Derrick.

Ava shut her eyes, feeling faint.

Now what?

• • •

"We have a few interviews from the camps," Detective Jensen Kenner stated. "We went to both camps near the recovery site and interviewed the employees. Everyone at Meadow Springs Camp liked Colleen Mallery. Claimed she was a sweet girl. She'd just graduated from OSU with a history degree but didn't have a job lined up, and she was thinking about getting her master's. I guess there wasn't a big job market for history majors at that time."

"I doubt there is today," said Mason. He dug through the box. "Nothing else on the camp interviews? All these employee interviews say the same thing. Colleen was seen during dinner, she wasn't needed again until breakfast the next morning, and that she typically vanished for a few hours to read and relax after dinner. No one thought she was seeing a boyfriend?"

Kenner shook his head. "No romantic interests, according to the other employees and family."

"How come no one interviewed the students?" Ray asked.

"We did . . . to a degree. There were two hundred kids there. We asked for anyone to come forward who'd seen Colleen after dinner that night or anything suspicious. We had no takers."

Mason flipped open a folder. "Here's what I wanted to see." He'd found the huge roster of the kids attending rocket camp at Meadow Springs, and he ran his finger down the names. He scrolled six rows and stopped as the name jumped out at him.

Troy.

Just like Jayne said on the phone.

Found you.

Wait. The name directly underneath was also a Troy. He started to count.

"Shit. There're eight Troys on this list. What the hell? Didn't people have any imagination when naming their kids back then?" Frustration overwhelmed him. Their killer's name was on that list; he was certain of that fact.

"You think it was one of the kids?" Kenner asked, disbelief on his face. "They were children."

"This camp went up to age eighteen," said Mason, studying the list, spotting Carson Scott's, Aaron King's, and Joe Upton's names. "I knew it." He tipped the list for Zander and Ray to see. "They're all on here."

"Eighteen is plenty old enough to kill," said Zander.

"But . . . this particular murder . . ." Kenner trailed off, shaking his head. "This was horrific."

"I agree," said Mason. "And I've seen three similar cases in the last week. I'd like to prevent the next. We need to pare down this list and do it damn fast."

"Eliminate the younger kids," suggested Zander. "The age range started at thirteen, right? Chances are a thirteen-year-old didn't hang out with three boys heading into their senior year."

"This doesn't list ages."

"Are there any photos?" asked Ray. "Any candid shots or group shots from the camp? We saw his profile and build today. Maybe we could see a resemblance."

"There should be some general photos in there," said Kenner. "I remember seeing group shots, but they aren't labeled with names."

Mason found eight black-and-white eight-by-ten photographs that looked like they'd been developed in a home darkroom. Three were from the second camp in the area, but the other five were labeled MEADOW SPRINGS. They were formal group shots, ones where the kids lined up in rows with a board that stated the camp name and year. The first was all staff, but the rest were grouped and labeled by age. He held the one of the seventeen-to-eighteen-year-olds close to his nose as he studied the small faces. The quality wasn't great.

"Hang on." Kenner stepped out of the room.

Ray and Zander peered over his shoulders. "He's in there somewhere," said Ray.

"But there're no names," countered Zander. "We already know his face. We *need* a last name."

"Call the camp," said Mason. "See if they still have old records. Maybe theirs are broken down by ages. Maybe they have some photos with identifications."

"I'm on it." Zander pulled out his phone.

"Meadow Springs went out of business a decade ago," said Kenner, entering the room. He had a small, clear, rectangular object in his hand. "The place sat empty for a few years before a new group bought it. You're gonna have to do some digging. Who knows if the new owners got the old records? I guess they might be able to put you in touch with the previous owners."

"Shit," stated Mason. Another speed bump.

"Exactly," agreed Kenner. He handed Mason the rectangle. "Try this."

It was a magnifier. Mason set the photo on the table and the three-by-five piece of plastic directly on top of it. The image jumped in size and big smiling faces grinned at him. "Perfect," he breathed.

"Easier than moving my reading glasses on and off when I'm at my desk," Kenner commented. "Tried bifocals and hated them. This works like a charm."

Mason slid the rectangle across the photo. Grainy faces emerged and vanished as the block moved.

"Go back," said Ray, leaning over the table.

He slid the block back an inch and spotted a familiar face at the same moment Ray exclaimed, "There!" *Carson Scott.*

Carson stood in the back row. He was taller than 90 percent of the other kids. His smile as distinctive then as it was today. *Was last week.*

Ray leaned closer as Mason studied the boys standing closest to Carson. "Is that Joe Upton?" he asked, placing a finger on the block. Mason studied the young face. All the older images he'd seen had been of Joe at a much heavier weight.

"I think that's him," asserted Ray. "Look at the eyes and shape of his nose."

Mason agreed. Joe stood three people away from Carson in the back row. He took a closer look at the boys between them, searching for Aaron King. He spotted him in the next row forward. "Aaron's in the row before Carson. Same general area, though."

Where is the man from the convenience store video?

He slid the block to the far right and stopped. The last boy in the row was the tallest.

A tingle started in his stomach. "This is him."

Ray stared and Zander came around the table to study the image. Both men started to nod.

"He's tall," said Zander. "Like the man yesterday. And has the same narrow face. I think you might be right."

"Now, how do we get a last name?" asked Mason. "There has to be a faster process than hoping that the old camp records exist."

"We can run a search on all the Troys on the list," Zander said. "We'll eliminate the younger ones, look for ones that have died, or moved out of state. We should be able to get driver's license pictures pretty fast. We'll take a closer look at the ones who are still in the area first."

"Searching Facebook might be even quicker as far as photos," added Kenner. "You wouldn't believe what people will post on their pages and leave wide open for anyone to look at. I wouldn't automatically eliminate the counselors. Are there any Troys on that list?"

"One," said Mason. "We can check him along with the rest."

"What about Laura King?" suggested Ray. "Weren't she and Aaron together in high school? Or at least knew each other? Maybe she'll remember a guy named Troy whom Aaron kept in touch with."

"I'll start with our databases," Zander said. "Mason, why don't you contact Laura King, and Ray, you do the Facebook search." He glanced at Detective Kenner. "Mind if we use your conference room for a while?"

"Go right ahead. I'll look online, too," Kenner offered.

Zander and Ray whipped out their laptops and Mason stepped out of the room to use his phone and call Laura King. He kept the photo of their three victims in his hand and squinted at the grainy image of who he hoped was Troy.

She answered on the third ring. He identified himself. "I'm trying to find out if Aaron might have had a friend during or even after high school whose first name was Troy. They would have shared an interest in rocket building, but I don't think he went to the same school."

There was a long pause on the other end.

"I don't know, Detective," she said slowly. "Troy's a rather common name, and Aaron had given up the rocket thing by the time he was finished with high school. That FBI agent took the box with the old yearbooks and rocket memorabilia. Seems like there were some photos in there. Did you look at those?"

Mason had. Several times. "They didn't have names on them. We're trying to figure out the last name of a rocket enthusiast named Troy that Aaron may have met at a summer camp."

"I can't think of anyone," she said. "I'm really sorry."

They ended the call, and Mason bit the inside of his cheek. *A dead end.* It'd been a bit of a stretch. He thought it was pretty rare that friends from high school kept in touch. *Friends?* Or would you avoid a person you'd committed murder with? Hell. He'd stay as far away as possible from a guy who knew that about him. And there was no way he'd introduce him to his wife or family. He'd been barking up the wrong tree by calling Laura King.

So what do you do with people you want to forget?

He went back to check on Ray and Zander's progress.

Ray had pulled up the original Fremont Bridge video and convenience store video for Detective Kenner to watch. Together they were searching every Troy from the roster through social media.

"Oh, Lord. Look how many Troy Johnsons there are on Facebook," Ray moaned. "Let's do the less common names first."

"Laura King doesn't remember a Troy," Mason announced. He pulled out a chair and parked next to Ray, studying his screen. Ray had already crossed two Troys off the list and put question marks by two more. "What's with the question marks?"

"It means I can't see a photo. Either they've posted pictures of their favorite sports team as their primary photo, or a dog or something. They haven't been ruled out," Ray replied.

Ray clicked on a name and a small photo of a man's face popped into view against a larger photo of a snowy mountain range. The man was Asian. "I wish they were all that easy to eliminate." He drew a line through another name and passed the information on to Zander.

Each line felt like one step closer to finding Ava.

Please don't let us be too late.

He didn't want to consider the possibilities.

"What about this one?" Ray opened a picture of a man standing at a river, holding three huge fish on a line. His face was shadowed by a hat brim but his white grin was huge.

Mason stared. "I can't tell. He looks tall, but there's nothing to compare his height to. Any other pictures?"

Ray made a few clicks. "No. No images of people. Just fishing and outdoorsy stuff."

"Put him on the maybe list." Frustrated, Mason turned back to the murder book from Colleen's death. He flipped to the autopsy section, preparing his stomach to study her pictures and read the dispassionate statements from the medical examiner.

His jaw clenched as he studied the photos. Colleen had been burned. The examiner theorized that the murderer had thought he could eliminate the evidence or body by fire. It takes a hell of a lot of heat to burn up a body. Most people don't realize that a cremation takes over two hours at more than fourteen hundred degrees.

Teenagers wouldn't know that. A teen might think a simple fire could get rid of all his problems.

He turned through the autopsy report, looking for the hand-labeled diagram of Colleen's injuries, wanting know what the ME had seen on her back. The stark outline of a female form was labeled with abrasions on her back and the backs of her legs.

No blanching in a daisy pattern.

The medical examiner noted that lividity had formed in her lower extremities, concluding that she had been hanged soon after her death. She hadn't lain still in one spot like the current victims. Mason frowned. So why had their killer created the daisy pattern on the backs of his victims if it didn't match anything in the original death? Seeking something that referred to daisies or a similar pattern, he sped through the rest of the medical examiner's notes.

Colleen's wrists had been slit, but the cause of death was attributed to strangulation. Petechiae had formed in her eyes and her hyoid bone had been broken. Both were common results of strangulation.

She'd been sexually assaulted.

But by whom?

All of them? One of them? He scanned further in the report. The medical examiner had found one semen sample.

Mason's stomach unclenched a bit, relieved that the girl had been spared the indignity of what could have been a gang rape.

Christ. She suffered rape, strangulation, and burns, and I'm pleased she was raped only once?

He shook his head. In this job, he took his relief where he could find it. Sometimes the minuscule victories kept the worst cases from tearing him apart.

Semen sample? "Was the DNA from the semen sample put in the system?" Mason asked Kenner.

He nodded. "We never got a hit. I assumed a DNA profile had never been submitted from the rapist in another crime."

Mason grimaced. *Which one raped her?* Their suspects had pretty clean histories except for Derrick Snyder. But even his past crimes didn't guarantee a DNA sample had been processed. Or entered correctly. The system wasn't perfect.

He continued to read. Colleen hadn't had the ball gag, but she'd had a large rock in her mouth. There were fresh chips in her teeth believed to have been caused by the placement of the rock or her biting it. Mason rubbed at the back of his neck, imagining the rough grit of rock against his molars. How long had she been conscious? The report stated that Colleen had been dead before the slitting of her wrists or the attempt to burn her.

Two more small victories for Mason to cling to.

Were they trying to disguise it as a suicide? All the different abuses to her body spoke of someone panicking, or a group with too many ideas about how to cover their crime. No mention was made in the murder book that more than one perpetrator had been present. He read through the last notes from the lead detective, inferring that they'd been seeking one man.

They were so far off.

But who would have guessed that this heinous crime might have been done by a group of high school students?

27

Zander listened with his phone tucked between his ear and shoulder, scribbling on a notepad, excitement rising in his stomach.

One of these has got to be right.

"Okay. Send it to me in an email, too," he told the agent at the other end. He ended the call and turned to the three men in the Yamhill County conference room. Detective Kenner and Ray were eyeing him with cautious optimism, but Mason looked tense with concern. The man hid it well, but if Zander was half out of his mind with worry about Ava then Mason was triple that.

"We've got two good leads from the Troys on that camp list. Both these guys are thirty-five, have long histories of living in this area, they're over six feet tall, own white vans, and own rural property."

"Yes!" Ray punched the air.

"He's emailing me their license photos."

"What are the names?" Mason asked.

Zander glanced at his list. "Troy Johnson and Troy Beadle."

The other three men went back to the laptop screen where they'd been checking the names against Facebook photos. "We already know there're too many Johnsons to locate the right one,"

Ray muttered. "Let's look at Beadle." He tapped the keyboard, and Zander went around to look at the screen.

"No personal photo," said Mason grimly. "Apparently he's a nature photo lover. Goddamned rivers and sunsets. Ray had marked him with a question mark."

Zander's phone buzzed as it received email. He opened the attachments and studied the license photos. Mason moved closer and looked at the screen.

"It could be either one of these guys from what we saw on that video today," he said after a moment. "I can't rule out one."

Zander agreed and passed his phone to Ray and Detective Kenner. One of the men was nearly bald on top, but both had a narrow face shape. Zander didn't see a way to eliminate one, either.

"Both own white vans?" Ray asked. "That's a coincidence."

"Beadle owns two. He's a house painter, so that makes sense. Johnson owns a small motorcycle repair shop. Again, owning a van makes sense so he can transport parts. Beadle lives out toward Scappoose, and Johnson lives on the other side of the Portland area outside of Sandy. Beadle owns three acres and Johnson owns a two-acre lot."

"So they both work in rather solitary professions," said Mason. "And both have property. Special Agent Euzent said they'd have a place where they could hold their victims. And the solitary professions don't surprise me. Coworkers notice when you're gone. Work for yourself and you set your own hours and do what you please. In my mind, both fall into the profile."

"Families?" Kenner asked.

"Both divorced."

"Arrests?"

"None."

"And the locations both work," observed Ray. "Both are within driving distance of the bridges where we've found the bodies. The Sandy location is obviously closer to the Bridge of the Gods, while the Scappoose location is closer to the Vernonia bridge. And Carson

Scott was found smack in the center. I wonder what bridge he has picked out for his next victim."

"We need to visit both homes. Tonight," Mason stated, glancing at the clock on the wall, fidgeting like he'd had a dozen cups of coffee. "I don't care if it's ten o'clock. This guy likes to visit bridges in the middle of the night, and we know he's got two victims. We need to go *now*."

"Agreed," said Zander. "We're working with Clackamas County and Columbia County sheriffs to get cars immediately on both scenes. They have orders to set up outside the properties and not go in until we get there. I don't want county cops rushing in without us there. I've activated our SWAT teams. They should be on both scenes within the hour. The scattered locations make them a bit far to get to."

"I want to take the Scappoose one," Mason stated, studying the driver's license photos again. "I've got a feeling about him."

"I'll go to Sandy," Zander agreed. "Ray?"

"Scappoose," he answered promptly.

Zander nodded. An odd sense of dread passed through him. He didn't like splitting up their group, but it made sense to cover both locations simultaneously, as time was ticking by. He didn't have a gut feeling about either suspect, but he understood Mason's need to investigate the one that was resonating with him. They had to find their killer tonight.

"Well, shit," said Kenner, looking annoyed. "I'd go along with you, but I've got no reason to be there. Dammit! I'd like to put this one to bed." The man scowled and Zander sympathized. It sucked to step back when an investigation suddenly grew hot. And this lead on the Bridge Killer was a scorcher.

Mason shook his hand. "You'll be the first to know what we find."

"Someone better keep me updated. Now I'm not going to sleep all night."

"We sent out alerts to every county and city in the area to keep an eye on their bridges tonight and tomorrow night. I think he's going to try to leave a body. If we're lucky, he doesn't know that Ava's in law enforcement. Hopefully he believes we think some woman has been grabbed and that we haven't made the connection to the Bridge Killer. Everybody know where they're going?" Zander asked.

"Yep," answered Mason. "Let's go get Ava." He held Zander's gaze. "One of us will find her tonight. I know it."

Zander glimpsed the first light of hope in Mason's eyes.

He prayed the detective was right.

• • •

Mason pulled his car in behind the Columbia County cruiser. A county car sat on either side of a driveway on the narrow rural road. It was after eleven P.M. and the rain had started again. He'd floored it most of the way from the sheriff's office. Driving the straightest route possible had meant a lot of time on unlit, winding country highways. Ray had spent most of the time on the phone, gathering what information he could about their suspect and passing it on to Mason. He'd even read the six Yelp reviews of Beadle Painting.

Customers were very pleased with Beadle Painting.

But was he their Bridge Killer?

"Current on his property taxes," Ray had muttered. "No one can find any other photos of him online. I find that to be suspicious."

"I don't have photos of me online," stated Mason.

"Have you looked?" asked Ray.

"No, but I haven't put anything up."

Ray tapped on his phone. "If I look at Google, there's a half dozen of you from that press conference at Christmas."

Mason nearly drove off the road. "What?"

"And more from the Coed Hunter case. Hey, here's one of both of us!" He held his phone out to Mason.

"Jesus Christ. Don't show me while I'm driving. How do I get rid of those?"

"Beats me."

Mason put the photos out of his head as he stepped out of his car, leaving his headlights on in the dark. He grabbed a heavy jacket out of the backseat, swearing at the rain. The two deputies headed his way, and he glanced around. The area was isolated. Nothing but fir trees. He would have driven right past the driveway if the county cars hadn't been present. Two tiny red reflectors on metal poles marked the edges of the driveway. If you missed the turn, you'd end up in the drainage ditch along the road. He squinted down the driveway. It curved into the woods and vanished. No buildings were visible.

No FBI SWAT team yet, either.

Shit.

The deputies approached, their flashlights shining on Mason and Ray, clear plastic rain gear covering their uniforms and hats, and introduced themselves. "We've been here forty-five minutes," said the taller one. "No one's come or left."

"Did you go up the driveway?" Mason asked.

The deputies glanced at each other. "We were told not to. We were told to wait for the FBI—they didn't say anything about OSP being involved."

Mason grimaced. "Task force. We're deep in it with the FBI on this case." He glanced at Ray. "How far out is their SWAT team?"

"They say at least twenty more minutes."

"Has Zander reached the other location yet?"

"Not yet."

Mason figured Zander's drive was a bit longer, but at least part of it would be on the freeway.

The four men looked at each other.

"What are you expecting to find up there?" asked the second deputy. He reminded Mason of a thin Jack Black.

"Not sure. Either we're going to wake up a hardworking painter who plans to be on a jobsite at seven A.M., or we're going to find the Bridge Killer with his latest victims."

"Holy shit!" Jack Black took a step backward. "They didn't tell us nothing. The last time we sat on a house and waited for the FBI, it was for a guy who was selling secondhand child porn videos on the Internet. They knocked on his door, and he walked out with his tail between his legs. A fucking sick wimp."

In the dim light and rain, Mason could see the excitement in the deputies' eyes. "We're gonna wait until SWAT gets here," he told the men. Beside him, Ray shuffled his feet. Mason eyed him. "What?"

Ray glanced up the driveway. "We could take a look. I've got the Google map of the area. I know where the house and two outbuildings are. There's one close to the driveway just after that curve, then the house, and then a large building farther back behind the house."

Mason stared at him, adrenaline pounding in his head.

Just look.

If Ava's not here, we need to get to Sandy and meet Zander.

"Dammit," Mason muttered. He looked at the deputies. "You been here before? Any calls to this place?"

"None. Completely quiet. We get called to a place about a half mile from here at least once a month, but this guy has never made a peep."

Mason looked up the driveway again. A faint glow around the curve told him the property at least had some lighting. "Okay." He pointed at Jack Black. "You come with us and your buddy can wait for the FBI. Ears and eyes open." He raised a brow at Ray, who grinned, knowing he'd planted the idea in Mason's brain.

"Won't hurt to do a quick recon," Mason said. "Can you dim your flashlight a bit? We'll take ours but leave them off for now." The deputy put his fingers over the face of his flashlight, cutting its output by 75 percent.

The three of them trudged up the packed-dirt driveway. Gravel crackled occasionally under their feet but the woods were mostly silent. The rain fell in a heavy mist that soaked everything without the noise of a pounding storm. The deputy's dim light showed them where to put their feet. Mason wished the moon were out.

Listening and watching carefully, they moved to the edge of the driveway as it curved around and brought them in view of the buildings. The deputy switched off his light. Ray's summary had been correct. A spotlight over the door of the first outbuilding lit up the area, and a small ranch-style house sat fifty yards away. Three pale outdoor lights shone from the home. Mason moved to the outbuilding and down the side facing away from the house. He stepped to a window and peeked inside. The deputy flicked on his flashlight and illuminated the inside. A John Deere tractor, at least fifty big white paint buckets in neat rows, and a dozen ladders filled the building.

No Ava.

Mason looked carefully, checking for cupboards or anywhere else to hide a person.

"Looks clear," said the deputy.

They moved toward the end of the building and peered around, eyeing the house. It was quiet. Mason wondered if the outbuilding behind the house was used as a garage where Beadle parked his two business vans. He gestured for the deputy to shine his dim light on the ground between the house and the building holding the tractor. The ground was flattened by tire tracks that led around to the back of the house and the second outbuilding. "Let's look in the second building."

"Are we going to check the house?" the deputy whispered.

Mason took a breath. "I think we'll wait for the FBI's SWAT team. If we can clear the outbuildings, that should be sufficient."

He wanted to go pound on the door and ring the doorbell a dozen times.

Someone was going to be livid with him for stepping onto the property without waiting for SWAT. He didn't need to push his luck. Conflict warred in him. *What if the next five minutes mean Ava lives or dies?* He blew out a breath. She could be in the other outbuilding; he wasn't twiddling his thumbs.

Keeping to the edge of the woods, they moved toward the back of the property. The second shed was slightly smaller than the first but had the same bright spotlight over the main door. They spotted a white van parked beside it.

His heart rate jumped at the sight of the van. "Look like the video?" he whispered to Ray.

Ray squinted and shook his head. "I can't tell. The light doesn't illuminate the front. The body of it looks about right."

The shed behind the house didn't have any windows to peek through. Mason led the group, keeping just inside the tree line of the surrounding woods, circling about ten yards away from the back of the smaller shed. Still no windows. They moved farther. The other side of the shed didn't offer a way to look inside, either. They'd have to use the door.

"Crap," Mason muttered. The three stepped out from the woods. The shed was now between them and any view of the house. They moved closer and got a clear look at the van.

"Looks the same," said Ray. "Same make and model that we saw." He cupped his hands and peered through the window. "I can't see into the back. It's too dark. There are a lot of papers on the dash and floor. Some painting supplies."

Mason's heart started to sink. *Are we in the wrong spot?*

He stepped close to the shed, leaned an ear against it, and held his breath for a solid ten seconds.

Silence.

"We need to look inside. Stay here while I check the door." Hugging the side of the building in the dark, he softly walked forward, and peeked around the corner and into the bright spotlight. The door had both a bolt and a huge hanging lock.

What was locked inside? Paint sprayers? Another van? Ava?

He moved back to Ray and the deputy. "It has a big lock. Without bolt cutters, we aren't getting in."

"I have bolt cutters," said the deputy at the same time that Ray replied, "We need to wait for SWAT."

Mason nodded. "It's time to wait." He turned and eyed the silent house. "It doesn't appear to have a basement, and none of the windows are covered. I don't think anything is being hidden in that house. This is the only building where it looks like something could be hidden."

The deputy's radio crackled quietly. "FBI is here."

The three of them glanced at the house ten yards away. "Let's head back." They jogged silently back the way they'd come, trying to see by the light of one dim flashlight.

"What do you think?" Ray huffed quietly to Mason.

"I don't think anyone is here," Mason said. "I hope Zander is having better luck than us."

. . .

Fifteen minutes later, the SWAT team had determined that the house and both sheds were empty. They'd rung the doorbell at the home and listened for noises inside with some special hearing equipment that Mason wanted for OSP. A simple blow to the door had opened it up and the house had been cleared within minutes while snipers kept watch on both sheds.

Then they'd cut the lock on the first shed and examined the John Deere. When they reached the second shed, they'd called for the detectives after determining no one was present.

Ray and Mason made the walk up the driveway again, this time along with Special Agent Parek, who'd accompanied the SWAT team from Portland. Parek had been working the command center for the Bridge Killer case and had attended all the briefings with

Mason and Ray. When they'd jogged down the driveway from the property, Parek had given them an odd look but held back any comments as the SWAT team got organized.

The SWAT team leader gestured toward the inside of the second shed. "Looks like someone has been busy in there."

Mason, Ray, and Parek looked inside and froze.

"You better call for a forensics team," Mason muttered to Parek. "Ray, call Zander. Tell him we struck gold."

No one was in the shed, but a metal ring about a foot in diameter, in the shape of a daisy, lay in the center of the floor. A small bouquet of real daisies lay next to it. Hair covered the floor next to an odd grouping of plywood and two-by-fours.

Mason squinted at the hair at the end of the plywood closest to the door. It was all short and brown. As if someone had been lying on the wood when his or her head had been shaved. His gaze traveled to the foot of the plywood. More hair on the floor.

But this time it was long and Ava's color.

He spun, pushing Ray out of the way, and took three staggering steps, gasping for breath and trying to hold on to the contents of his stomach. He bent over, his hands resting on his thighs, his head hanging.

I can't be certain it's hers.

He could feel his fingers running through her hair.

He'd know her hair anywhere.

"Mason?" Ray spoke behind him. "You good?"

"Yeah," he croaked. "Give me a minute." He breathed heavily through his nose several times and straightened. "She was here. He's taken her somewhere. That means he's ready for the next step."

"You don't know that," Ray stated firmly.

"Get the word out. Everyone needs to be watching the bridges in their communities. *Everyone.*"

"Parek just made another call to do that. We'd already sent out one alert, so everyone knows something is up."

"I need to take another look," Mason said firmly, heading back to the shed.

"Here." Ray handed him a pair of booties. He'd already slipped on a pair. Mason covered his boots, thankful that he didn't have to run back to the supply in his trunk. Parek was pacing a few yards off, talking earnestly on his phone. Mason and Ray stepped into the shed.

"It's his torture chamber," said Mason. "Look. He ties them up here." Under the makeshift plywood table were several large paint buckets. Inside, Mason spotted duct tape and the padding he'd seen on the wrists of the other victims. Surgical tape, scissors, and wet towels filled the other buckets. Some were streaked with blood.

"Here's what made the blanching on their backs," said Ray, crouching to get a closer look at the metal daisy. "I don't know if he had enough time to get a pattern this time. How long did Dr. Rutledge say it took for the lividity to fix?"

"I don't remember," said Mason. "Seems like it was supposed to take quite a while."

"He would have had to kill—" Ray broke off and slammed his mouth shut.

Mason gave him a grim look. "Killed them immediately. I know. And unless he's got another ring, he couldn't have put it on both."

"And there's only one table. I've had the feeling that he doesn't work that quickly. What do you think the real daisies are for? He's got the metal ring that looks like a daisy and now real ones?"

"Isn't it known as a flower of death?" Mason asked, uncertain where his memory had pulled the association from.

Ray's face brightened and then fell as he thought the statement through. "That does sound familiar."

Mason nodded and looked closer at the long hair at the far end of the table. It still looked like Ava's color and texture. But there wasn't very much of it. He studied the table. Why was her hair at a different end from the short hair? The table had posts at the other end that he assumed were to brace arms. It didn't make sense for

Ava's hair to be at this end. *Unless she wasn't on the table.* A tiny spark of hope bloomed in his chest. *There's hardly any fresh blood. Not at all the amount I would expect from slashing someone's wrists.*

He carefully checked the floor. The room was empty except for the implements of torture in the center of the room. He discovered the insulation around the door had been replaced. Someone had previously ripped it out. *Trying to escape?* Had the Bridge Killer allowed his victims to be loose in here? Or had one gotten free from his bonds and tried to escape?

Ava.

If anyone could think or talk her way out of a tight situation, she could. She had the training and brains to analyze what her captor was thinking and use it to her advantage.

If she could talk with him. What if she was gagged?

In one corner, someone had torn at the insulation. There was a small pile on the floor, and he saw it'd been ripped from a low area on the wall. As if someone had been sitting with their hands tied behind their back and had picked at the insulation. He squatted and looked closer.

Shiny.

He pulled a pen out of his pocket, pushed the pile of insulation aside, and felt his heart slam into his throat. Ava didn't wear much jewelry. Mainly conservative earrings and the occasional necklace. But she often wore a silver ring with a scrolling thistle design, and it was on the floor in front of him. She'd told him it was a copy of a ring from a favorite novel. Something Scottish.

She'd been sitting in the corner. For a period of time. Long enough to rip out the insulation and leave a sign that she'd been there. Had she hoped he'd be the one to find it?

Mason breathed a little easier.

Maybe she hadn't made it to the table.

"Whatcha got?" Ray asked.

He couldn't speak, so he moved out of Ray's view and indicated the pile and ring.

"That Ava's?" Excitement raised Ray's voice.

Mason nodded. "I hope she sat here most of the time." He poked at the wall of insulation with his pen, looking for anything else she might have tucked in the wall or left behind. A long stray hair was stuck in the insulation. He let his gaze wander over the carpet in the corner, hoping to find some sort of mark or message. He slowly backed out of the corner, noticing that Ray was doing the same examination of the rest of the floor and walls.

There was no other sign that Ava had been there. The hole in his gut tore wider as he stood over the long strands near the table. He wanted to pick some up and tuck them in his pocket. He glanced guiltily at Ray, and discovered he was being watched. Ray's expression showed he knew exactly what Mason was thinking.

"I'm sorry, man," Ray said with pain in his eyes.

Mason looked away. He hated pity.

"Hey!" Parek appeared at the door to the shed. "We've got a bridge sighting."

28

Ava sat on the bridge, her back against the van's tire as she watched Troy work on the ropes around Derrick's neck. The ride to the bridge hadn't been that long, but it was dark and she wasn't positive where she was. The two-lane bridge stretched over a narrow body of water. To one side she could see a few floating homes and what appeared to be floating garages for boats. On the other side was a boat dock. No people.

Troy had parked the van across the two lanes, creating an effective block for any traffic. A small car could drive around, but any sane person would question why the bridge was blocked. From her side of the van, the land beyond the bridge stretched out. She could faintly make out groves of trees and distant hills. She scooted toward the back of the van and peeked around. The land at the other end of the bridge abruptly sloped upward into forested hills.

"Don't move!" Troy shouted at her, his hands full with Derrick.

She moved back to her position by the front tire. Troy had answered a few of her questions but some had drawn confused looks. He seemed to think she should know exactly what he was doing and why. He'd grown agitated when she'd asked him to let Derrick go.

"This is what you wanted," he'd answered, with a stunned look on his face that rapidly morphed into anger, reminding her of the Hulk. "You told me to do this!" Ava had quickly placated him but then worried about asking the wrong question. She didn't need him angry and now thought carefully before speaking.

"Where are we?" she asked in a low voice.

Troy glanced up. He had Derrick on his stomach on one of the raised sidewalks that lined both sides of the bridge, holding him down with a knee in his back as he tied the rope. He'd already fastened one end of the rope to the metal guard that ran the length of the bridge. Derrick sobbed, often choking behind his gag. "This is the bridge to Sauvie Island."

Ava nodded. She'd driven once to the island that sat in the Columbia River ten miles west of Portland. She had friends who swore by the beaches, places to bike, and fresh produce available on the tiny island. She remembered rural farms and narrow roads and the single bridge that'd led to the piece of paradise. It seemed unreal that such a peaceful area existed so close to the big city. She didn't know if there were any police stations nearby.

Troy had chosen a very quiet bridge for this victim. When she'd looked around the front of the van, she'd realized that vehicles driving past the bridge on the country highway wouldn't notice the van. The gentle crest of the bridge gave them some visual protection. Someone would have to turn onto the bridge or be looking hard from the highway to notice it. It was the dead of night; traffic was scarce.

She stared toward the island. Could she make a run for it? She immediately rejected the idea. Her hands were still tied and her sense of balance would be severely affected. Sharp pain ricocheted from her upper arm to her brain if she shifted just right.

Physically she was outgunned.

That left mental. And she was trying desperately to keep her wits sharp. She was exhausted and brain-numb from watching Troy torture Derrick. He hadn't let her look away. Every time she'd averted her eyes, he'd screamed for her to watch.

When he'd put her in the van, he'd stroked a hand through her hair and apologized for cutting it. The swings from adoration to rage in his eyes were terrifying.

Who was Colleen?

She'd figured out Troy was on a mission to avenge Colleen, but why did he believe Ava was she? She must resemble Colleen, and he'd called Jayne the "fake Colleen." But where was the real one?

There was no way in hell she would admit she wasn't Colleen. He'd truss her up like Derrick and wrap a noose around her neck, too. The gasoline can sat a few feet away, drawing her gaze more often than she liked. What were his plans? Was he going to douse Derrick and light him up? Before or after he hanged him?

The cop part of her brain wondered why Troy had veered from his pattern and not slit Derrick's wrists. Was he starting to crumble? Or had her pleas made him change his plan? Had Colleen witnessed the other murders and egged him on?

Satisfied with his knot work, Troy stood and picked up the gas can. He loosened the lid and started to pour its contents over Derrick's legs. Derrick screamed behind his gag.

"No!" Ava shouted, leaning forward as if she could stop him. "Don't! Please don't!" Fear pumped through her muscles, and she struggled to stand up.

Don't light him on fire!

She shifted to her knees and pushed up onto one leg as Troy stopped pouring and turned back to her.

"Sit down!" His face contorted, becoming an evil mask. "This has to be done!"

Ava went back to her knees but pleaded in his direction. "Don't burn him! I don't want you to!"

"Yes, yes, you do. We already worked it out." He continued to pour and the odor slapped Ava in the face, making her nose and eyes sting. He soaked Derrick's back and head as gasoline spilled off the man and puddled on the ground. Small streams ran from the body and filled the cracks in the concrete. He set down the can and dug in his pocket.

"Noooo!" Ava shrieked at him, lunging toward him on her knees.

"*Shut up!*"

. . .

Troy'd had enough of Colleen's mouth. They'd worked out every detail of the plan to punish the others, and now she changed her mind? He'd agreed to not slit Rick's wrists, and because of it, he'd had to deal with Rick's bawling and thrashing. Hanging a dead body was much easier than hanging a live one. Since she'd appeared in person, Colleen had made everything more difficult.

He took a threatening step in her direction, and she scooted back against the van, clamping her lips together. Her face blurred and tilted, and he rubbed at his right eye, trying to get her back in focus. "Let me finish this!"

"Don't burn him," she urged again, her voice lowered this time, wrapping its sound around the part of his mind that'd wanted her for too many years. She'd always been his ideal woman. When he'd stumbled across her yesterday, he'd nearly cried.

He finally had her.

But she wasn't acting like herself.

He blinked, and her face righted. "I'm not going to burn him yet." He had to get Rick over the edge of the bridge first. He couldn't move a burning body. He strode to the back of the van, opened the cargo doors, and pulled out a large piece of plywood. He rested it against the railing of the bridge, making a ramp. Rick saw what was happening and started to squirm away. Troy stood still and watched him. The man was pathetic. He could scoot about four inches at a time with his ankles and wrists tied. Did he believe he could escape? He was tied to the railing. He'd choke himself on the ground if he went much farther.

Troy bent over and dragged Rick to the foot of the plywood. He shoved and pulled, rolling the man a few feet up the ramp. He paused to catch his breath, bracing Rick's body with his own, and cursing himself for changing his plans, for allowing Colleen to influence him. He glanced back at Colleen and jumped as he met her gaze.

She was standing directly behind him.

She kicked at the back of his knee, and Rick slid on the ramp. Troy lunged at her while attempting to keep Rick in place with one hand. She leaped backward out of his reach, but went no farther, seeing his struggle to keep Rick in place.

"Put him down," she begged. "I've changed my mind."

"No!" Troy shifted and pulled Rick halfway back up the ramp. "He has to pay for what he did to you!"

"I forgave him," Colleen pleaded. "Now untie both of us."

"No."

Colleen darted to the rail of the bridge, and Troy's hands went cold. She awkwardly stepped on the first bar of the three-barred rail. She looked down at the water and took a deep breath. "I'll jump if you don't let him go."

Troy stared. He couldn't move. Colleen couldn't die; she'd finally returned. "No," he ordered. "You don't want to do that for a piece of shit like this. He's not worth it. Remember how he hurt you?"

"Yes, he hurt me, but killing him doesn't fix it."

Anger rushed through him. "This was all about fixing it! You told me we would both be at peace if I did this! I've been in agony for years over what I watched happen to you. I did nothing to stop it!"

"Now you can stop it. You can stop me from dying again. Here's your chance." She lifted a foot to the second railing, balancing her hips against the top rail. The slightest shift of her weight would send her over the edge.

Troy looked down at the water. The bridge wasn't as high as the other ones he'd used. She'd easily survive the fall, but how would she swim with her hands tied? What if the fall knocked her unconscious? He let Rick slide a few inches back down the plywood. "Don't jump," he begged. "I can't help you if you jump."

Headlights shone on the three of them.

. . .

Mason saw her. Headlights lit up the three people through the drizzling rain. Ava stood on one of the railings of the Sauvie Island bridge with her hands tied behind her back, and looked like she was about to jump over the edge.

She was alive.

She wavered on the railing, looking their way, and moved a foot down to a lower bar.

"Thank you, God," Mason muttered as he stepped out of the car into the light rain.

"Amen," said Ray.

Ahead of them, Special Agent Parek spoke on the phone as he stood behind the protection of his car door. The FBI's SWAT team had followed them to the bridge and had huddled up behind Mason's vehicle to form a plan. Their three cars and an assault vehicle had stopped just before the truss of the bridge, fifty feet away from Troy Beadle and his victims. Mason spotted Derrick Snyder thrashing on a ramp and breathed a sigh of relief that Troy hadn't killed his victims before hanging them like he'd done before. Derrick was moments away from going over the edge. Mason could see the rope around his neck that was tied to the railing. Ava stepped off the rail and faced the vehicles. She collapsed to her knees on the bridge and hung her head, her shoulders shaking.

What had she gone through?

Ray and Mason joined Parek.

"I've got more support coming," said Parek. "The team that was headed to Troy Johnson's house is coming this way. We canceled them before they got there."

"Good thing," said Ray.

Parek glanced over their shoulders at the SWAT team. "Let's find out how they want to handle this. There's no law enforcement on the island, so no one can come from the other side of the bridge to help."

"I hope the island residents stay away. We've got nothing to keep one of them from driving into the middle of this," said Mason.

Parek nodded. "We need to handle this as quickly as possible. Multnomah County's river patrol is headed our way via boat. They can land on the island and keep people back." He paused. "They're sending their dive team, too."

"Good idea," Ray said as Mason silently shuddered. He wasn't fond of rivers and lakes. Give him a nice chlorinated pool. He looked downriver. The water was black, and he couldn't see the outlines of the banks. Visibility in the river would be impossible at this time of night.

"Let's start talking to him," said Mason. "Let's not mention Ava is FBI until we find out if he already knows that fact. Does your SWAT team have a negotiator?"

Parek shook his head. "I asked for one. He's on his way, too. Either of you done it?"

Ray and Mason looked at each other. "I've done some," admitted Mason. "We can see how he reacts to me." He put all thoughts of a tense standoff last Christmas out of his mind. His son and Ava had emerged safe. That was all that mattered.

Except when I dream my son's throat is slit and I'm powerless.

Parek eyed the cowboy hat. "I think that'll work in your favor here. Gives you a good-ol'-boy flavor. Hopefully he'll buy it. I'll go talk to SWAT."

"Let's cut the headlights except this vehicle," suggested Mason. "They're too intimidating."

"On it," replied Parek.

Mason nodded. He turned his attention to the three figures on the far side of the bridge and cupped his hands around his mouth. A bullhorn would have worked better, but he didn't want to spook Beadle. "Hello!" he yelled. "I'm Mason Callahan with OSP. Can you put the man back on the ground? We don't want anyone to get hurt." Three sets of headlights cut out as he spoke.

"Stay back," yelled Troy.

Troy backed up a step, and Derrick Snyder slid to the bottom of the ramp.

"Nice," Ray breathed.

Troy pulled a gun out of his jacket and pointed it at Derrick, and at the same time stepped backward between the open cargo doors of the van, leaving them with a view of his weapon and hand.

"Oh, shit," said Ray in the next breath. He and Mason stepped into the weak protection of the door of Parek's vehicle. Mason heard a rumble of voices from the SWAT team as they spotted the gun.

Dammit. The weapon put everyone on high alert.

"We'll stay back," Mason shouted. "What do you plan to do?"

Troy ignored him, but it sounded like Troy was talking. Mason could hear his voice but not the words. Ava's head jerked up at something Troy said, and Mason could see her lips move as she answered him.

"Troy! We don't want anyone to get hurt. What can we do to help you?"

"Get lost!"

"I can't do that, Troy. We can't walk away when we see someone's about to be hurt, but we can help you end this safely. How about you let us take him? He's got several warrants out for his arrest. He won't be walking the streets for a while."

The man with the gun briefly peeked around the corner of the cargo door.

Now I've got your attention.

"Let's keep you out of this," said Mason. "Let us arrest him. He won't be dead, but I guarantee he'll be miserable."

Ray snorted.

Ava spoke again, looking at Troy at the back of the van. With her and Mason both coming at him with the right words, they were bound to get through to him.

"He'll be locked up for a long time," said Mason. "And we can help you get what you wanted from him."

Troy laughed. "I need him dead. He needs to suffer for what he did to Colleen." He gestured at Ava with the gun.

"Crap," mumbled Ray. "Good thing you didn't use her name. Colleen's dead. But he's calling Ava by her name?"

"Is Colleen hurt?" Mason asked, his voice nearly cracking.

Ava shook her head as Troy replied, "No."

Mason felt his spine relax ten degrees. *Now get her out.*

"How about we get Colleen out of there? Then we can figure out what to do with the other guy." Mason reviewed his previous words, trying to remember if he'd used Derrick's name. If Troy had Ava's name wrong, Mason wasn't going to push his luck and assume he had Derrick's name right.

"No!" Troy shouted. Ava said something to him, but Mason couldn't hear Troy's reply.

He sucked in a deep breath. It wasn't going to be simple to get Ava away.

Parek spoke from behind him. "SWAT has two snipers trained on the guy. We need him to put away that gun. They said their bullets will pierce the cargo doors of the van, but they'd rather have an open shot."

"No one's shooting anyone," stated Mason, glaring at Parek.

Rain streamed down the agent's face. *Get a hat.* "Ava's too close. You tell SWAT to keep it in their pants."

"They will. No one's shooting without orders, but I wanted you to know it was an option."

"Crappy option."

"Agreed," said Parek.

Mason turned his attention back to Ava. *How can I get her out of there?*

•   •   •

Ava couldn't move. She hadn't realized how drained she was until she saw the vehicles and Mason's silhouette in the headlights. That hat made him recognizable anywhere. She'd nearly fallen backward off the railing when she spotted it. Now Troy was hiding between the cargo doors with his weapon trained on Derrick. Ava had a clear view of Troy, but she assumed Mason and the SWAT team could only see his feet.

They'll fire if they have to.

She knew they'd give negotiations a chance, but if Troy looked like he intended to shoot, they'd take him down. She licked her lips, knowing they'd watch her as an indicator of Troy's behavior. Right now he was sweating badly. Even in the light rain, she could see sweat on his temples and upper lip. His tension had ratcheted up a hundred points since the FBI had arrived. At first he'd seemed angry but in control. Now he appeared nervous and antsy. And volatile.

His gaze jerked back and forth between her and Derrick as he wiped his upper lip. "What are they doing?" he hissed at her.

She looked at him calmly. "They're standing there talking. I don't see any weapons. The men from the SWAT team vehicle are waiting far behind the three men at the front." She spoke in a low voice, hoping to take the edge off his tension. "I've seen things like this before. They're going to talk to you for a while. They don't want to look bad on the news because they shot someone without asking questions first."

"They want me dead. They probably know what happened." Troy's voice rose an octave and his left hand balled into a fist.

"I don't think so. They want to come out of this looking good. For them that means no dead bodies. What do you think about letting them arrest him?" She nodded at Derrick. "I told you I thought that was a good idea. That way you're not to blame for anything that's happened to him."

Troy frantically shook his head. "That's not how it's supposed to go." He ran a hand across his forehead and flicked away the water. "We know what needs to be done."

"I think we should—"

"Stop talking!" he shouted at her. "I need to think!" He closed his eyes and tipped his head back but kept his gun pointed at Derrick's.

Ava looked toward Mason. He was too far away for eye contact, but she slowly shook her head, hoping they would understand she meant *Don't fire,* not *This isn't going well.* She saw his hat dip in an abrupt nod.

Troy appeared to be thinking through his options. Now she needed to guide him to pick the right one. Thank goodness Mason had caught on that Troy believed she was Colleen. If Troy knew she was an FBI agent, she didn't know what he'd do. She'd been lucky that Derrick was too scared to tell Troy who she really was.

"Troy," she started. "Do you think you could untie my hands? I can't feel—"

"I said, *Don't talk!*"

She pressed her lips together and glanced at Derrick. He lay on the ground, a soaking mess of rain, tears, and gasoline. Would the rain be enough to keep his clothing from lighting? His petrified gaze met hers and his chest heaved with each breath. He'd been close to going over the edge, and he knew it. He also knew he wasn't out of the woods.

"How about you let one of them go, Troy?" Mason shouted. "You don't need both of them."

Troy muttered under his breath and shook his head resolutely but didn't answer. He glared at Derrick. "I'm never going to get him over the edge with these guys here. They'll shoot me before it happens."

"You're probably right. Why don't you let them arrest him?" Ava said calmly.

Derrick nodded, making a squealing noise behind the gag.

Troy smirked at Derrick. "You'd like that, wouldn't you? That'd be a nice easy end for you. You forget you're supposed *to suffer!*" he snarled. Derrick turned his face to the concrete.

Ava eyed the distance between Derrick and Troy. Maybe twelve feet? Troy would be dropped by bullets in a split second if he rushed to heave Derrick over the edge. Should she encourage him to do it? She knew the SWAT team; there'd be two snipers with their sights on the cargo door.

Troy shoved his gun in his waistband, reached into the van, and grabbed a box smaller than his palm.

Matches.

She held her breath as he lit one, flicked it at Derrick, and laughed. The match fizzled on the ground two feet from his face. Derrick shook his head and tried to inch farther from Troy.

Will the rain keep him safe?

Fuel catches fire on top of rivers.

Troy flicked another match at Derrick. The man flinched and the flame extinguished on the concrete.

"Troy, stop it," begged Ava.

"No one stopped him when he burned you, Colleen."

What happened to that poor girl?

"But I'm okay now. Please let the police take him away."

Troy shook his head and rubbed at his right eye with the back of his hand as he frowned. "It was all supposed to be better today. Once I get across this bridge, I'll have peace. I need to finish this and things will return to normal."

Across the bridge?

Ava glanced behind her at the end of the bridge on the island. What was he expecting? "Across this bridge, Troy? What's over there?"

"Not a real bridge. The steps that make the bridge to forgiveness. I've completed three of your steps. I need to finish the fourth and fifth and it will be over."

"Fifth step?"

He gave her a pitying look. "I know I'm part of your plan."

Alarm shot through her. "The plan is over, Troy. I want it to end. It's not going how I expected." She paused. "How were you going to do the fifth step?"

He shrugged, glancing at the gun in his waistband.

He's suicidal. He doesn't care if the FBI shoots him. He's only protecting himself at the moment because he wants to finish Derrick.

"Troy, I don't want you to hurt yourself."

"It's okay, Colleen. I know you say that, but I see it in your eyes." He smiled at her. "You've been good to me, but I always knew you wanted me dead. No one goes through what you did and offers forgiveness. They say I'll be dead before the year's out anyway."

"Who says that?"

"The doctors. It's too big. They can't take it out, and I don't want them to treat it."

"Treat what?"

He tapped his temple. "The tumor."

His speech. His vision issues. Is the tumor real?

"But I'll reach my goals first. I have to accomplish something with my life and bringing you revenge has given me a purpose." He removed the gun and pointed it at Derrick again. "Just because I can't kill him the way we agreed is not a reason to give up."

Ava saw his hand tighten around his gun.

Time to act.

She scrambled back to her feet, nearly tipping over onto her face. *I'm going to end up with a broken nose.*

Troy took a step in her direction. "Get down!"

She turned and ran toward the side of the bridge, throwing herself against the railing as she tried to find her footing to hoist herself up.

"Colleen!" Troy screamed behind her.

29

All Mason's nerves fired at once as Ava wrestled to her feet and veered toward the edge of the bridge. She slammed into the rail and started to scramble up, leaning forward to keep her balance with her hands tied behind her.

His heart stopped. Mason took two running steps and his collar abruptly choked him. He whirled around to see Ray's incensed face. "You can't run out there!" he shouted with the back of Mason's coat collar in his grip.

"Get down," shouted Parek. "He's out!"

Mason turned back to the bridge and saw Troy rush from the protection of the cargo doors toward Ava. Mason instinctively ducked, expecting to hear shots from the snipers.

No shots. He watched as Troy threw himself at Ava and hauled her off the railing. She fought back, swinging her head at his jaw and kicking backward with her heels. Troy jogged sideways, keeping Ava between him and the snipers, and leaped into the back of his van. The cargo doors slammed shut.

"They didn't take the shot," muttered Mason.

"Did she do that to draw him out?" asked Ray. "And we blew it?"

"Happened too soon," said Parek, glancing back at the SWAT team. "They hadn't received official clearance to shoot yet. We didn't think the situation had degraded to that point."

"She just risked her life to give them the shot!" Mason shouted at Parek. "Now look where she is!"

Parek held his gaze. "She moved too soon. Not our fault."

"God damn it!" Mason looked back at the white van. The side of its cargo hold was solid metal without windows. He couldn't see anyone through the passenger window in the cab. What was Troy doing to Ava in the back?

"We need to regroup," said Parek. "When the other team gets here—"

Their heads jerked as an engine started. The van's tires squealed as Troy stepped on the gas and yanked the steering wheel toward the other end of the bridge. The van jolted forward and the wheels grated as it attempted the sharp turn. Smoke blew from the back tires as they left tread on the bridge. The van made the turn and hurtled away from the men.

"Let's go!" Parek slid into the driver's seat of his vehicle and slammed the door.

Mason's brain froze. *Go with Parek or drive my own car?* Ray turned him toward his own car and pushed, making the decision for him. Mason heard the crack of a gun from the direction of one of the snipers.

Tires squealed and Mason turned around in time to see the van abruptly swerve to the left, its front tire flat as it hurtled toward the low railing near the far end of the bridge.

"NOOOO!"

Time seemed to slow as he watched the van plow through the barrier. He bolted to the near side of the bridge, gripped the rails, and looked over. The van tipped over the edge and fell nose-first, landing on the far bank of the Multnomah Channel.

The roar in Mason's head drowned out the crash.

The van toppled onto its side and rolled, tumbling down the steep bank and into the water.

The splash was deafening.

Ava!

Mason started to run. His heart pounded in his head and his boots slammed the pavement. He strained for oxygen, sprinting as he'd never run before, keeping one eye on the white van in the water. He emerged from under the arched truss structure, gauging the distance to run to the island road on foot and loop around down the bank of the channel.

Too long. Not enough time.

He stopped where the van had plowed through the guardrail. The drop to the bank was a good twenty feet. He'd break a leg. He looked to his left. If he doubled back, he'd land in the water if he jumped. But it was higher.

He stared down. The nose of the van had sunk. Black water covered the windshield and crawled toward the roof. No one emerged from the van.

Do something. Now.

Mason dashed back to the start of the truss, kicked off his boots, yanked off his coat, and climbed to the top of the guardrail. To his left he heard Ray shout; Mason tuned him out.

He threw off his hat, took a breath, and jumped.

. . .

Ava couldn't see.

Troy had flung her into the van, and she'd landed on her back— her breath knocked out. Troy had jerked the cargo doors shut and crawled over her toward the front of the van. She'd tried to head butt him, and he'd punched her in the face. She'd lain on the floor, gasping to get her lungs functioning. He'd started the van, and she'd been thrown to the side as he turned and floored the gas. Both her shoulders and her head screamed in pain as she was tossed around in the back of the van.

She'd tried to catch her balance so she could scoot to the front and stop him. She'd press the brake pedal with her head if she had to. Before she could get her bearings, the van crashed and tipped forward. After a full second of weightlessness, she fell and slammed into the backs of the front seats as the nose of the van hit the ground. She lost her breath again as blackness engulfed her vision.

She felt water. Her eyes flew open and she blinked, trying to see.

It was pitch-black inside the van and water soaked the floor. The van bobbed and swayed and tipped forward again as the nose started to sink. She scrambled to get into a sitting position and braced her legs against a solid metal beam across the floor. She heard water fill the front of the van, and she strained to see Troy.

"Troy?"

There was silence except for the rush of the filling water.

Ignoring the pain in her shoulder, she tried to yank her numb hands from her bindings. The van lurched downward, and she nearly tipped over. "Troy?" she screamed. She scooted toward the back end of the van and tried to find the door release behind her back with her numb hands. She could see the inside of the doors in her mind. There was a handle halfway up on one of them.

Her hands were useless. She'd never get the door open.

She tried to feel with her elbows but the numbness extended most of the way up her arms. She whirled around and felt at the door with her mouth, using her tongue and lips and nose to find the handle.

There.

She opened her mouth and tried to slide the handle inside her cheek. She clamped down on the metal handle with her jaw and felt a molar chip. She pulled. The handle slipped out of her mouth, and she fell onto her rear and tumbled backward the length of the cargo area to the front seats. Water soaked her to the waist. She lunged to her feet and worked her way up the angled floor to the cargo doors. She pressed her face against the cold metal doors, gasping to catch her breath.

How long before the water fills the van?

She located the handle again and carefully bit down. A hand grabbed her waistband and wrenched her backward. "Troy?" she screamed as she landed in the deepening water. "Open the doors!"

"No! It's better this way. We're both supposed to die." His voice was oddly calm in the pitch black.

"Fuck you!" she shrieked. "Like hell I'm going to die in here. Open the doors!" She pressed her back against the side wall of the cargo space and inched toward the rear doors.

"I'm really sorry, Colleen," he said. "I don't want to hurt you again."

"Here's your chance to help me, Troy. You can save me this time."

"No, it's too late. It can't be undone."

"Open the doors!" She lunged forward and her head connected with his chest, sending them both plunging into the rising water. She swallowed a mouthful and coughed and gagged, shooting water out through her nose. Her legs kicked, seeking purchase, and she flung herself out of the water. There was two feet between the water and the cargo doors. The front seats were now underwater. Troy thrashed in the water as the van did a stomach-churning tilt and the angle steepened.

Can I tread water with no arms?

She didn't want to know. She pressed her cheek against the cargo door, her lungs sucking for air, bracing her legs against the beam on the floor, knowing she couldn't open the door, and that she would drown in the dark.

· · ·

The impact of hitting the river knocked the breath out of Mason. Underwater, he looked up toward the night sky and kicked as hard as he could. Just as he thought he would have to breathe in a lungful of water, he broke through the surface of the channel and gasped for air. The back of the van bobbed in the river fifteen feet away.

Ava!

He pumped his arms into a crawl stroke. Reaching the van, he crawled onto the cargo doors, feeling the van sink deeper from his weight. He shifted onto one door, grabbed the handle of the other door, and flung it open.

"Mason?" Ava shrieked.

She was just inside the door. He bent over and grabbed her under her right armpit and heaved, hauling her upper body out of the van and onto the other door. She shook as she hugged the metal door with her torso, sputtering a mess of sobs and curses. He pulled at the ties around her wrists, but knew he needed a knife. Suddenly she tensed and screamed as she was jerked back into the van by her legs. Mason lunged but couldn't get a grip on her. Screeching, she vanished into the wet black hole of the cargo area.

He bent over the opening, trying to see into the back of the large van. Faint lights from the bridge showed her thrashing with Troy Beadle as he tried to hold her head underwater. The water level rapidly rose, bringing the two of them closer to the doors. Mason reached in and grabbed Troy's collar, slamming his head into the closed cargo door. He jerked the man's head back and forth, trying to get his hands off Ava's neck.

Troy's hand shot up to grab Mason's wrist, and Ava's head popped out of the water and she gasped for breath.

"Mason!"

The water level grew even with the doors. Its air bubble gone, the van accelerated toward the bottom of the channel. Mason's perch on the closed cargo door rapidly sank, and Ava's head went under the water. He wrenched his wrist out of Troy's grasp and grabbed blindly in Ava's direction. He caught her hair and yanked with all his strength as he pushed off the cargo door with his feet.

Last shot.

The van sank away, and Mason pulled her head above the water. Ava spit water out and sucked in a shuddering breath. He pulled her tight to him, treading water with his legs and one arm. "Kick your feet," he ordered.

"We're going to sink!" She thrashed in his arms.

"No. I've got you. I won't let go."

"Where is he? Where'd he go?" She craned her neck, trying to look at the black water.

"He's gone." Mason scanned the water, not believing his words, but desperate to put her at ease. "I'm going to roll you onto your back; just float, okay?"

"No!" She kicked and tried to bury her face in his neck, pushing him deeper.

"Ava! Hold still!" he ordered.

She froze and he rolled her over, looping one arm under her armpit. "I've got you. It's not far to the bank."

Ray's welcome face appeared in the water. "Need a hand?"

Mason wanted to kiss him. "Take her," he demanded, pushing Ava at Ray as he felt something touch his foot. Ray looped an arm around her neck and reached out with a long stroke to swim them back to shore.

Take her out of reach.

Treading water, Mason stared down and tried to see through the murk, his heart pounding against his chest.

He waited for the demon.

Nothing else touched his foot. He scanned the surface of the water, wondering how long Troy could hold his breath and how far away he could swim.

Is Troy gone?

30

Three days later

The giant crane lifted the van out of the channel and water rushed out of the open rear door, streaming back into the river. Ava gasped and looked down.

Mason felt Ava shudder and pulled her tight against him. He watched tears run down her face. She cautiously glanced at the crane and then looked away again. She repeated the behavior several times and each glance ripped at his heart a little more.

"I can't believe I was in that," she whispered.

Mason and Ava watched from the banks of the Multnomah Channel. Spectators packed the side of the road, and Mason and Ava blended in with the crowds, avoiding the press and large police presence. They'd spotted Zander and Parek supervising the removal of the van. She'd told Zander she didn't want to watch the van be pulled out of the river, but this morning Mason had noticed she couldn't sit still. He'd ordered her into his vehicle and they'd driven silently to the site.

He hoped he'd done the right thing by making her come. He'd thought seeing the van be pulled from the waters would purge some of her nightmares. Twice last night she'd woken up screaming, convinced she was drowning. She'd thrashed her arms, believing they were still tied and that she was sinking under the water. He'd struggled with his own nightmares. The ones where he plunged into black water and couldn't find her. Or the one where his last-ditch grab for her hair failed, and Troy Beadle dragged her to the bottom of the river.

The first night, he'd sat at Ava's bedside in the hospital, and dreaded that the man had escaped in the dark and would come after her. But divers had recovered Beadle's body the morning after the incident.

Should I have dived after Troy?

Could he have saved him?

No.

"Holy crap, would you look at that," said a spectator to Mason's right, snapping photos of the dangling van with his phone. "Drowning was too good for that asshole."

Ava straightened and looked at the man. "Damn right." She winced as she adjusted the sling on her left arm. Her ordeal had damaged a muscle attachment, and she was scheduled for surgery tomorrow. Her surgeon had wanted to operate immediately, but she'd told him to wait. She wanted to catch her breath and get her feet back under her.

And monitor Jayne's progress. Her left arm had been badly burned in the house fire.

When Ava had heard what'd happened to Jayne, she had been unable to sit still in her hospital room until she'd seen her sister. Her twin was in the burn unit. The hospital had turned over Jayne's valuables to Ava. They'd consisted of three one-dollar bills and a ring dangling on a gold necklace.

"She didn't sell our mother's ring," Ava had whispered. "I didn't believe her when she said she'd kept it. I thought for sure it was long gone. Even though she'd hit rock bottom, she didn't part with it."

"But she was fine with stealing it," Mason had countered. He'd never forgive Jayne McLane. She'd hurt Ava too many times.

"Both our left arms are injured," Ava had said softly to Mason. "I never know if it's coincidence or fate when something happens like that. Whatever befalls one of us seems to echo in the other."

Ava had started to ramble while on strong pain-killers later that day. "It's unavoidable," she'd slurred. "I can't change what's supposed to happen. I've tried my hardest, but sometimes I think it'd be easier to let go and simply let genetics take over . . . instead of constantly fighting to be the exact opposite of everything she is."

She'd closed her eyes and fallen asleep, leaving Mason speechless. Within twenty-four hours she'd cut the pain-killers back to a minimum, saying she couldn't think straight and didn't mind the pain in her shoulder. She'd exposed the most damaged part of her heart to him. Did she remember? He silently renewed his promise to help her carry the load with her twin, to do everything he could to relieve some of her burden.

"I've seen enough," she whispered to him on the riverbank. "Let's go home."

Mason nodded and opened the vehicle door for her. She winced as she slid into the seat, protecting her shoulder, and leaned her head on the headrest.

She closed her eyes.

. . .

A knock on the door startled Ava awake from her nap on the couch. She sat up, ignoring the pain shooting through her arm, and answered the door. A worn-looking Zander stood on the front porch.

Do I look that exhausted?

Probably worse.

She self-consciously touched the chopped side of her hair. A good cut and new short style would even it out, but she hadn't found the energy to make the appointment.

Ava asked him in and they sat in the living room. She blinked the sleep out of her eyes and offered him a drink, which he refused. He sat stiffly on the edge of the chair, and she wondered what news he had.

"Where's Mason?" he asked.

"I can hear him talking to the dog," she said. "They must be out back."

Zander sat silently for a minute, his hands twisting.

"What's happened? What's wrong?" Panic crawled up her spine.

"Nothing." His eyes widened and he raised his hands. "Calm down. Nothing's happened."

"Oh." She leaned back against the couch in relief. "You looked so uncomfortable. I was certain you had bad news."

"No. It's just . . . I mean . . . seeing you like this . . ." His words stumbled over themselves. "I was worried about you."

Ava's vision cleared. *He has feelings for me.* And she'd had no clue. She took a closer look at Zander Wells, liking everything she saw. *Why didn't I see it?*

Bingo rushed into the room and plunged his head into Zander's lap. Zander laughed and scratched his ears, a smile breaking across his face. Ava looked in the direction Bingo had come from and her heart did a double beat at the sight of the man standing there.

That's why.

She'd been waiting all along for this man. Fate had kept her blind to any others, knowing they weren't right. She and Mason *fit perfectly.*

"Hey, Zander," said Mason. "Bingo told me someone was here." He met Ava's gaze and a question passed through his eyes as he sat next to her on the couch.

She shrugged her good shoulder at him.

She didn't know why Zander was here. Mason had taken time off to help her recover and neither of them had spoken much to the FBI except to deliver statements about what had happened on the bridge that night. Both had avoided the news channels. She knew

Mason had spoken with Ray, but she hadn't asked any questions. She hadn't wanted to hear about Troy Beadle.

Until now.

"Dr. Rutledge sent over the autopsy on Troy Beadle," Zander started. He raised a brow at Ava, and she nodded at him to continue. She was ready.

"Cause of death was drowning."

No surprises there.

"He had a huge tumor in his brain. Checking with his doctors confirmed what he'd told you, that he wouldn't live out the year. *But it wasn't untreatable.* They'd given him several treatment options. He'd chosen to do none of them. They weren't great options but they would have given him a few more years."

"Could the tumor have affected his behavior? Made him do what he did?" Mason asked.

"Hard to say," Zander answered. "His recent medical history says he had vision and speech issues. I don't think doctors could say for certain if the tumor affected his recent actions. It's possible, but too hard to quantify."

Ava exhaled. "Why? Why would he pass up help for his tumor?" She immediately answered her own question. "He thought he was supposed to die. He chose it as penance for his role in Colleen's death." She shuddered. It'd be years . . . if ever . . . before the terror of three days ago subsided.

She could still feel him cutting her hair, smell the rusty blood in the carpet, and hear Derrick's screams. In the shed, she'd believed she was to be his next victim.

And I almost drowned.

Water. Dark. Troy.

Mason's arm slid around her; she was shaking.

Zander nodded. "You're probably right. We've been in contact with her parents. They're relieved to have some answers after all these years. I don't know how much it helped. Their daughter still died in a horrible way. That hasn't changed.

"The Bridge Killer's victims' families are glad to have some answers. None of them appeared to know about the murder these men committed years ago. These men truly took their secret to their graves."

"I don't know how someone could function with a secret like that," said Mason. "How could Carson Scott move into politics knowing what he'd done in the past? I guess everyone handles it differently. Aaron King obviously had anger issues, and Joe Upton curled up and hid his face from the world."

"While Derrick Snyder continued to ruin other people's lives," added Ava.

"He'll be paying for some of it now," Mason said. "Yamhill County is putting together a case against him for Colleen's death, and he has to answer to the Portland police for a dozen different crimes. I predict he'll be locked up for the rest of his life."

"Troy Beadle's van had a pulley system welded into the frame. Our theory was right about how he hung Joe Upton by himself," said Zander.

Ava remembered the beam she'd felt with her feet across the bottom of the van. In the dark. In the water. A quake shot through her nerves.

"We found Carson Scott's Explorer and Aaron King's truck parked in the woods on Troy Beadle's acreage," added Zander. "Their cell phones were in the house along with some of their cloth- ing items. And Euzent was right on the money with Troy Beadle being a neat freak. I've never seen a guy's house that clean. Even the cans of food were in neat rows."

Zander stood.

"I wanted to get you caught up and see if you needed anything." He looked at Ava and then at Mason. "Looks like you're in compe- tent hands."

He made a fast but polite exit.

Mason shook his head as they stood at the window watching Zander leave. "Man, he had it bad for you."

Ava looked at him in surprise. "You knew? I had no idea until today."

"A man knows," he said mysteriously.

She wrinkled her nose at him. "Men can rarely see what's right in front of them."

"I saw," Mason said, turning her toward him and pulling her against his chest. He lifted her chin. "Angels sang in my brain the first time I saw you. I just didn't know what it meant."

She snorted. "I call BS on that one."

"Well, maybe it took a little longer than that. I'm happy someone placed us in each other's paths."

"Me, too."

"You're good for me, Special Agent McLane." His expression turned deadly serious. "I didn't ever expect to feel this way. When I saw you on the rail of that bridge, I was relieved that you were alive and completely terrified that I was about to watch you die."

"I'm sorry," she whispered. "The whole time I worried about what you were thinking. One of the reasons I fought him so hard was to keep you from suffering if something happened to me."

"You worried about what I was going through?"

"Hell, yes. I knew you'd be out of your mind."

"I wanted to kill someone. When I watched him throw you in the back of the van, I was ready to rip it open with my bare hands to get at you."

"You did." She remembered his stricken expression when he'd flung open the cargo door. He'd been prepared to go to hell and back to get her.

He nearly had.

He'd jumped off a bridge and fought off a killer.

For her.

"I'd do it all again," he promised, his voice husky. "I won't let go."

"Me neither," she said, clutching him tighter. "Thank you for loving me."

Mason laughed. "Agent McLane, you have no idea how easy it is to love you. And I plan to do it for the rest of my life."

She couldn't wait.

ACKNOWLEDGMENTS

Thank you to all my local readers who reach out to me because they like reading about the gorgeous Pacific Northwest in my books. I take a few liberties with our cities and landmarks, and some aspects are fictional, but I try to incorporate as much Northwest flavor as possible. I love hearing from you!

I must tell my girls that I appreciate their patience with a mom whose brain seems to vanish during random moments of the day. They're growing up so fast, but Amelia, you're not allowed to read my books yet. To my husband, Dan, I'm sorry that I couldn't figure out a way to incorporate zombies into this book, either.

Thank you to all my usual suspects. JoVon Sotak and Jessica Poore from my Montlake publishing team, and Charlotte Herscher, who always makes my books shine. Giant thanks to Melinda Leigh, who helped me figure out what on earth to do with a van in a stand-off on a bridge. Someone who listens to my moaning when I'm stuck in a manuscript is priceless.

ABOUT THE AUTHOR

Born and raised in the Pacific Northwest, Kendra Elliot has always been a voracious reader, cutting her teeth on classic female sleuths and heroines like Nancy Drew, Trixie Belden, and Laura Ingalls before proceeding to devour the works of Stephen King, Diana Gabaldon, and Nora Roberts. She won a 2014 Daphne du Maurier award for best Romantic Suspense for *Buried*, which was also an International Thriller Writers' finalist for Best Paperback Original and a Romantic Times finalist for best Romantic Suspense. Elliot shares her love of suspense in *Hidden*, *Chilled*, *Buried*, *Alone*, *Vanished*, and now *Bridged*. She lives and writes in the rainy Pacific Northwest with her husband, three daughters, and a Pomeranian, but dreams of living at the beach on Kauai. She loves to hear from readers at www.KendraElliot.com.